Discovering Dance

Gayle Kassing

Human Kinetics

Library of Congress Cataloging-in-Publication Data

Kassing, Gayle.
  Discovering dance / Gayle Kassing.
    pages cm
  Includes bibliographical references and index.
  1. Dance--Study and teaching. 2. Choreography--Study and teaching. I. Title.
  GV1589.K375 2014
  792.8071--dc23

2013040254

ISBN-10: 1-4504-6886-1 (print)
ISBN-13: 978-1-4504-6886-2 (print)

Permission notices for material reprinted in this book from other sources can be found on page vii.

The web addresses cited in this text were current as of December 9, 2013, unless otherwise noted.

Acquisitions Editor: Scott Wikgren; **Developmental Editor:** Bethany J. Bentley; **Assistant Editor:** Derek Campbell; **Copyeditor:** Joanna Hatzopoulos; **Indexer:** Sharon Duffy; **Permissions Manager:** Dalene Reeder; **Graphic Designer:** Nancy Rasmus; **Graphic Artist:** Nancy Rasmus; **Cover Designer:** Keith Blomberg; **Photographs (cover):** © Human Kinetics; courtesy of Morton Ranch High School, Katy Independent School District; Alexander Yakovlev/fotolia.com; Dragan Trifunovic/fotolia.com; © Golden Pixels LLC/age fotostock; **Photographs (interior):** © Human Kinetics, unless otherwise noted; **Photo Asset Manager:** Laura Fitch; **Visual Production Assistant:** Joyce Brumfield; **Photo Production Manager:** Jason Allen; **Art Manager:** Kelly Hendren; **Associate Art Manager:** Alan L. Wilborn; **Illustrations:** © Human Kinetics; **Printer:** Courier Companies, Inc.

We thank the Northside ISD Office of Fine Arts Dance Department in San Antonio, Texas, along with participants in the photo shoot for this book: Maia Cody, Alexandra Delgado, Anthony Esparza, Avery Heyse, Siena Pangtay, Jacquelyn Revilla, Ashley Rivera, Brittany Valdez, Jacqueline Aguirre, Tiffany Martinez, Elizabeth Sanchez-Lopez, and Shauna Havener. Thanks to Rose Laurel of Leapin' Leotards in San Antonio for providing dance wear and shoes.

Printed in the United States of America   10 9 8 7 6 5 4 3 2 1

The paper in this book was manufactured using responsible forestry methods.

Human Kinetics
Website: www.HumanKinetics.com

United States: Human Kinetics, P.O. Box 5076, Champaign, IL 61825-5076
800-747-4457
e-mail: humank@hkusa.com

Canada: Human Kinetics, 475 Devonshire Road Unit 100, Windsor, ON N8Y 2L5
800-465-7301 (in Canada only)
e-mail: info@hkcanada.com

Europe: Human Kinetics, 107 Bradford Road, Stanningley, Leeds LS28 6AT, United Kingdom
+44 (0) 113 255 5665
e-mail: hk@hkeurope.com

Australia: Human Kinetics, 57A Price Avenue, Lower Mitcham, South Australia 5062
08 8372 0999
e-mail: info@hkaustralia.com

New Zealand: Human Kinetics, P.O. Box 80, Torrens Park, South Australia 5062
0800 222 062
e-mail: info@hknewzealand.com

E6150

CONTENTS

PART III   Dance on Stage

PART IV   Dance for Life

Welcome to *Discovering Dance*. This textbook is designed for new or experienced students who are taking an introductory dance course. The book reviews and enhances the exciting activities you experience in your dance course. It functions as your guide in learning about dance and in learning about yourself in the process. To further extend your understanding of dance, the companion student web resource gives you more opportunities to explore dance topics presented in each chapter.

In dance class you learn about dance foundations, history and culture, genres, and career options. To aid in learning you participate in movement activities, study various aspects of dance through the eyes of a dancer and choreographer, and view dances from an array of dance genres and artists, historical periods, styles, and cultures.

Discovering Dance is divided into four parts. Part I introduces you to the foundations of dance that include the elements, processes, and principles that underlie all dance genres. Part II covers dance genres in society. The chapters delve into social, folk, and cultural dance genres. In part III you study dance on stage. This series of chapters examines ballet, modern dance, jazz dance, tap dance, dance entertainment forms, and dance production and performance. Part IV investigates dance as preparation for life. These chapters investigate college and career preparation in dance and associated areas, and dance in your life.

This book integrates 21st-century learning skills and practices for college or career preparation. Each chapter includes several topics that explore dance from different perspectives. The Discovering section introduces you to the chapter topic or a specific dance genre. The Exploring section provides ways to dig deeper into the history, culture, styles, and dance artists who contributed to the dance genre. In other parts of Exploring sections, you learn dance technique and the vocabulary of the genre. This understanding gives you the dance genre language with which to perform and create dance. Each chapter has a section titled Thinking Like a Dancer. This section is a way to step into the shoes of a dancer or choreographer so that you can learn more about the dance genre and its processes. Throughout the chapter are a number of activities. These activities include discovery activities, movement activities, response activities, and others for you to learn more about the chapter or the dance genre. At the end of each chapter a portfolio assignment outlines an extended project that you or the class can participate in.

Each chapter includes two special sidebars: *Did You Know?* expands on a topic from the chapter. *Spotlight* puts attention on a dance artist, personality, or company related to the chapter topics.

Finally, chapter review questions help you check your understanding of the content presented in the chapter. A comprehensive glossary supplies you with the major concepts, topics, people, and ideas presented in this book.

Discovering Dance provides a way to read and learn about dance that supports your dance learning and the dance activities in class. To find a variety of learning experiences and study aids (including extended learning activities, video clips, and web search suggestions) to help you discover, explore, and expand your knowledge and interests in dance, visit the web resource at www.discovering dance.org/student.

This text and web resource will guide you in discovering, exploring, and thinking as a dancer and a choreographer. Enjoy your dance discoveries!

Photo on p. 3 © DreamPictures/Blend Images/age fotostock

Photo on p. 4 © Andrey Kiselev | Dreamstime.com

Photo on p. 10 courtesy of ILL-Abilities

Photos on pp. 23, 40, 56, 226 from *Music Fundamentals for Dance* by Nola Nolen Holland, 2013, (Champaign, IL: Human Kinetics), Photographer: Dave Garson

Photo on p. 55 © AP Photo/Daily Herald, Bev Horne

Photo on p. 75 Tony Russell/Associated Press

Photo on p. 88 courtesy of Library of Congress

Photo on p. 89 © Roger Wood/ArenaPal

Photo on p. 113 © Ermess | Dreamstime.com

Photo on p. 114 © Alexander Podshivalov | Dreamstime.com

Photo on p. 128 © nikitabuida/Kalium/age fotostock

Photo on p. 132 © Anke Van Wyk | Dreamstime.com

Photo on p. 132 VWPics via AP Images

Photo on p. 139 AP Photo/Tampa Tribune, Cliff McBride

Photo on p. 169 AP Photo/The Herald-Palladium, Don Campbell

Photo on p. 191 AP Photo/The Herald-Palladium, Jody Warner

Photo on p. 225 courtesy of Darby Boyd

Photo on p. 230 courtesy of Jennifer Dawson, Terri Ware, and Silver Star Dancers

Photos on pp. 231, 245 Jim West

Photo on p. 237 © Roman Nazarov | Dreamstime.com

Photo on p. 238 courtesy of Judi Fey, photographer Scott Swanson

Photo on p. 252 AP Photo/The News-Times/Carol Kaliff

Photo on p. 261 Kyodo via AP Images

Photo on p. 262 © Sanches1980 | Dreamstime.com

Photo on p. 272 © Florin Prunoiu/age fotostock

Photo on p. 281 © Zero Creatives/age fotostock

Photo on p. 282 AP Photo/The Commercial Appeal, Brandon Dill

Sidebar on p. 42 based on Forklift Dance Company. Available: http://forklift danceworks.org/trash-dance.

Text on p. 51 adapted from *Blueprint for the arts: Dance, dance making*, (New York: NYC Department of Education), 37.

Sidebar on p. 172 based on www.dancemagazine.com/issues/December-2007/ iDANCE#sthash.WMK0BTUv.dpuf and other resources.

Sidebar on p. 214 based on http://www.about-tap-dance.com/most-taps.html.

Text on p. 220 adapted from L. Lewis, 2013, *Beginning tap dance* (Champaign, IL: Human Kinetics), 109-111.

Sidebar on p. 233 reprinted, by permission, from Riverdance. Available: http:// events.riverdance.com/entice-clients/facts.

Text on pp. 268-269 adapted from http://www.thirteen.org/edonline/concept 2class/mi/index.html.

PART I
Foundations of Dance

PART II
Dance in Society

PART III
Dance on Stage

PART IV
Dance for Life

one

Dance for All

ENDURING UNDERSTANDING: Dance is a part of humanity and culture.

ESSENTIAL QUESTION: Who dances?

LEARNING OBJECTIVES

After reading this chapter, you should be able to do the following:

- Identify your participation in dance.
- Differentiate between categories of dance.
- Explain the three processes of dance.
- Understand the artistic processes that relate to all arts disciplines.
- Recognize the underlying principles that relate to dance processes.
- Comprehend dance literacy and artistic literacy.

"Everywhere in each individual . . . there is a dancer—a dancer who wants to be released."

Rudolf Laban, a pioneer of European modern dance

Dance has always been an integral part of humanity. Today more than ever dance is popular as a social, recreational, cultural, artistic, or personal expression. People participate in dance at wedding celebrations, family parties, or community events. Taking part in traditional dances connects people to their culture and heritage. At school or in your community you may have taken dance classes or performed dances with a group. Or, you may have spontaneously danced on your own. Have you experienced dance in any of the following ways?

- Moving to music in your room
- Dancing with a partner at a social event
- Joining in a group folk or cultural dance as part of a celebration

ACTIVITY 1.1　JOURNAL

Your Dance Experiences

In your journal, list several ways you have participated in dance. Think about your dance experiences, then respond to these questions:

- Why do you dance?
- Where do you dance?
- What dances do you do?

As a class, post each question on a large sheet of paper, then write your answers on each sheet. After all students have posted their answers, summarize the class responses to each question. Then, record these conclusions in your journal:

- Did a majority of students have similar experiences? How would you characterize these similar ideas expressed for each question?
- Likewise, what experiences were unique?
- Compare your answers to the majority and minority of other answers posted.
- Where do you stand on each of these questions?
- Do any of the other ideas listed intrigue you enough to consider as a future dance experience or a topic you want to learn about?

- Executing a synchronized routine as part of a dance or drill team at a sporting event
- Doing an end-zone dance to celebrate a team's victory
- Taking part in a dance jam or similar spontaneous mass dance event
- Participating in dance fitness activities as part of a healthy lifestyle
- Performing dance works onstage

You may have participated in dance in one or more of these ways, or you may have experienced dance in ways not listed. Activity 1.1 explores questions about your experiences in dance.

Discovering Dance Categories

You have been moving since before you were born. As a baby and then growing up you learned everyday movements and expanded them through play, games, sport, and dance. Sometimes dance is similar to everyday movement from which people express themselves or communicate ideas, emotions, or themes. Some dance is fun, part of a social occasion, challenges you, tells a story, or teaches a skill. Dance can reconnect to family traditions or heritage and culture. Dance can be a way to be physically active and fit. It is an art form where movement unfolds through time and space. These are just some of the ways dance can be a mode of expression and communication. Dance is done for fun or as part of a social occasion, or used for physical fitness. Some dance tells a story or teaches a skill, reconnecting people to a tradition or culture. Each category of dance has unique characteristics, and some **genres** include various **styles**. Traditionally, **dance categories** include creative movement and dance, recreational dance, dance fitness, and concert dance.

Creative movement and dance is a dance category in which you explore movement. This exploration can enhance your understanding of the elements of dance as a movement vocabulary and a basic understanding of the process of making a dance. Creative movement and dance is a tool for selecting movements for a new work. A creative movement experience can be a guided exercise in a class, or it can be spontaneous movement that allows you to explore new ways to move or find movement ideas that express thoughts, emotions, or themes. Moving to music in your room is a creative movement experience in which you might express an emotion such as happiness. How you perceive and interpret an external idea through your personal movement is creative movement. For example, you could create movement about your appreciation of nature or the environment.

Recreational dance is a social activity in which people of all ages can participate. Recreational dances come from all over the world and include folk dances, cultural and historical dances, and social dances from the past and present. These genres of dance use a variety of steps, figures, and formations. Because recreational dances are performed with a partner or in a group, partnering techniques are essential to them. Recreational dance styles, performance, and music relate to the cultural roots, historical eras, and geographic areas from which the dances originate.

Dance fitness is a fun way to increase cardiovascular endurance, strength, and flexibility. A wide variety of dance genres support fitness. Dance-related fitness training systems, such as cardio dance and barre workouts, have exploded over the last couple of decades. Millions of people enjoy using dance as a fitness activity.

Concert dance is a category of dance performed as art and entertainment. Concert dance genres include ballet, modern dance, jazz dance, and tap dance. These dance genres predominately use specific vocabularies of steps. Concert dance spans classical and traditional to contemporary styles as well as blended genres and styles. Depending on the intended performance, some blended dance genres, forms, or styles cross two or more of these categories. For example, in musical theater dance the style of the musical, its characters, and the plot deter-

❗ ACTIVITY 1.2   DISCOVER

Creative Movement

The class works in pairs. With your partner, select three or four everyday movements, then link the series of movements together to form a movement phrase or longer sequence. When all couples are ready, share your movement phrases with each other to see the variety of ways people move.

To extend the activity, you can learn one or more of the other couples' dance phrases. Are these phrases new or similar to the ones you and your partner presented? Think about how the movements are different. As a class, discuss the similarities and differences between your couples' creative movements.

mine the types of dances. Dance teams focus on blended concert and contemporary dance styles for dynamic, synchronized routines. In entertainment and commercial settings such as theme parks, resorts, nightclubs, cruise lines, television, videos, and other settings, concert-based and blended dance genres contribute enormously to leisure attractions.

Exploring Dance Processes

Dance is both a process and a product. Three processes are fundamental for exploring dance: dancing, dance making, and dance appreciation (figure 1.1). These processes are interconnected for the dancer, the choreographer, and the audience. The products in dance are **dance works**. These works are shared to communicate personal, universal, and artistic values. Whether they are creations of major choreographers or they express the values and beliefs of a culture or historical era, these dance works may be considered works of art. Viewing dance works and then studying, analyzing, and responding to them is similar to studying literature or another art form.

The three dance processes have many connections to life, including celebration, social engagement, recreation, competition, education, fitness, art, culture, heritage, performance in various settings, and personal meanings that you decide are important in your life.

Dancing is the human body rhythmically moving with energy through space and time. To perform a dance, a dancer engages physical, mental, and spiritual attributes. Dance is a conduit of expression and communication, and movement conveys the

Figure 1.1 The three dance processes are interconnected.

message. A dancer learns to use movement to express an emotion, an idea, or a personal statement. Dancing can mean different things for different people and in different cultures. It can be tradition, recreation, fitness, art, entertainment, or a unique blend of styles for personal expression.

Dance making involves learning to use dance elements to create dance works. Some dance genres have inherent choreographic designs and structures; others are flexible, so the choreographer can determine a dance composition's form. When designing a dance work, a **choreographer** uses movements, applies the creative process, selects a structure, and employs devices to express an idea, emotion, or story or to communicate a personal statement. In dance making, the dancer and the choreographer may be the same person, or they may be separate people.

Dance appreciation is participation in a variety of dance-related activities in order to learn about and through dance. Appreciating dance comes from viewing, thinking about, and responding to dance works you study.

Because dance is a performing art, the primary focus of dance appreciation is on viewing dance performances. Dancers experience the performance while they are dancing, and often they view their own performances on video to learn how to increase their artistry. Students, choreographers, and audience members view live and recorded performances of others performing dance works. As a result of viewing many performances, they develop extensive visual memory banks of dance works.

To develop your visual memory bank, you can view recorded or live performances. Dance professionals create dance works for television and other media; students and ordinary people share their dancing with the public on television and the Internet. As a result, you can view almost any dance genre on the planet, and you can become familiar with famous dance works, artists, and companies. This easy access to dance has attracted people to view and learn more about dance. You can also view live community or professional performances.

Dancers perform, think about, and write about the dance processes.

You can gain further appreciation of dance and what dancers do as artists when you participate in dance classes. When you learn to compose dances to perform for class assignments, you appreciate the work of both dancers and choreographers. Dance appreciation helps you develop your dance literacy (see Thinking Like a Dancer, later in this chapter).

Underlying Principles

All of the arts include underlying principles that support their various styles. Knowing these principles informs you of standards used in the arts and helps you understand and analyze art works. Underlying principles may come from other disciplines. In dance, they include scientific information and accepted theories or standards used in other art forms.

The following **principles** support the three dance processes:

- *Dancing* includes movement science principles that support developing safe body movement and practicing correct dance technique.
- *Dance making* depends on using choreographic principles for designing a cohesive dance work.
- *Dance appreciation* includes understanding and analyzing dance works using aesthetic principles to determine the artistic value of a dance in relation to other dance works.

Dancers and choreographers use these principles in performing or creating dance works. Audience members use choreographic and aesthetic principles when they view and analyze dance works.

Dance and Related Arts Processes

Dance is one of the performing arts. Studying dance requires physical and intellectual skills through which you gain knowledge, skills, and attitudes that relate to movement, performance, and creating dance works. Although dance has its

---

ACTIVITY 1.3   EXPLORE

Benefits of Dance

How do you believe participating in dance processes will benefit you

- physically?
- intellectually?
- socially?
- emotionally?

Write a separate paragraph to answer each question. You can include this assignment in your journal. Then make a copy of the questions, and place them at the back of your journal to answer again at the end of the term. Compare the two sets of answers.

own specific processes, it shares these general **artistic processes** with media arts, music, theater, and visual arts:

- Creating
- Presenting, performing, or producing
- Responding
- Connecting or interconnecting by analyzing (within dance, other art forms, and community)

These artistic processes are grounded in the philosophical foundations of each art form, and experiencing them supports you in becoming an artistically literate person. Studying an art introduces you to various ways of thinking and problem solving as well as to skills, such as effective communication in various languages and working as a team, which will transfer to other areas of your life.

Participating in dance processes can benefit you in many ways. Doing, creating, viewing, and evaluating dance can challenge and change you physically, intellectually, socially, or emotionally. Some benefits are easy for you to recognize now as a dance student, and some of them will appear when you are involved in other academic disciplines or later in your career.

SPOTLIGHT

ILL-Abilities

ILL-Abilities is an international breakdance crew comprised of five dancers. The ILL-Abilities concept was created by Montreal-based dancer, Luca "Lazylegz" Patuelli. When founded, ILL-Abilities was an all-star team of differently-abled dancers with the goal to compete in the b-boy competition circuit as a real crew and the intention to show the world that anything is possible. After performing together, the crew quickly realized their potential to inspire audience members with dance and positive attitudes. Now, the goal for the crew is to spread positive thinking by sharing their stories with motivational entertainment programs and theatrical dance performances around the world. They are currently fulfilling their mission and spreading their message: "No excuses, no limits!" Visit their website, www.illabilties.com, to see videos of them in action.

Thinking Like a Dancer

The three dance processes provide you with ways of learning about and through dance. When you connect movement with learning about, creating, and studying dance, you essentially learn to think like a dancer, increasing your literacy in dance. **Dance literacy** is being familiar with and being able to speak and write about dance, dance artists, dance companies, and dance works—in essence, *thinking like a dancer*. All of the dance processes contribute to becoming dance literate.

Just as music has musical scores from centuries past, visual art works exist from prehistoric times, and dramatic works survive from ancient civilizations, dance has a huge heritage of oral, written, and recorded original and restaged performances. All works of dance from the past through today are part of **dance literature**. Viewing dance works is a way to access the performance literature of dance. Reading, writing, listening, and speaking are basic to all disciplines you learn, and they transfer to the arts, too. Your body and its movement is the medium for expressing yourself through dance. Reading, writing, listening, and speaking are ways to communicate your understanding, analysis, and responses of learning through and about dance, choreography, and dance works. When you analyze a dance performance or read a dance, you have to be literate in media and arts to understand it. This concept is not new; you use this literacy every time you turn on the television, use the Internet, play a video game, or attend a drama or dance performance. In these events you encounter an art or media form, find the central focus of the work, and recognize how the other aspects of the performance or experience interrelate or support the work. As a dance literate person, you think about questions such as these: What role does the music or sound play in the dance performance? How do the visual designs of lighting, set, and costumes enhance or detract from the performance? What aspects of the performance do you believe contribute to the work? What aspects of the performance do not support the overall presentation?

Dance is a multimedia art form, so when you think like a dancer, you also begin to think like a multimedia artist, broadening your knowledge about dance and other arts. As you learn about visual arts, music, drama, and other arts media, you develop artistic literacy. **Artistic literacy** is having the knowledge and understanding you need in order to participate authentically in the arts. In other words, when you are artistically literate, you can use what you know about arts and media to express your ideas and respond to art creations.

ACTIVITY 1.4   RESEARCH

Dance Literature

To gain a sense of the wealth of dance literature, take a quick Internet tour. Search for the Library of Congress dance sites, such as American Memories, then move on to related topics such as folk arts or musical theater. Or, do an online search of the New York Public Library dance collection to get an idea of the vast number of dance resources. Then move on to other arts-related collections that exist in libraries, museums, and other places. You will find archival documents, film, video recordings, articles, costumes, paintings and other visual art works, and more about dancers, dances, and dancing.

Summary

This chapter introduced you to the many ways that dance can connect to you and others. Its deep historical and cultural roots connect you to the past and the present, and using it as personal and artistic expression in your life connects you to the present. Dance has many categories and genres. It can be recreation, fitness, creative and artistic expression, or entertainment. Through dance processes you can participate in, view, and learn about dance to become dance literate and enrich your life in many ways.

Your first portfolio assignment is to set some goals for your journey through the *Discovering Dance* course. To help you set those goals, answer these questions in your journal:

- What do you want to get out of this course?
- What do you hope to achieve in dance by the end of the term?
- What role do you think dance will play in your life after this course?
- How do you define dance?
- Why study dance?

REVIEW QUESTIONS

True or False

1. The three processes in dance are dancing, dance making, and dance appreciation. _____

2. Dance literature relates to learning various dance techniques and styles. _____

3. All of the dance processes contribute to dance literacy. _____

Multiple Choice

1. _____ Which of the following artistic processes relate to all art forms?
    a. apply, present, respond, relate
    b. create, perform, respond, connect
    c. read, create, perform, discuss

2. _____ Principles that underlie dance processes are
    a. dancing, dance making, and dance appreciation
    b. movement, choreography, and aesthetics
    c. technique, etiquette, and safety

Short Answer

1. List three benefits of participating in dance processes. How do the benefits you gain from participating in dance carry over to other arts or other disciplines you are involved in?

Matching
Match the term with its definition.

1. _____creative movement and dance
2. _____recreational dance
3. _____dance fitness
4. _____concert dance
5. _____dancing
6. _____dance making
7. _____dance appreciation

a. Dance forms that increase cardiovascular endurance, strength, and flexibility

b. Explores movement to understand the elements of dance and choreographic processes

c. Folk dances, cultural and historical dances, and social dance

d. Human body rhythmically moving through space and time with energy

e. Participation in a variety of dance related activities

f. Dance genres performed onstage as art and entertainment

g. Composing dances

 To find supplementary materials for this chapter such as worksheets, extended learning activities, and e-journaling assignments, visit the web resource at www.discoveringdance.org/student.

Safety, Health, and Wellness

two
two

ENDURING UNDERSTANDING:
Safety, health, and wellness are key to dancing for life.

ESSENTIAL QUESTION: How do safety, health, and wellness apply to dancers?

LEARNING OBJECTIVES

After reading this chapter, you should be able to do the following:

- Recognize the difference between movement as physical activity and movement as dance.
- Develop your body knowledge to ensure dance safety through proper warm-up and cool-down techniques.
- Demonstrate body science to practice dance safety using correct dance technique.
- Apply proper alignment to move correctly and efficiently, executing correct dance technique.
- Interpret dance fitness and conditioning principles to gain and maintain physical fitness.
- Understand the mental demands of dance.
- Plan good nutrition and self-care for optimum dance performance, health, and wellness.

"It takes an athlete to dance, but an artist to be a dancer."

Shanna La Fleur, dancer

Dancing is physically and mentally demanding. You need strength, flexibility, endurance, and overall fitness for dance class and performance. You develop these attributes through conditioning in dance and other movement-related disciplines.

Dance technique is grounded in scientific knowledge of how the body moves. Applying knowledge from movement sciences helps you to develop ways to move effectively and efficiently and prevent injuries. A strong body and safe dance practices connect to overall health and well-being.

Dancing safely requires you to know how your body works, develop kinesthetic awareness, condition your body for dancing, follow dance protocols, and practice good habits for mental and physical wellness. Because dance is physically and mentally engaging, staying in excellent physical, intellectual, and psychological condition helps prevent injuries and ensures that you can keep dancing for a long time.

❗ ACTIVITY 2.1 DISCOVER

When Does Movement Become Dance?

To explore how movement becomes dance, try this exercise with your class: List some ordinary movements you have done since childhood, such as walking, running, galloping, sliding, or skipping. First, all students spread out through the dance space. With or without music, walk around the space, then softly tag someone on the shoulder. Tagging is a cue to change to another movement. If you have been tagged and you have tried all of the ordinary movements you listed, start over; this time, change a characteristic of each movement to make it new. Altering your movements in this way takes your movement from an everyday function to a unique creative movement style.

Here are a few options to get you started:

- Change your movement speed from fast to slow or slow to fast.
- Make your movements sharp and strong or soft and flowing.
- Alter large movements into small or vice versa.
- Add arm movements to complement your movement.
- Think about and express through your body an emotion or feeling you get from doing the movement.

Once you are finished with the exercise, find a partner and reflect on this question: Do you believe the movement you created was dance? Tell your partner at least three reasons why you believe your movement is or is not dance. Then share some of your movements, and ask your partner to share his or her opinion about whether or not they are dance.

As you do this activity, think of the questions *What is dance?* and *Who is a dancer?* When you are finished, jot down your responses to these questions, then share them with the rest of the class in word clouds or posters. Everyone can read and think about the responses posted. How do your answers compare to those of your classmates?

Write a one-page paper on this topic. In the first two paragraphs, outline your answers to the questions *What is dance?* and *Who is a dancer?* In the next paragraph, expand on your opinions. Share one or two ideas about each of these topics with another student or a small group of students. Then, on a second page, write a paragraph that explores ideas others have shared about the two questions that you do not agree with, and provide reasons for disagreeing. End the paper with a conclusion about what you have learned from this activity. You can post your answer in your journal or as part of your portfolio.

Discovering Dance as Movement and Movement as Dance

Movement is inherent to the body. The bones, muscles, and joints work together to move the body so that it can perform everyday activities, sports, or artistic dance movements.

Dance is movement, but not all movement is dance. To distinguish dance from movement, you must answer the fundamental questions *What is dance?* and *Who is a dancer?* For example, when you watch a dancer execute movement, what are some of the attributes that set the dance movements apart from other types of

Dance and the athlete:
A winning combination

Successful performers in sport and dance share many of the same skills and gain many of the same benefits from their practice.

Dance builds an athlete's mind.

- Confidence
- Discipline
- Artistry
- Focus
- Dedication
- Teamwork
- Competitiveness
- Sense of accomplishment

Dance builds an athlete's health.

Ballet brain

Both dancers and athletes must be able to perform quick turns and changes of direction without getting dizzy. New research suggests that over time, ballet training reduces gray matter density in an area of the cerebellum involved in processing signals from the balance organs of the inner ear. This makes ballet dancers less able to feel dizziness.

Cardiovascular health

Long sequences of jumps, runs, leaps, and high kicks build excellent cardiovascular endurance in dancers.

Dance builds an athlete's body.

- Agility
- Aerobic fitness
- Speed
- Flexibility
- Coordination
- Balance
- Anaerobic fitness
- Muscular strength

Flexibility and injury prevention on the football field

The ballet position "turnout" rotates legs and feet from the hips and helps strengthen smaller, more injury-susceptible muscles. Doing jumps and leaps increases ankle and foot flexibility, which enhances agility.

On the football field, John A. Bergfeld, the Cleveland Browns' medical advisor, noted that groin injuries decreased in the season following ballet training. He believed that the training had taught the players awareness of their pelvis positioning and that this had reduced injury potential by increased range of motion in the hips.

F Y I

Ballet training has been part of pro football since the 1970s. Some big-name players have taken ballet to up their game:

Willie Gault   Lynn Swann   Herschel Walker   Walter Payton

movement? What abilities does the person need in order to create the movement so that it is dance? The answers to these questions are a matter of debate in the dance community.

Exploring Safety, Health, and Wellness

Collectively safety, health, and wellness create a holistic view of how your body and mind work when participating in dance. Before you can synthesize them, however, you must first explore the distinct topics that support them. The following sections represent concepts that support safety, health, and wellness in dance. Understanding anatomy, fitness, kinesiology, alignment, safety, and mental and physical preparation will help you move and dance well throughout your life.

Basic Anatomy

The amazing human body houses many systems that support life. This section focuses on bones (skeletal system), muscles (muscular system), and joints, because they are key components of anatomy and of movement.

Skeletal System

The skeleton is the framework for the body. It includes 206 bones of various sizes and types (figure 2.1). The skeleton's main function is to protect organs and to anchor the skeletal muscles. These muscles pull two or more bones closer together or apart.

Muscular System

The muscular system (see figure 2.2) includes smooth muscle (muscle you don't control), cardiac (heart) muscle, and skeletal muscle (muscle that connects to bone). Every time you perform a conscious movement, you use skeletal muscle. Skeletal muscles connect to the skeleton, and they contract and stretch to perform various movements. Performing weight-bearing exercises such as dance movements, conditioning, or weightlifting exercises increases the strength and endurance of the skeletal muscles and the density of the bones.

These groups of skeletal muscles help to move and sculpt your body in various ways for dancing:

- *Core muscles* give the trunk (torso) spinal stability and abdominal strength for the waist and lower back, which is a critical part of body alignment.
- *Leg and foot muscles* support your body in poses and create movements on the floor and in the air.
- *Arm and hand muscles* express movement and gestures, but they can also support your weight, hold props, or lift another dancer.

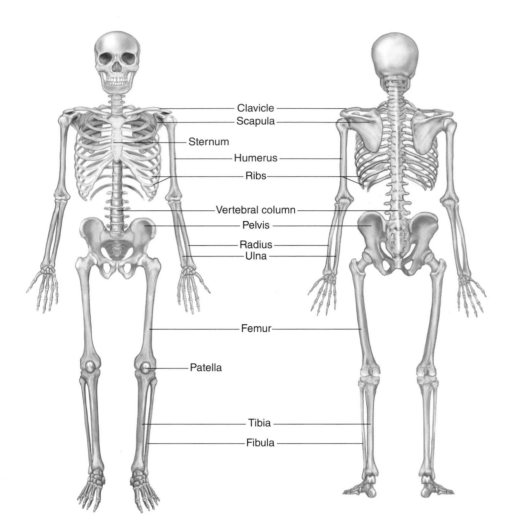

Figure 2.1 Skeletal system.

- *Neck muscles* support and work with the head and the body interdependently in creating total body movement.

All of these muscles work in synergy to create poses and movements that are technically and stylistically correct to achieve artistry in movement.

Joints

Joint types identify how the joints move, their strengths, and their limitations. Understanding joint actions can help you recognize how the body works and know the movement possibilities in various parts of the body during dance. Dancers stretch muscles within their **range of motion (ROM)**, the amount of movement you can make at a joint. Some types of joints are more applicable to dance movement than others. They are summarized here:

- *Ball-and-socket joints* have the most extensive **range of motion**. The body has two ball-and-socket joints, the hip and the shoulder. In the hip, the head of the femur (thigh bone), which is shaped like a ball, fits into the deep socket in the hip bone. This arrangement allows for the leg to outwardly rotate in the hip socket for ballet, modern dance, jazz dance, and other dance genres. In the shoulder, the humerus (upper arm bone) fits into the socket in the shoulder blade. Because the shoulder joint is shallow, it has the greatest range of motion and is therefore the most mobile joint.

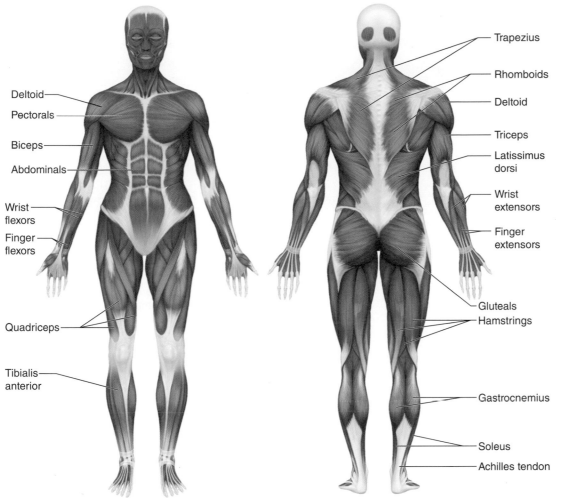

Figure 2.2 Muscular system.

• *Hinge joints* move only in one direction. Elbow, finger, knee, and toe joints are hinge joints. The knee is the largest hinge joint in the body and is considered a modified hinge joint because it not only bends but swivels on its axis. When the knee is not bearing weight, the lower leg and foot can turn side to side. Other hinge joints do not swivel.

• *Gliding joints* move mostly in sideways directions. The spine includes gliding joints in the cervical (neck), thoracic (middle back), lumbar (lower back) vertebra.

• *Pivot joints* have several functions depending on location. For example, the pivot joint at the top of the spine allows the head to swivel and bend, whereas the pivot joints in the forearm and lower leg allow the wrist and ankle to twist.

Connective Tissues

In order for muscles to move the bones, they must be connected. Two types of tissue connect bones and muscles. A **ligament** is a strong band of tissue that connects bone to bone. A **tendon** is a strong band of tissue that connects muscle to the bone (figure 2.3).

Dance Fitness

Dance and other forms of exercise develop strength, flexibility, and endurance. Some measures of these components are natural outcomes of dancing.

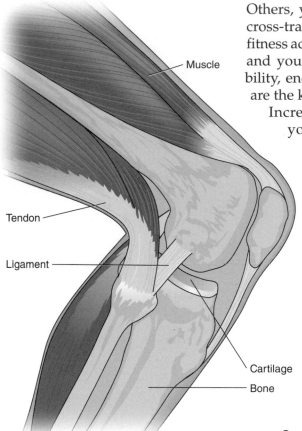

Others, you acquire or increase through cross-training—using a variety of other fitness activities that benefit your dancing and your quality of life. Strength, flexibility, endurance, and body composition are the key components of dance fitness. Increasing your fitness means that you strengthen your bones and muscles, gain flexibility and range of motion in your muscles and joints, and increase your endurance (ability to do something for a long time). Good dance fitness means you have the cardiovascular strength and endurance needed to sustain long movement sequences or dances that require a lot of energy to perform. Your fitness is tested during performance, but it is tested even more during rehearsals when you repeat a movement or dance many times to refine it.

Figure 2.3 Connective tissues.

Knee joint

Muscle

Tendon

Ligament

Cartilage

Bone

Strength

Strength is defined as the amount of force a muscle can produce. You need strength to dance. Using correct technique, doing conditioning exercises, such as sit-ups or push-ups, and weight training contribute to the strength of your muscles and bones. Core, leg, and arm strength are essential for safe dancing. Although some strength building is inherent in dancing, cross-training can help you get stronger. Scientific studies support strength training for dancers as part of dance fitness (International Association for Dance Medicine and Science 2011).

Flexibility

Flexibility is the ability to move a joint throughout an entire range of motion. Flexibility is an essential part of dance training, and you increase it through stretching. When and how you stretch affects the quality and safety of your stretching. To prevent injuries, your body must be properly warmed up before stretching. The end of class is a good time to stretch, because your body is warm. Some classes include stretching as part of a cool-down at the end of class, but you can also stretch on your own immediately after class while you are still warm. How you stretch is important to ensure the integrity of your joints, so be careful not to overstretch. Before you stretch, you need to determine how flexible your body is. You know your body, so you can assess whether you are very flexible or not very flexible or somewhere in between. Knowing your body's limits helps you know what, how, and how much to stretch. The first step is to learn and practice the stretching routine your teacher presents in class.

Endurance

Endurance is the ability to perform a movement for a long time. Although dance is basically an anaerobic movement form, you need a lot of endurance to perform a 90-second ballet variation, a 10-minute folk dance, or a 45-minute dance work. The longer you move at a moderate pace, the more you build aerobic capacity for increased endurance (International Association for Dance Medicine and Science 2011). Together, strength and endurance training are important components of dance fitness.

Body Composition

Body composition literally means what composes your body. Your body is made up of bone, muscle, fat, and other tissues in addition to water. In exercise science, body composition refers to the proportion of fat mass to lean muscle tissue in the body. The ratio of lean muscle to fat affects dance performance and overall health. Body composition is often expressed as a percentage of body fat in relation to the mass of the entire body.

Dancers requires both strength and proper positioning to safely execute a lift.

The World Health Organization indicates that a healthy range of body fat percentage for females is 17 to 25 percent and below 15 percent for males (International Association for Dance Medicine and Science 2011). **Eating disorders** such as bulimia and anorexia nervosa are of concern to health, safety, and wellness. Bulimia is a disorder characterized by binge eating and then purging. Anorexia nervosa is a disorder characterized by severely restricting food intake and an extremely low body fat percentage and body mass.

Body composition varies depending on the person and type of activity. The best body composition for dancers is one that allows them to jump, turn, endure grueling rehearsals, and get through intense performance schedules while maintaining their overall health. To perform well and stay healthy, all dancers need adequate nutrition, hydration, and rest (International Association for Dance Medicine and Science 2011).

FITT Principle

When creating a routine to enhance your fitness, it is helpful to have a set of exercise guidelines. No matter your fitness goals, the **FITT principle** helps you get the most out of your exercise program. FITT stands for frequency, intensity, time, and type.

Frequency refers to how often you do the exercise, fitness routine, or a physical activity such as dancing.

What Is Your Personal Physical Best?

Determine your physical activity interests and levels, then set goals for yourself. Like all goals, these goals should be written with attainable steps that will contribute to your physical fitness. Dance contributes to your physical fitness, and you have additional options, too.

To enhance your fitness levels, you can increase your time spent dancing to contribute to strength, flexibility and endurance, and body composition. You may already participate in activities that contribute this way, but you may want to try some others. For example, you can try yoga for overall strength and flexibility, Pilates for core strength and flexibility, weight training for muscle and bone strength, or a different dance fitness routine, and combine it with walking and running to develop enhanced cardiovascular endurance.

Sample one or more of these options, and determine which one is most appealing to you. Take into consideration whether you are most interested in gaining strength, increasing flexibility, or expanding your endurance. Find a fitness activity offered in your school or community and try it out. You may wish to take one or more classes or a short session to decide if this option is what you are seeking. Visit the web resource to conduct a personal fitness assessment and determine your goals.

Intensity is how much strength it takes to accomplish the workout or class. For example, in weight training it refers to how much weight you lift. In dance it could be how many times do you jump or leap or do strenuous exercise that takes a lot of strength and energy to perform.

Time refers to how long your workout or class lasts. Sometimes this is a static period because classes are a specific amount of time, but you can increase it with training sessions outside of class. Learning and rehearsing a dance increases the amount of your practice time.

Type refers to the specific exercise you are doing, such as dancing, swimming, running, weightlifting, and so on.

The FITT principle relates well to dance and dance conditioning. Participating in classes or rehearsals is a starting place for dance fitness. Beyond class, rehearsal and performance schedules increase frequency, intensity, time, and type. Additional types of training should be balanced with your dance schedule. Intensity and time extend with your studies and progress as a dancer. You may be studying a variety of dance forms, or you may be participating in only one dance genre. Learning more than one dance form extends your knowledge of dance and your abilities to think in different dance languages to express yourself physically and intellectually.

Basics of Kinesiology

Dance, like other movement forms, is a physical skill, so principles of kinesiology apply to it. **Kinesiology** is the science of body movement. Kinesiology principles applied to dance include these techniques:

- Jumping and leaping
- Pointing

- Turning and spotting
- Falling and rising
- Contracting and releasing
- Breathing
- Ankle and foot movements
- Leading and following
- Isolations

Overall, principles of kinesiology underlie other areas of dancing such as the development of your kinesthetic sense, learning correct movement techniques, using proper alignment, and other movement principles that weave through all dance genres. To understand how movement and body science work together each of these areas of dance will be explored.

Kinesthetic Awareness

No matter what movement techniques you use, your senses inform your brain about body positions such as standing or sitting or when you are in a straight or curved body shape. When you move in various directions or speeds, your senses tell you where your body and body parts are in relation to each other and in relation to space. Being aware of your body and body part positions while you are motionless or move is known as using your **kinesthetic sense**.

Dancers acquire this deep intuition of body knowledge when motionless or moving through proprioception or person perception that comes from the nervous system as a whole and through your kinesthetic sense that is informed by sight and other senses. When you develop a **kinesthetic awareness**, you develop a consciousness of muscles, bones, and joints in relation to space and you become aware of the entire body or a body part as it moves through space. To acquire and cultivate a kinesthetic sense, you need to feel how your body and body parts are positioned or move in space and notice the feedback you receive from these positions or movements.

For your body to learn correct positions or dance techniques, you have to observe, perceive, and sense your body as a whole and your body checkpoints of muscles, joint positions, and bone placement in your torso, legs, arms, head, and neck. Sensing body parts and their relation to other parts and to the entire body moving through practice becomes an automatic checking and adjustment process done subliminally; you do not notice or think about it. Once you acquire a kinesthetic sense, it allows you to concentrate on other aspects of dance performance.

Developing your kinesthetic sense through dancing increases sensory and body awareness. This awareness establishes in your memory an understanding of optimal positions to aid in injury prevention and to meet criteria of performing various dance genres. Moving with awareness entails calibrating your kinesthetic sense so that as it develops you acquire a sense of your body in directions, how body parts relate to other body parts, and how your body relates to the bodies of others sharing the dance space.

When learning proper dance technique, you use your kinesthetic sense to tune into your body position and movement and then memorize the sensory information so that you know, for example, that your arm is in the correct position

ACTIVITY 2.3 EXPLORE

Your Kinesthetic Sense

Stand in front of a mirror using what you consider good posture; with your legs and feet facing forward under your hips and shoulders. Take a minute to see where body parts are in relation to each other in this position. Take a deep breath, and close your eyes. Focus and sense the position of your head, neck, torso, arms, legs, and feet in relation to standing in correct posture. In this position, bend your knees as much as you can while keeping the full foot on the floor, then straighten your knees.

Open your eyes and repeat these vertical down and up movements. Focus on where body parts are in relation to each other as they move down and up. Beginning with your head and neck, sense each body part and their positions or movements as you bend and straighten your knees.

Next, standing in correct posture with your legs and feet facing forward and under your shoulders and hips, lift both heels to balance on your toes and balls of the feet, and then lower your heels to the starting position. Take a minute to sense where body parts are in relation to each other at the beginning, during the up and down movements, and at the end. Focus and sense the position of your head, neck, torso, arms, legs, and feet in relation to standing in correct posture as you move up and down.

Finally, run several steps, then leap into the air, landing on one foot; hold the ending position. Before you start, check your body position. During the runs and the leap, focus on body and body part positions as you move across the floor, move through the air, land, and hold your position.

In each of these movements you used your kinesthetic sense. You sensed your body and body part positions standing still, or moving parts of your body around a stable base, or moving the body through space. As a dancer you must continually develop this awareness. When the movements become embedded in your body, you continue to use kinesthetic sense to increase clarity and quality.

forward or to the side without looking to check that the position is accurate. Your kinesthetic awareness expands exponentially when you are doing a duet in which you and your partner work together in various positions, move together in the space, complement each other's movements, or accept each other's weight during performance. Likewise, moving with a group of people, your kinesthetic awareness increases as your movements interact with their movements in the dance space.

Alignment

Dance requires using correct posture, or **alignment.** In daily life, proper posture is the basis for a healthy back. In dance, good alignment of body parts creates ease and efficiency in body movement. A dancer continually checks and rechecks alignment before, during, and after an exercise or step and throughout a dance combination to ensure that it supports correct dance technique. Self-checking your alignment while you move in class will help you become conscious of it. However, dance class is not the only time to check your posture. Sitting, standing, or rising are good times to do your alignment self-check throughout the day.

Achieving good vertical alignment requires correctly positioning the parts of the body. The following checklist lists the steps for doing a self-check on your alignment. Do these steps in the order listed. Before doing your self-check, take a deep breath in and out. Then direct your attention first to your center of alignment, the pelvis.

1. The pelvis is held in a neutral position (neither forward nor back) and centered directly over the legs and feet.
2. The spine stretches vertically upward from the pelvis; the tailbone drops downward to help center the pelvis.
3. The abdominal muscles engage and lift to stretch the area between the hips from the ribs.
4. The rib cage is relaxed and in a neutral position (neither expanded or contracted) so that you can breathe easily.
5. The shoulders are level, relaxed downward, and aligned over the pelvis.
6. The neck stretches upward from the shoulder girdle.
7. The head is centered on top of the spine; the eyes focus forward.
8. The arms and hands hang out of your shoulders naturally and slightly in front of the body.
9. The legs stretch; the feet are positioned under your hips.
10. Both feet share the body weight equally. The entire sole of the foot rests on the floor with all toes stretched along the floor in the **full-foot position**. All five metatarsals and the center of the heel of each foot connected create a foot triangle. The body weight should vertically be centered over the center of the foot triangle.

When you are in dance class or even during everyday movement, keep these body part positions in mind like a map to guide you toward correct dance alignment. A copy of this checklist and a detailed description of how to achieve each of these parts of correct alignment appear on the web resource.

Alignment is assessed from the front and the side of the body. After viewing your alignment from the front, stand with your side facing the mirror and do a side-view alignment check.

Imagine drawing a straight vertical line starting from your earlobe, then moving to the middle of the tip of the shoulder joint, the hip joint, just in front of the middle of the knee, and just in front of the ankle joint (figure 2.4). If you can't visualize this position, have a partner take your photo, then try to identify each of these points to check your vertical alignment from the side. If you notice that a body part doesn't fall on this vertical line, then examine it more closely or ask your teacher for guidance.

Dance Safety

Your dance safety begins before you enter the studio and requires physical and mental checks while you dance. Practicing dance safety crosses all dance forms and includes a variety of components. Following are some general guidelines, procedures,

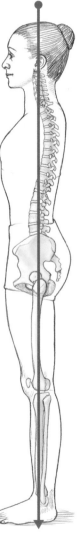

Figure 2.4 Proper skeletal alignment.

ACTIVITY 2.4 EXPLORE

Sense Your Alignment

Repeat the activity titled Your Kinesthetic Sense, this time while sensing your alignment. Begin by standing in parallel first position, and bend your knees while keeping your whole foot on the floor. Check your alignment—the position of your pelvis, torso, shoulders, head, and neck—in your starting position, as you move down, as you move up, and the ending position. Try this activity several times.

When you move vertically downward and then upward or upward and then downward, picture an elevator. Elevators don't swing back and forth; they simply move up and down on one track. If you sense your movement shifting forward or back at the beginning, as you move, or at the end, then use the elevator image to help you sense the vertical rising and descending movements you want to attain.

For the next step in this activity, if you are in the dance studio use a barre. With both hands resting on the barre, raise your heels so the toes and metatarsals remain on the floor. Do a series of these rises and returns to a full-foot position to determine whether your path was vertical or whether you shifted your weight over your foot triangle before moving upward. Or, on the descent, did you come down and then shift your weight backward to your heels off your foot triangle? If you noticed either of these shifts, then center your body vertically over your foot triangle before the rise, and try to keep the descent vertical to return to the beginning position.

and rules that apply to all dance. Your teacher will present specific guidelines for dance class, specific genres, and other events.

Dance Wear

Dancers wear specific clothing and shoes to dance class to allow their bodies to move without restrictions and for support. Dance wear may or may not be form fitting, but it should reveal the body lines made in certain forms of dance. In a dance class, your teacher should be able to see your body lines to determine whether you are using proper alignment and technique. Your teacher will provide you with dance wear guidelines for your classes.

Dance grooming includes hair styles and jewelry, which your teacher will specify. For safety, dancers with long hair generally secure it close to the head. If long hair is loose or in a ponytail, it can swing around as the body moves and hit the face or another dancer. For similar reasons, dancers usually don't wear jewelry to dance class. A bracelet, watch, or ring can connect with you or another dancer near you as your arm moves. If jewelry or props will be part of an upcoming dance performance, you should wear the jewelry or practice with the prop during rehearsal to get used to dancing with it safely.

Dance Class Etiquette

As with all classes and other social situations, dance class has some general rules of etiquette to support an efficient and effective learning experience. Many of these rules are traditional and demonstrate what is considered good manners, and they often are part of dance safety. In addition to this general overview, your teacher will provide you with specific information about arriving to class, being ready to dance, asking questions during class, leaving the class, and other topics that relate to your particular school setting. Following are some specific skills that all dancers practice.

A partner can help you find or sense a correct position.

PERSONAL AND GENERAL SPACE   As part of safe dancing you have to use your kinesthetic sense and other senses to establish your spatial awareness. **Personal space** is the space you occupy while either standing or moving through the dance space; it is like a bubble that surrounds you. **General space** is the dance space you share with other dancers and their personal space; it is like a big bubble housing small bubbles. Obviously the dance space can be large to accommodate everyone dancing, but sometimes the dance space is confined. In either situation the general space and each person's personal space must change to accommodate the physical space and the number of dancers moving within the space. In this situation, you must be continually aware of these changing parameters and how they affect your movement and that of other dancers moving in the space.

ⓘ ACTIVITY 2.5   DISCOVER

Your Personal Space

This activity is as easy as stretching your arms overhead, out to the sides, and down to the floor in various directions while standing in one place. With your arms outstretched to the sides, turn around within this bubble you have created that is your personal space. Dance is most often a group activity, so you have to respect other people's personal space while moving in place or through the dance space. In your personal space, move your arms and extend your legs in different directions. Then, do these movements again as you travel through the dance space. Move in a variety of directions while making sure you don't invade the personal space of others.

WATCH, LISTEN, DO Learning in dance class requires that you bring your body and mind to class. In dance classes, the teacher presents exercises, steps, movements, or problems to which you respond through movement or oral or written responses. When learning movement, keep in mind these three easy steps: watch, listen, and do.

When the teacher presents movements or steps, dance students watch to learn the movement. The teacher may place the class in a variety of formations or groups for a learning experience. While you watch a movement, you need to listen to the instructions for the movement and how the movement and the music (if used) relate. As you watch and listen, you must remember to prepare for the final step, doing. Doing is where you mentally and physically put it all together as preparation to execute the movement sequence or do it with music.

Once you have done the movement once, you still have more to learn. Mentally self-check whether you did all of the movements and if they connected to the music. You can do this self-check during the movement as it is taking place and again afterward as you rerun the mental video of yourself doing the movement. Learning to use self-checks helps you become responsible for remembering the movement. Applying both self-corrections and teacher corrections helps you to make the movement better.

Remembering and applying the teacher's technical corrections or feedback helps you self-check your performance.

Physical Preparation

Dance class can be physically challenging. During class you practice dancing safely to prevent dance injuries, but sometimes injuries do occur. Preparing your body for class with warm-ups and using proper technique during class are essential to injury prevention and therefore dance safety. Cooling down returns your body to normal from the exertion of dancing and gives you time to stretch your muscles. Both warm-ups and cool-downs safely prepare you for the next time you dance.

Warming Up and Cooling Down

Dancers warm up before dance class, rehearsal, or performance. The purpose of warming up is to raise the core temperature of the body and its parts through a series of exercises that prepare you to move. Warm-ups are a series of exercises that elevate the heart rate and include gentle overall body stretching to prevent strain or injury in the major muscle groups. Cooling down is a series of exercises done after dance class, rehearsal, or performance. The purpose of cooling down is to slow down the heart rate from dancing and stretch to prevent stiffness.

The dance class warm-up and cool-down can be general, or they can contain specific components. General exercises support all dancers in a dance class, but you may choose some specific ones to meet your body's needs. Exercises related to a particular dance genre prepare your body for specific classes, rehearsals, or performances.

Warm-up formats vary depending on the class and the amount of class time. Some warm-ups begin with increasing the heart rate through movements travelling around the dance space, while other warm-ups focus on gentle stretching movements of body parts to warm up the entire body. A warm-up can be a separate section that begins the class, or the warm-up exercises can blend together with executing dance movements and exercises, too.

Cool-downs may be part of the end of dance class or personal time after class. Cool-down exercises contribute to slowing down your heart rate and include stretching and personal reviewing of movements, steps, or combinations to help you remember how to correctly perform them.

In a beginning dance class, warm-ups and cool-downs are teacher led to help you learn them as part of the dance class. Later you can develop personal warm-ups and cool-downs for practice during other times before and after dancing.

Stretching

When you stretch before class or after class, you need to use proper body position to stretch the correct muscles, and you need to know how much to stretch. If you just stretch without paying attention to body position, you may not achieve your goal and could increase your potential for injury. The American College of Sports Medicine (ACSM) recommends flexibility training a minimum of 2 or 3 days per week, holding each stretch for 10 to 30 seconds to mild discomfort; 3 or 4 repetitions per stretch.

Another factor depends upon where you are in the flexibility range. If you are very flexible, then stretching does not have the importance to extend your range of motion that it does for a person who has little flexibility. Rather for the flexible person, the goal is maintenance of flexibility and acquiring strength to support it. For example, these two components will support your leg extension while giving you the core muscles to use in a leap or a huge jump.

Treating Dance Injuries

Because of the nature of the activity, dancers are prone to injury. Preventing injury is achieved through practicing dance safety and correct technique. Dancers routinely may encounter strains, sprains, or tendonitis, among other minor injuries. If you have an injury, immediately report it to your teacher and determine whether you should see a health professional.

Minor dance injuries from too intense dancing are common and may be treated with the commonly used **PRICED** (previously called RICE) method (International Association for Dance Medicine and Science 2010), **which** stands for the following:

P = Prevention of injuries by practicing correct techniques

R = Rest and refrain from dancing or other movement activities

I = Ice applied for 20 minutes at a time

C = Compression of the body part

E = Elevation of the body part

D = Decision if you need to see a health care professional

The decision of whether you need to see a health care professional should be considered soon following the injury to ensure proper recovery.

Mental Preparation

As with any other course in school, in dance class you process a lot information, so you need to clear your mind. Preparing your mind is just as important as preparing your body for dance. Mental preparation includes putting away thoughts about the previous class you attended, your daily to-do list, and any social or personal issues that claim your attention. Mental preparation allows you to focus on learning and enjoying the experiences you will have in dance class.

Stress is part of everyday life, which often includes demanding situations. Negative stressors are causes for *dis*tress, while positive stressors can lead to *eus*tress. Eustress is a heightened sense of excitement you can get from demanding but positive situations such as participating in adventure activities, the arts, and dance. Negative stressors can be physical, emotional, social, or environmental, such as a difficult break-up, not getting enough rest, or being sick. Deep breathing, relaxation exercises, regular physical activity, and laughter are some ways to cope with distress. Specific stress reduction exercises are included on the web resource for this chapter under the heading Additional Resources for Students.

SPOTLIGHT

Diana Dart Harris

Diana Dart Harris is an author and dance educator with a degree in exercise science. Her blog The Healthy Dancer includes a variety of topics related to healthy dancers, injury prevention through correct technique, and good nutrition. She writes to help dancers understand the science behind technique, health, and wellness topics. Her blog has have become popular reading for dancers and teachers. Diana believes that all dancers should be healthy ones and that dance can benefit everyone.

Thinking Like a Dancer

Dance wellness includes nutrition and hydration, rest and recovery, and self-care. As a dancer, you should be aware of how these components of wellness help you become physically and mentally prepared to dance and to enjoy the experience. After you read the following sections, reflect on your lifestyle, then consider what changes you can commit to in each of the dance wellness areas.

Nutrition

Nutrition is the food you eat that fuels you as a dancer. The right balance of carbohydrate, protein, and fat is necessary not only for dancing but for maintaining and rebuilding the body for continued healthy dancing.

As a dancer, you should consume 55 to 60 percent of your calories from carbohydrates, 12 to 15 percent from protein, and 20 to 30 percent from fat. If you are training, rehearsing, or performing at a high level, then carbohydrates can increase to 65 percent of your diet (IADMS 2005). You should eat meals around 1 or 2 hours before dancing.

To learn more about good nutrition and how it relates to dance and other physical activities, view the MyPlate website at www.choosemyplate.gov. This website provides information sheets about nutrition that can be helpful when selecting what you eat. The SuperTracker link provides the following:

- A Food-A-Pedia link to learn more about the food selections you make
- A Food Tracker link to learn about the nutrients and calories for the foods you eat
- A Physical Activity Tracker link where you can key in a dance genre and find information about how many calories you are burning while dancing.

Hydration

Adequate hydration supports healthy body functioning. You use up a lot of energy and sweat in dance class, so drinking enough water is essential for optimal performance during class and recovery afterward. On the average, one cup of fluid every 15 minutes is recommended (IADMS 2005). Keep track of the beverages you drink for a week, then take a look at your list. How many soft or sports drinks, milk, juice, or other beverages do you drink a day? How much water do you drink? Look at the number and types of calories in your drinks. Do they provide what you need to grow, maintain, and replenish your body? If you consume soft drinks or sport drinks more than water, then rethink what you drink.

Rest and Self-Care

Dancing takes physical and mental energy to learn, perform, and enjoy. To balance these intense physical and mental sessions, dancers must have adequate rest and ensure they practice self-care to keep in peak condition.

If you look and feel tired or perform poorly, you might not be getting enough sleep. Sleep is an important component of good health. During sleep, the body repairs itself and the mind rests. A good night's sleep provides benefits such as better stress management, eating better, and ability to learn better. To be at their best, teenagers and young adults need about 8 1/2 to 9 1/4 hours of sleep on a school night. Short naps can work to recharge you during the day. However, getting enough sleep at night is what keeps you healthy, smart, and energized to dance.

Self-care means paying attention to yourself in diverse settings. It is all about the physical, physiological, emotional, and spiritual sides of you as a person. Each area needs self-care for you to function well and handle a variety of situations in a balanced way. Physical self-care includes eating good food, exercising, sleeping, and doing fun activities such as dancing. Psychological self-care involves expressing yourself, reflection, learning to say *No* when you need to preserve some time for yourself, or trying new experiences. Emotional self-care entails spending time with others you enjoy being with, laughing, playing, and finding ways to constructively express anger. Spiritual self-care requires making time for spiritual activities, expressing gratitude, and helping others. All of these self-care aspects contribute to a balanced person who can function well in school or the workplace and enjoy a high quality of life.

Summary

This chapter explored the many components of safety, health, and wellness and how they apply to dancers. It began by exploring the difference between physical activity and movement as dance. Body knowledge sets the stage for understanding how your body works for practicing dance safety in all dance genres. Understanding body science is the basis for applying kinesiology principles for correct technique. Dancers practice fitness and conditioning principles to gain strong, supple bodies. Developing your kinesthetic awareness is an important component of personal spatial awareness and sharing the dance space with others. Alongside the physical demands are mental demands of performing dance that require attention for the dancer to work at a high level of efficiency and wellness. The healthy dancer is fueled by good nutrition, adequate hydration, rest, and self-care to attain optimum dance performance levels.

Formulate your health and wellness plan. Write a portfolio entry with your responses to the following instructions. Then, select some aspects to concentrate on and write about during the term. The following list includes health and wellness topics for you to think about in relation to your personal needs and lifestyle. In addition, you are asked to set some goals related to your overall health and wellness.

- *Conditioning exercises:* List three to five conditioning exercises or physical activities you believe would benefit your development in dance to support aerobic capacity, muscular strength, flexibility, and endurance.

- *Nutrition and hydration:* Summarize your calorie journal for hydration or nutrition or both, and determine whether there are areas you want to change to improve your nutrition or hydration over the term.

- *Stress:* Describe some of the negative (unhealthy) stressors in your lifestyle. Research two or three ways to reduce unnecessary stress. Try these activities, and decide whether you think these stress-reduction activities are effective, or if you need to seek others. Write what you learned about personal stressors, and identify effective activities to control stress.

- *Rest:* Record how much sleep you get each night during a week. Include a paragraph that estimates how much sleep you think will make you ready for the physical and mental requirements for your day.

- *Self-care:* List one or two self-care activities you do now in each category. Then identify one or two self-care activities you want to try during this term.

Write three to five mental and physical goals for becoming a healthy dancer during this course. Select two or three of your goals and determine how to implement them into your daily routine to enhance your health and wellness. Write your goal statements and outline in a sentence or two and your strategic plan for implementing them. In a week or two, reread your goals and implementation plans, and write a reflection on how well your plan is working or if you need to revise the plan.

REVIEW QUESTIONS

Multiple Choice

1. _____ For overall fitness during class and performance, dancers need
   a. strength, timing, and coordination
   b. motivation, flexibility, and stamina
   c. strength, flexibility, and endurance

2. _____ A ligament is a band of tissue that connects
   a. bone to bone
   b. muscle to bone
   c. muscle to muscle

3. _____The muscle group that gives the trunk and spine stability and abdominal strength for the waist and lower back is called the
    a. spinal muscles
    b. torso muscles
    c. core muscles

4. _____The three steps in learning dance are
    a. observe, talk, and do
    b. watch, listen, and do
    c. listen, do, and think

5. _____What is the purpose of a warm-up in dance class?
    a. personal stretching of the body to prepare for the class
    b. a time to socialize with classmates prior to the class
    c. raising the core temperature of the body and its parts

6. _____Kinesthetic sense is best described as
    a. muscles, bones, and joints sense as the body moves
    b. perception of how your inner body functions
    c. movement within personal and general space

7. _____Adequate hydration includes such fluids as
    a. water and milk
    b. sports drinks and soda
    c. juices and caffeine drinks

True or False

1. Dance technique is grounded in scientific knowledge of how your body moves as a dancer. _____

2. All muscle groups work independently to create poses and movements. _____

3. The purpose of the cool-down is to reflect upon what you have learned in class. _____

4. Anatomy is the science of movement. _____

5. The FITT principle stands for frequency, intensity, time, and type. _____

6. Dance class etiquette is comprised of general and specific rules for good manners in class. _____

Fill in the Blanks

1. The three major components of your body are _____, _____, and _____.

2. Dance wellness includes the three components of _____, _____, and _____.

3. PRICED is part of dance wellness and stands for _____
_____.

4. Three areas of injury prevention to implement into your practice include
_____, _____, and _____.

Matching

1. _____personal space
2. _____body composition
3. _____dance wear safety
4. _____range of motion
5. _____hinge joint
6. _____strength
7. _____flexibility
8. _____ball-and-socket joints
9. _____alignment
10. _____intensity

a. Move only in one direction

b. Appropriate clothing, shoes, hair, and jewelry

c. Amount of movement you can make at a joint

d. Space you occupy either standing or moving through the dance space

e. Good posture in dance

f. Bone, muscles, body fat, and all other body tissues

g. Amount of force a muscle can produce

h. How much strength it takes to accomplish the workout or class

i. Ability to move a joint gained through stretching

j. Move through extension, flexion, and rotation

To find supplementary materials for this chapter such as worksheets, extended learning activities, and e-journaling assignments, visit the web resource at www.discoveringdance.org/student.

Elements of Dance

ENDURING UNDERSTANDING: The elements of dance are used in all dance genres and styles.

ESSENTIAL QUESTION: What are the elements of dance?

LEARNING OBJECTIVES

After reading this chapter, you should be able to do the following:

- Recall the elements of dance.
- Understand movement principles.
- Apply music basics for dance.
- Recognize qualities, effort actions, styles, dynamics, and personal interpretation.

"Basic dance—and I should qualify the word basic—is primarily concerned with motion. So immediately you will say but the basketball player is concerned with motion. That is so—but he is not concerned with it primarily. His action is a means towards an end beyond motion. In basic dance the motion is its own end—that is, it is concerned with nothing beyond itself."

Alwin Nikolais, 20th century American modern dance choreographer

VOCABULARY

accent
beat
body actions
body shape
dimension
directions
dynamics
effort
effort actions
levels
locomotor movements
measures
movement principles
movement qualities
nonlocomotor (axial)
  movements
observation
pathways
rhythm
rhythmic awareness
rhythmic competency
space
tempo
time
transitions

Dance is a language that dancers use to move, think, and respond. Dancers learn specific movement languages that are part of dance genres, forms, and styles so they are able to express themselves clearly, concisely, and with fluency. Movement and steps could be considered the words, and grammar could be considered the rhythm. You combine these elements of dance to create movement sentences. When joined together these sentences become paragraphs and sections of a dance.

In this chapter you will learn the elements that are basic to all dance. Although all dance genres use the same dance elements, different genres might place a different emphasis on one or more of the elements.

Discovering the Elements of Dance

Dancing is the body moving in space and through time with energy. All dance uses the same basic elements in similar yet specific ways. The words emphasized in the following list present an easy way for you to remember the purpose of each element.

- The body or body parts is *what* moves.
- Space is *where* the dancer moves.
- Time is *when* the dancer moves in relationship to the music.
- Energy is *how* the dancer performs the movement.
- Relationship can be with *whom* or *what* (because dancing is often with another person, other people, or an inanimate object or a prop).

Each element of dance contains specific ways to move. These added dimensions provide possibilities to explore. Experimenting with the elements and how they combine in various ways interconnects and extends movement ideas. In this chapter you will encounter how these elements can evolve and expand to express your intention. You already do this when you present your thoughts and ideas to communicate to another person. When you dance, you transfer your perceptions and thoughts through bodily movements.

ACTIVITY 3.1   DISCOVER

Ways to Move

To get a sense of the basic elements for various ways to move, create an 8-count movement sequence with a beginning, middle, and end. Determine the *what, where, when,* and *how.* Then share your movement sequence with another student or in a small group. Repeat the movement sequence you have created, but change one or two of the elements *what, where, when,* and *how.* Then share your movement sequence with another student or in a small group. Or show your first and second movement sequence, and ask for a response to the question: Comparing one movement sequence with the other, which movement sequence do you think is the best and why?

Exploring the Elements of Dance

The elements of dance are the primary parts of dance. They include body, space, time, energy, effort, and relationships. Dancers use these elements to experiment with and then refine movement.

Body

Body actions are actions of the whole body, body parts, or body shapes. Being aware of the actions of the body in a pose or movement is part of gaining kinesthetic awareness of your body in space (see chapter 2).

Body shapes involve creating shapes that are curved, straight, twisted, angular, wide, or narrow (figure 3.1). Body shape designs are symmetrical (both sides of the body replicate the same shape) or asymmetrical (the shape of one vertical half of the body is different from the other).

Space

Space is the area through which the dancer moves. The dancing space defines **general space**, which all dancers share for their movement in the studio. Each dancer occupies **personal space**, which is the space your body takes up while standing still or moving through general space. The space your body occupies is **positive space**. The space around you that is not occupied by another person is **negative space**. As you move in your personal space through the general space, you adjust your movement to travel through negative space. Moving through space you encounter these other spatial elements that contribute to your movement:

- **Directions** in space include the basics of moving forward, backward, sideways, on a diagonal, in an arc, in a circle, or up and down.
- **Levels** can be low (from lying or sliding across the floor to kneeling level), middle (from knees bent to standing), or high (from standing to air movements) in the space (figure 3.2).
- **Pathways** are the routes created by the movement that is straight, curved, diagonal, indirect, or direct. Pathways can combine direction and levels on the floor and in the air.
- **Dimension** is how small to how large the movement is.

Movement through space is what dance is all about. Dance uses two basic types of movement: **nonlocomotor (axial) movements** in which body parts move around a stationary base, and **locomotor movements**, which enable you to travel across the floor. Nonlocomotor movements include bending, stretching, and twisting. Locomotor movements divide into even and uneven rhythms. Even movements are walk, run, hop, jump, and leap. Uneven movements are slide, gallop, and skip.

Time

Overall, the concept of **time** relates to the length of the dance determined by the dancer, choreographer, or the music. Other aspects of time include these basic elements of music:

Figure 3.1 Body shapes: straight, curved, twisted, angular, narrow, or wide.

- **Beat** is the underlying pulse of the music.
- **Rhythm** is the pattern of beats or sounds. Feeling and indicating the beat by using a simple word such as *pat* while touching your shoulders or knees is a way to check your beat awareness. The ability to walk to a steady beat

Figure 3.2 Levels: low, middle, and high.

develops basic timing and beat competency. Recognizing the beat and moving to the beat builds rhythmic competency (Weikert 1989). Listen to an example of a steady beat on the web resource.

- **Tempo** is the speed of the movement or the music. Tempo can be slow (adagio) to fast (allegro) to very fast (presto). Listen to an example of tempo on the web resource.
- **Measures** are groups of beats that are separated into intervals and have a primary accent (figure 3.3).
- **Accent** relates to emphasis on a beat or group of beats.

It is easiest to perform movement you create using your personal interpretation of its rhythm. Most often in dance, sound or music accompanies movement. The music creates the rhythm for you or the group to match your movements to the beats. The most difficult rhythmic activities are when people move to a beat they produce. Practicing basic timing and beat competency through walking and then dancing leads toward attaining **rhythmic awareness** when you hear and feel the rhythm. **Rhythmic competency** is when you have the ability to perceive and keep the rhythm automatically.

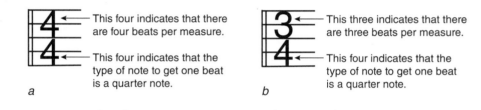

Figure 3.3   Examples of measures: 4/4 time (a), and 3/4 time (b).

Energy

When you dance, you feel the amount and type of energy as you move through the space to the music. Energy, sometimes called *effort* or *force,* creates the quality of movement. You can express energy in two ways: movement qualities and efforts.

Movement qualities release energy during different time spans to give each quality distinct features.

- *Pendular* movements have a light swinging quality.
- *Sustained* movements emit energy at a continuous rate as you move a body part or the body.
- *Suspension* describes the moment off balance before catching your fall.
- *Collapse* is a quick discharge of all energy in a body part or the entire body.
- *Vibratory* discharges energy in quick, repeated releases, most often using small body parts.
- *Percussive* delivers sharp, forceful movement, quickly halted, and punctuated by a sound. Without the sound, the term for this type of energy release is *abrupt*.

Effort is another term to describe energy or force. **Effort** combines time, weight, space, and flow in various proportions to create various blends of energy components.

- *Time* is measured from very fast to very slow.
- *Weight* varies from light to heavy.
- *Space* stretches from small to large.
- *Flow* of movement spans from bound to free.
- Movements are either *direct* or *indirect* movements or paths.

Twentieth-century movement analyst Rudolf Laban developed a system of describing movements by their effort patterns used in dance, sport, and everyday activities. **Effort actions** describe types of exertion; they designate a series of sudden or slow movements that are light or strong and use a direct or indirect path.

- *Dab* (sudden, light, and direct)
- *Flick* (sudden, light, and indirect)
- *Punch* (sudden, strong, and direct)
- *Slash* (sudden, strong, and indirect)
- *Glide* (slow, light, and direct)
- *Float* (slow, light, and indirect)
- *Press* (slow, strong, and direct)
- *Wring* (slow, strong, and indirect)

Notice the three patterns in the effort actions in the previous list. Changing from one movement to the next requires transitions. **Transitions** relate to use of

- *space,* such as change of levels or direction,
- *time,* or the speed you execute a movement, and
- *energy or effort,* where you control weight, flow, and other changes.

Transitions between movements affect the overall quality of movement in a movement sequence or dance. Making transitions seem fluid and effortless takes a lot of experience. Learning how to determine the intensity needed for an effective transition comes from trying more than one way to do it and practicing many times for seamless performance.

ACTIVITY 3.2 EXPLORE

Effort Actions and Movement Qualities

Divide into groups, and move to a corner or a place in the space. The teacher will provide you with a large sheet of paper that has a quality or effort action listed on it. Describe the term using your own words to characterize the effort action or quality. Or, draw a diagram to provide a visual representation of your findings about this term. Share your poster with the class.

Next, relate the quality or effort action term to various elements of dance. For example, explore body parts doing this effort action or quality. Try timing or speed changes for executing the quality or effort action. How does the effort action or quality react to spatial changes? After you and your partner have experimented with the quality or effort in relation to these elements of dance, together design a four-movement phrase using the effort action or quality, and explore each of the elements you just investigated. Share your movement phrase with the class.

Relationships

You can create relationships in a number of ways, such as between body parts of a dancer or with other dancers, groups, or objects. Creating and departing from these relationships give dancers many ways to use space, time, and energy or effort. Prepositions such as over, under, around, through, against, in front or behind, near or far, in or out, and on or off describe another aspect of relationships. With a partner or a group, additional relationships involve the following:

- Types of meetings: meet and pass, meet and part, meet and stay, meet and follow, or meet and join
- Lead and follow actions
- Directions: back to back, side to side, front to front, and other variations

This huge variety of movement options may seem overwhelming to read or remember, but once you get the elements of dance as a movement language into your body and motor memory, they will become more intuitive through practice. Eventually you will begin to think like a dancer, using movement as a language.

Movement Principles

Movement principles underlie dance genres, which are made up of the elements of dance. The movement principles are concepts based on body science applied for correct dance technique and performance (see figure 3.4). The anchor for movement principles is alignment, while balance functions as a static and a dynamic principle that connects to all of the movement principles.

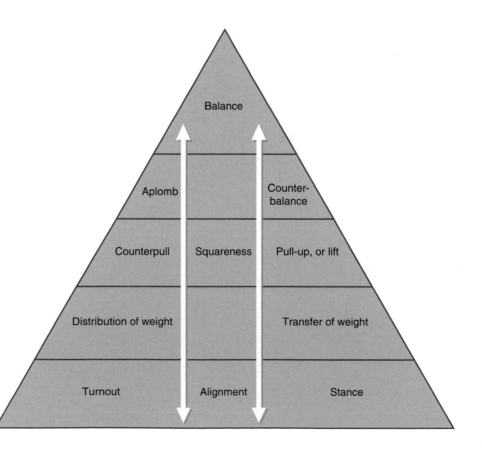

Figure 3.4 Movement principles. Begin reading at the base of the pyramid, and move upward.

Some of the following movement principles are more apparent in some dance forms than in others.

- **alignment**—The proper posture that allows the dancer to stand and move efficiently.
- **turnout**—The outward rotation of the legs from the hip joint. It is a feature of several dance genres (figure 3.5).
- **stance**—The weight of the body distributed on both feet and one foot and changing weight during movement (figure 3.6).
- **distribution of weight**—The weight distribution over both feet, the full foot, or three-quarter relevé.
- **transfer of weight**—The change of weight from two feet to one foot, one foot to two feet, or from one foot to the other.
- **counterpull**—The nonmuscular sense in which the body appears to resist gravity by pulling upward as the body descends.
- **squareness**—The hips and shoulders are level and parallel to each other as part of establishing frontal alignment (figure 3.7).
- **pull-up (lift)**—Stretching the legs upward from the floor while engaging the abdominals and extending the lift upward to lengthen the torso to the sternum. This upward sense is part of centering the dancer's vertical alignment (figure 3.8).
- **aplomb**—The vertical line on the side of the body that the dancer imagines when moving vertically up or down.

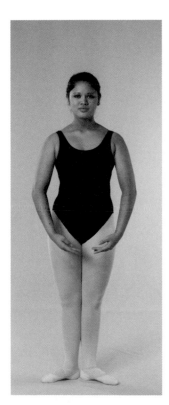

Figure 3.5 Turnout.

Figure 3.6 Stance: both feet *(a)*; one foot *(b)*.

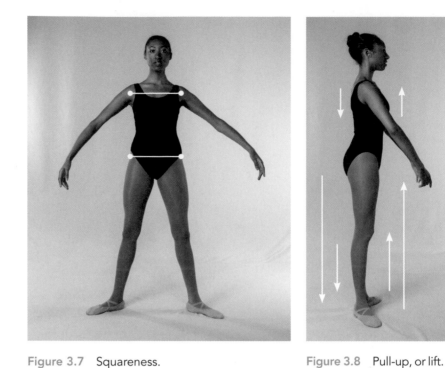

Figure 3.7 Squareness.

Figure 3.8 Pull-up, or lift.

- **counterbalance**—The upward and forward tilt of the torso when the working leg extends above 45 degrees behind to alleviate stress on the middle back (figure 3.9).
- **balance**—The dynamic principle of subtle adjustments the dancer uses while standing or during movement.

These movement principles apply to executing exercises, steps, positions, and poses. Hence, they apply to shorter and longer movement sequences and dances.

Figure 3.9 Counterbalance.

Dynamics

Dynamics is a combination of movement, energy, effort, and time. Dynamics change movements and their intensities throughout a statement, section, or dance, providing endless possibilities for expression.

Exploring the elements of dance separately and in combinations is learning the fundamental vocabulary for the language of dance. Expressing yourself through

SPOTLIGHT

Margaret H'Doubler

Margaret H'Doubler, an American dance education pioneer, founded the first college dance major program in the United States at the University of Wisconsin in 1936. She created and described the dance elements as the basis for dancing and dance making. Her work in dance education combined the scientific aspects of dance with the expression of emotion through movement.

the many languages of dance fluently and eloquently as an artist develops over time; it takes a strong commitment to continually expand your skills.

Thinking Like a Dancer

Dance movements or steps combine elements of dance in a variety of ways. They can be unique to each dance genre or shared by several genres. Inventing movement and learning the steps of a dance genre require thinking like a dancer—using movement as language.

Learning Movement Languages

Dancers become fluent in movement languages of dance genres, forms, or styles. They pick up movement language variations from choreographers, viewing and performing great works, or inventing movement and creating their personal style. Just as a linguist can translate one language to another, dancers are able to translate their observations, action words, and dance terms from one dance language into another. Dancers work to preserve the innate characteristics of the dance form and stylistic characteristics that are unique to the dance genre. The accomplished dance artist can quickly and flawlessly attain these highly complicated intellectual and motor skills. Acquiring these skills requires concentration and dedication to many aspects of the movement such as spatial use, timing, efforts, and movement qualities in learning to perform dance. This continued focus on details is how an artist refines a work.

Dance technique is the skill with which the dancer executes movements, steps, positions, and poses in a dance genre. When you use technique, you apply kinesthetic and movement principles along with other principles.

Observation is the process of perceiving through the senses. It includes viewing movement while listening to verbal instructions and the music for the information needed to execute the movement. Learning observation skills helps you to replicate movement or grasp the information to create new movement. Using observation skills is vital for memorizing movement and doing it correctly to music. As you move, you do some complex thinking to prepare for doing a step and prepare for transitioning to the next movement. These processes require a visual and physical (motor) memory to remember sensory movement changes. You should observe the subtle adjustments during transitions between movements to ensure that you can perform the movements consistently while keeping within a particular genre or style of dance.

◆ ACTIVITY 3.3 EXPLORE

Physical and Mental Rehearsals

Physical and mental rehearsal techniques are the basis for learning longer sequences of movement and dances. Developing a memory bank of movement is a continuous activity in learning a dance language and becoming fluent in it.

During your class, memorize a dance combination. After class, physically practice it by yourself or with a partner. Then sit down in a quiet place and mentally rehearse the combination. Visualize the combination. See yourself dancing the combination using complete body, arm, and leg movements. Then, visualize doing the movement to the music. Repeat the physical and mental rehearsals of the combination until you feel confident you can perform the combination. At your next class meeting, perform the combination.

Dancers use kinesthetic and motor memory as they dance. Cultivating mindfulness helps you focus on the movement, concentrate on using correct techniques, and apply movement principles. Mindfulness also helps you develop and expand your visual memory as a responsible dancer. It is amazing the amount of information a dancer's visual memory can store and retrieve to perform later. Sometimes dancers can recall entire dances that they and others learned and performed years ago. This complicated set of skills requires a clear mind as well as strong observation and memorization of movement, its nuances, and changes that come about through practice, rehearsal, and performance.

Practicing Roles of Performer and Audience Member

In dance class you practice your role as a performer when you present your dance sequences to another person, a group, or the class. Likewise, you take the role of an audience member observing these movement segments as an individual, a member of a small group, or a member of the class. The responsibilities of these roles help you develop as a dancer and a dance observer, and expand your dance literacy skills.

Performers must know the movements, their space pattern, timing, qualities or efforts in each movement, and their relationships to other dancers—essentially, the elements of dance. When you dance as a member of a group or with a partner, each person has responsibility for the movement they will do. Many times during a dance, your relationship with other dancers creates a picture or a memorable movement sequence that takes teamwork, timing, dynamics, and precision to accomplish. Moving as a group you can acquire similar breathing patterns and often share energy and movement qualities in executing movements. Using your peripheral vision helps you move while avoiding collisions.

As an audience member in class, you have more responsibilities than sitting and enjoying the dances. In class you have to be open and attentive to the movement sequences your classmates produce. Sitting quietly you can direct your focus on the dance. While you observe the movement, you are also thinking like a dancer and gaining dance literacy skills. You memorize movement sequences and capture the elements and how they were used to express the message. Discussion of the dances often follows their viewing. Making a response about another person's movement sequence requires some basic protocols that show respectfulness for the person and the work they have created.

As an audience member, you must learn to respond appropriately and productively to a dance performance. The following three steps open a dialog to talk about the dance work.

1. First, pay a sincere compliment to the choreographer about the movement sequence or dance.
2. Ask one or two questions of the choreographer whose work you viewed. You can rephrase possible questions for reflection in your own work for the work you just viewed, like this:
   - How might I make a specific movement or phrase more interesting and relevant to the dance?
   - Should the dance be revised, and if so, in what ways?
   - What other ways might there be to think about this dance?
3. Include a suggestion for the choreographer's reflection and consideration.

Responding to another person's work requires sensitivity to the person and the work. Before you speak, think through what you plan to communicate, and ensure that your response is respectful.

ACTIVITY 3.4 JOURNAL

Reflect on Your Movement Experience

Your teacher will provide you with several music selections and ask you to move to the music. All you have to do is move to the music using your rhythmic awareness and personal space as you move through the general dance space.

Dancing is a holistic experience where you tap into your perceptual movement source. Yes, you can turn off thinking about what you are doing and just express yourself through the movement. After the group experiences moving to a music selection, first talk about the music and its tempo, its rhythm, its style, and other distinguishing characteristics. Second, discuss how the music influenced your movement through space; your use of speed; your energy, efforts, and movement qualities; and your movement dynamics.

After the movement experiences, sit down and reflect on how you would describe two of your movement experiences. Write a paragraph to describe the various types of movement you did to explore two of the music selections provided.

Summary

Getting a grasp on the elements of dance gives you infinite possibilities of movement from which you can select to create or analyze dances across history and from any part of the world. This is the dance vocabulary, or language of dance, that is used in the processes of dancing, dance making, and dance appreciation. Seeing their definitions in words, looking at a photo, or viewing a video clip of an example are not the same as your own experience—having a deep understanding in your body and mind about what the elements are. Absorbing these elements of dance allows you to move toward fluency in dance so that you can express your emotions and ideas through movement.

Draw a concept map or diagram, or create a table that presents the elements of dance in a way that will solidify your understanding of the different parts or dimensions of each element. In a paragraph, identify the elements you believe you need to study more and why. Then, write a paragraph outlining how you plan to tackle this challenge.

REVIEW QUESTIONS

Multiple Choice

1. _____Dance is best defined as
   a. the body moving in space, and through time, with energy
   b. actions of the whole body, body parts, or shapes
   c. pathways in space where the body moves, jumps, or turns

2. _____A transition in movement relates best to
   a. changing from one style to another
   b. moving effortlessly to the next movement
   c. using various speeds of movement

3. _____In movement principles the anchor principle is
   a. counterpull
   b. balance
   c. alignment

4. _____A combination of movement, energy, and time best describes the term
   a. dynamics
   b. indirect movement
   c. dance style

True or False

1. The elements of dance are the basic building blocks of dancing and dance making. _____

2. The space your body occupies is negative space. _____

3. Dance technique is the way a dancer executes a dance genre. _____

4. Observation is the same as motor memory. _____

Matching

Match each movement quality to its definition.

1. _____ pendular
2. _____ suspension
3. _____ collapse
4. _____ vibratory
5. _____ percussive
6. _____ abrupt
7. _____ sustained

a. Quick discharge of all energy in a body part or entire body

b. Moment off balance before catching your fall

c. Sharp, forceful movement, quickly halted without sound

d. Quick, repeated releases of energy through small body parts

e. Sharp, forceful movement, quickly halted, and with a sound

f. Having a light swinging quality

g. Continuous release of energy at the same rate

Match each movement principle to its definition.

1. _____ alignment
2. _____ turnout
3. _____ stance
4. _____ transfer of weight
5. _____ balance

a. The weight of the body distributed on both feet and one foot

b. The proper posture that allows the dancer to stand and move efficiently

c. The outward rotation of the legs from the hip joint, a feature of some dance forms

d. The subtle adjustments the dancer uses while standing or during movement

e. The change of weight from two feet to one foot and one foot to two feet

Short Answer

1. List the three steps for opening the dialog to discuss a dance work.

 To find supplementary materials for this chapter such as worksheets, extended learning activities, and e-journaling assignments, visit the web resource at www.discoveringdance.org/student.

Basics of Dance Composition

ENDURING UNDERSTANDING: A dance has specific movements, steps, and patterns that may communicate or express an idea, emotion, or theme.

ESSENTIAL QUESTION: What processes and structures make a dance?

LEARNING OBJECTIVES

After reading this chapter, you should be able to do the following:

- Remember the process for making a dance.
- Explain choreographic principles and structures.
- Describe major choreographic works of dance performance literature.
- Understand aesthetic principles in relation to dance composition.
- Execute dance sequences as creative and expressive works.

"In dance, in composition, in sculpture, the experience is the same: we are more the conduit than the creator of what we express."

Julia Cameron, American writer, filmmaker, and author of *The Artist's Way*

When you go to an art museum, you view paintings or sculptures. Sometimes you see people standing in front of a painting for a long time. Often they walk and stand at different places in relation to a sculpture to absorb the meaning, composition, and aesthetics that the art work embodies. When you attend a music concert, you listen to the music as it unfolds to convey an emotion, a theme, or a vision of the composer. Viewing a dance is a multimedia experience. In a dance work, dancers move through time and space using various movement qualities and efforts to express an emotion, a theme, or an idea to the audience. The choreographer created the dance to inspire or elicit a response from the audience.

To create a dance, you have to know and understand the elements that are your materials for movement invention. You learn to manipulate these materials through a creative process while you use choreographic principles of design and structure to convey a personal statement through movement. Composing a dance is similar to composing in other art forms. Musicians compose musical scores, playwrights compose dramas, and visual artists create works of two- or three-dimensional art. This chapter introduces the basics of dance composition, the processes, and the structures used to design and develop choreography. The chapters in part II will present choreographic structure in relation to various dance genres.

! ACTIVITY 4.1   DISCOVER

Movement Invention

Begin by thinking about new ways of moving than what you normally do. Your teacher will guide you through this exploration. Here is an overview:

To begin this exploration, create and hold a body shape at a high level until your teacher cues you to move through the space to a new place where you create a low-level shape. Then hold this shape until your teacher cues you to move through the space to create a new high-level shape. You can keep moving, changing levels and body shapes any number of times.

Before you begin, take a moment to review the options for dance elements to try during your movement invention experience. The elements of dance are listed in chapter 3 of your book, they may be written in the concept map project you made, or they may be posted in your classroom. In your movement invention session choose a variety of elements of dance from each category during your experiment.

Body shapes: stretched, bent, curved, twisted (rotated)

Locomotor movements: even (walk, run, hop, jump, and leap) or uneven (slide, gallop, and skip)

Try the activity again. Select movements and body shapes that contrast with what you previously did. In this contrasting movement order you could incorporate the following to explore new movement qualities:

- Nonlocomotor (axial) movement into the body shapes: movement qualities such as springing into a high body shape that you hold, or melting into a low body shape on the floor
- Locomotor movements at different speeds
- Different pathways (straight, curved, or zigzag)
- New energies or efforts while moving in and out of body shapes

Your continued experiments with new movements increase ways to express yourself and expand your movement possibilities. What you have just experienced is sometimes called free movement, body storming, spontaneous movement, movement invention, or what musical and theater artists and dancers call **improvisation**.

Choreographer

The term *choreographer* comes from the Greek term that literally translates as "dance writer." The term did not come into use until the 18th century. Even through the early 20th century in some dance genres, the term *dance arranger* or *dance supervisor* or a similar term was used to denote the choreographer.

Discovering Dance Composition

The primary source of movement in a dance work is the **choreographer**, the person who creates the dance. If you were to step into the shoes of the choreographer, then the source would be *you*—your imagination, your experiences, and your movement. The source of movement for any dance can be internal or external. Movement can originate from your personal feelings, emotions, beliefs, or perceptions about a topic or the world. Outside sources for choreographic ideas could be nature, a popular trend, a social or political statement, or a universal truth, to name just a few.

Discovery is the adventure of going down new pathways or trying new things, then reflecting and deciding whether what you have learned fits or challenges you as a person and as a dancer. The movement discovery activities in this chapter provide new ways to find or extend your movement resources for creating dances. Dancers and choreographers use these types of activities to acquire new movement choices in their work.

Personal movement resources come from your internal body knowledge and past experiences. Your knowledge and experiences contribute to your **somatic awareness of movement.** Here are some ways to help you find and tap into these movement resources:

- As you explore movement, slow down to experience it, use your sensory awareness, and feel the nuances of each part of the body and how it relates to the movement.

- To awaken your kinesthetic awareness, become aware of your body and what parts move. These movements may create new sequences, designs, or surprises related to your movement.

- Breathe through the movement to find its energies, efforts, effort actions, and movement qualities.

- Allow your movements to release into gravity or gain support from gravity.

- Release muscle tension from parts of your body while you explore new movement options.

- Add to the somatic movement experiences with rest or **constructive rest** so that the body can process these experiences. Master teacher Eric Franklin describes constructive rest as resting in supine position (on your back with your knees bent, feet on the floor with arms resting across the chest). This relaxed position is a way to improve posture and concentrate on deep and relaxing breathing techniques to stimulate body awareness.

As you continue to view dance and experience your movement inventions, the movement resources in your body and mind are constantly increasing. Learning to connect to these resources is an enriching experience. As you participate in composing dance sequences as part of larger dance segments such as studies and then dances, you gain a deeper understanding of movement as creative expression.

Exploring Dance Composition

Dance composition is learning how to make a dance. During the dance composition process you explore a movement idea by creating dance movement or selecting steps in some dance genres, then you manipulate these elements and materials of dance into movement modules of various lengths to compose a dance. To understand how to use your tools for composition, you need to be familiar with choreographic design principles, structures, and devices. For a dance work to have solidarity and value, the choreography should connect to aesthetic principles that underlie art works.

In the Movement Invention activity, you invented two contrasting dance phrases (a short series of movements that connect into a pattern) or longer sequences. In the next activities you will create a **movement sequence** (a group of movements that form a unit), and then you will develop a **movement statement** (similar to a sentence). All of these movement segments contain a beginning, a middle, and an end. Coupling movement sentences together builds a dance segment similar to a paragraph in writing. Regardless of how long or short it is, a dance composition focuses on the beginning, the middle, the end, and on the movement between these points. Creating and composing the movement is one part of the **choreographic process**. Checking to ensure choreographic principles underlie the dance modules requires you to analyze your composition during the process and when it is complete. Table 4.1 lists the basic choreographic principles that underlie a dance composition.

The following sections lead you through the choreographic process as you compose your movement segments.

Table 4.1   Choreographic Principles

Elements	Structures	Designs	Devices	Relationships
Space Time Energy Efforts Relationships	Musical forms (AB, ABA, rondo, theme and variations) Narrative Other forms	Body shapes Pathways Symmetrical or asymmetrical Relationships (sequential, successional, oppositional, complementary)	Repetition Altering direction, facing, level, dimension, tempo, rhythm Quality or effort action	Solo Duet Group

Creative and Choreographic Processes

Different dance scholars present similar creative and choreographic processes. Some scholars write about the creative process, while others write about the steps to create a dance. Both processes underlie making a dance.

The **creative process** in dance making requires a period of preparation in which you collect ideas. This preparation time should include time for developing choreographic ideas; in other words, you need to figure out the central idea and how to approach it. Next you have to experiment with movement for a deeper insight into the movement ideas. In later sessions, you evaluate the movement and determine what works and what does not work as part of the dance work. The final step in the process is elaborating on the movement ideas you have selected.

Another dance composition process uses similar steps. First, observe the world around you, and explore ways of imitating or symbolizing what you have observed using bodies and movement. Working by yourself, do movement explorations and collect external experiences by observing the work of others. During the composition process, group reflections and discussions provide feedback that should be sorted out as to how well it applies or transfers to the dance in progress. In creating a dance, use your synthesized information from exploration and reflection. After the performance, a final group reflection helps to analyze the process and the product. Then extend the group reflection to a journal of what you learned and what ideas have been sparked for future choreography.

You should know the reason behind your writing activities in relation to your movement activities. Choreographic journaling has been part of dance composition courses since at least the last quarter of the 20th century, and this type of journaling continues today.

In academic dance courses, you usually keep choreographic journals to collect written records of your observations, movement experiments, research, and findings as you go through the dance composition process. Often you write about personal goals in the class and challenges you have faced during a course. You also write about how as an individual or in a group you responded to the process or what you learned from it to help you frame or propose your next project.

With the creative and choreographic processes in mind, the next step is to survey your ingredients for making a dance. In chapter 3 you learned about the elements of dance that play a central role in creating a dance. However, other ingredients also contribute to dance composition.

Sources of Movement

Creating new dance movements comes from exploring and experimenting with movement possibilities. Exploring new ways to move may take you out of your comfort zone. As you mentally and physically record these experiments, keep in mind that they may or may not turn out to be movements you want to add to your movement memory bank. But don't let that stop you from experimenting. Although it does involve taking movement risks, your experiments are being done in the safe setting of a dance class.

Improvisation is creating movement or movement invention for making dances. Using different stimuli creates new movement. Internal stimuli could include exploring your spontaneous individual movements based on touch, auditory, or visual sources. External stimuli could come from music, a work of art, nature, or an everyday task.

When a group is looking for solutions to a problem, they often brainstorm, and together they consider a number of options. Improvisation is similar to brainstorming; in fact, it has been called *body storming*. You can practice body storming by yourself or with a group. Doing movement improvisation with a group can

⊕ ACTIVITY 4.2   EXPLORE

Create a Movement Sequence

Using the locomotor movements from chapter 3, select two, three, or four even and uneven locomotor movements, and join them together into an 8-count movement sequence. Often movement sequences are parts of a longer movement statement. If a sequence appears to be complete, it may be referred to as a *movement statement* or *sentence*. This activity has two parts.

Part 1

Decide the order of the locomotor movements. Practice your movement sequence until you have it memorized. To add variety to the movement sequence, here are some ideas to try:

First, do the movement sequence as you created it. Repeat the sequence once at slow speed, then repeat it again at a faster speed. Changing the speed or timing on movements changes your energy or qualities of movement. Memorize these movement sequences in the order you chose.

Think about what energy, effort, or qualities you used in these repetitions and how they changed. Review the list of effort actions or movement qualities from chapter 3, and identify which ones you used. If you find a couple of undistinguishable efforts or movement qualities, try the movement again to clarify them.

Part 2

Now select two, three, or four different even and uneven locomotor movements or basic steps presented in chapter 3; these movements should be ones you are less comfortable with. Use these movements to create another movement sequence. Practice and memorize your new sequence. Again, perform the sequence four times using two or three different speeds. Then, do the first movement sequence followed by the second, or longer, sequence.

Reflect on these ideas about both movement phrases or sequences:

- The locomotor movements or steps you chose
- The differences in speeds
- How the energy, effort, effort actions, or movement qualities changed

How does the first movement sequence compare or contrast to your second movement sequence? Identify at least two similarities and two differences in movement, energy, effort, effort actions, and movement qualities when you changed the speed of your movement.

Summarize your reflections either on paper or in your mind. In a small group, take turns doing your two movement sequences following one another. Then present to the group your summary of the similarities and differences between the two movement sequences you created. Ask the group, "What did you see as similarities and differences after viewing my two movement sequences?"

Listening to the feedback of your peers may give you new ideas to try or to incorporate into your sequences. Observing others perform their movement inventions may give you more ideas to store away in your movement memory bank for future use.

be a lot of fun, and it allows you to gather or share new movement ideas. While improvising, use the somatic movement awareness principles and Laban effort actions. Experiment with how these important actions connect to space, time, energy, and weight to create new dynamics in your dancing.

During improvisation, the teacher can provide valuable feedback or suggestions about the movement or poses being created.

Sources for improvisation can be visual, words, poetry, tasks, senses, or someone else's movement or dances. These movement experiments or improvisations have several forms:

- **Free-form** improvisations are self-expression based on the premise of you moving and responding to music. This type of improvisational study can be a movement response to auditory, visual, textural, or a combination of stimuli.

- **Semi-structured** movement experiments solve a problem, answer the question, or have different points that the teacher or you determine as the criteria for composing the work.

- A **structured improvisation** is an experimental movement sequence that is loosely structured and practiced. Quite often a group work, the choreographer identifies movement sections or specific movement pictures that the group has developed during practice. These sections or pictures give the work an overall form and an artistic focus.

When you view or discuss an improvisation, you need a framework to help keep the discussion focused on the composition instead of on personal likes and dislikes. One system for discussing dance is known as **RADS**, which stands for using the following components: relationships, actions, dynamics, and use of space. Try it after a movement invention session or apply it as a self-analysis to your own movement improvisation.

Improvisation is a creative way to extend your personal movement repertory and styles. Practicing the many forms of improvisation helps you tap into your own creative force, enhancing your experience as a dancer and as a dance maker.

Dance Structures

Although the choreographic process is creative and involves exploration, eventually a completed dance work needs to have structure—a recognizable overall form. Some structures come from other arts. Because music often accompanies dance, musical forms such as the following can give dances their structure.

- **AB form** and **ABA form** present contrasting sections of music. AB form is a binary (two-part) form. ABA form is a tertiary (three-part) form. In ABA form, the first and third parts are musically identical.

- Theme and variations is a more complex form. The structure has multiple parts: $A_1A_2A_3A_4$ and so on. The A_1 is the theme section of the music followed by several variations on the theme. Often this musical form ends with a repetition of the original theme.

- Rondo form is even more complex with more sections: ABACAD. This structure begins with a main theme, A. The next section is a different movement theme, followed by a return to the main theme. After each new movement theme, the theme returns to A.

- Canon and fugue are still more complex.

In addition, for telling stories through dance and movement, these structures support dance composition:

- Narrative structures create a story-based or dramatic choreographic form. In this form the dancer is also an actor to convey a character or a role through movement, gesture, and facial and body expression.

- Open (free) structures rely on the dance or the idea to create the form of the dance work.

Trying each of these structures over time will expand your dance composition experiences. Sometimes the idea, the music, or the story line will dictate which form works best for a dance composition. However, not all music has to directly accompany the dance. Later you can experiment using sound collages or sound-scapes to support your dance composition.

ACTIVITY 4.3   EXPLORE

Creating Movement Statements

Learning to use the elements of dance and manipulate them to create compositions is learning to make dances. You made two movement sequences. At the end of the last activity you put the two sequences together. This activity explores and extends sequences into movement statements.

Building a movement statement is similar to writing a sentence. A dance statement uses the structure of a beginning, a middle, and an end to present a complete idea. A movement statement usually contains 8 to 16 counts. For this movement statement, focus on its parts in the structure.

Beginning

When you begin a sentence, the first word is capitalized. Your "capital letter" begins where the movement begins. Decide whether to begin your movement statement with an entrance into the dance space or to begin in the dance space in a body shape. Then, respond to the appropriate set of questions and instructions:

Entrance

- Enter the dance space from which side?
- On the side near the front or the back or from a corner?
- Try several even or uneven locomotor movements before you select one.
- Decide on a straight, curved, or another pathway.
- Where does your entrance movement end?

(continued)

Body Shape Pose

- Explore several body shapes (vertical, angular, curved, or twisted) at various levels.
- What are you are seeking in this opening shape? A dramatic shape, an expressive shape, a pose you have seen in sculpture, a shape prompted by a character in a movie or a book, or a shape inspired by nature or everyday life?
- When you select a body shape, be sure you can comfortably hold the pose for several seconds at the beginning of your movement statement.
- The shape you choose provides the options of nonlocomotor movement followed by locomotor movement. For the locomotor movement ideas, read the entrance information in this section.

Middle

Before developing the middle section, first create two new body shapes that contrast each other and are at different levels. If you used a body shape for the beginning of your dance, these new shapes should be different but can have some similarities.

Composing the Middle Section

- Choose even or uneven locomotor movements to connect the beginning shape to the two new body shapes in the middle section.
- Select locomotor movements and pathways as the way to move between one middle section shape and the next.

Experiment with different locomotor movements, levels, speeds, movement qualities, and pathways to move between the body shapes. Explore several ways to move into different shapes. Decide if the movement in and out of the body shape pose feels right and adds visual interest between the body shapes.

If you are unsure about this middle section, show your work to another person for feedback.

Sometimes you have to play with the poses, movements, and transitions to give them seamless connections or transitions.

End

The ending section of your movement statement is similar to the beginning. Select a locomotor movement that connects from your last body shape pose to exit the dance space.

Review your movement statement in your mind by visualizing the movement and shapes and qualities from the beginning to the end. Determine whether you believe you have created a cohesive and complete movement statement or you want to change any part of it.

On a blank sheet of paper draw a diagram of your dance statement from the beginning to the end. You can draw your body shapes and make symbols for the various locomotor movements and their pathways. Insert a key in your drawing for each locomotor movement.

Then, looking at the visual representation of your movement statement, go through it and answer these questions:

- What did you like?
- What would you change?

- What parts worked?
- What parts need revising?

Write your notes on a separate sheet of paper. Using these ideas, revise your movement statement. When you have completed the revision, change your diagram or redraw it, and write your responses to the same questions.

Choreographic Designs

Dance is a moving, visual art that communicates meaning. The elements for choreographic design are body shapes and movement, which you explored in chapter 3. When composing a dance, you choose whether the shape of the body is vertical, angular, curved, or twisted depending on the dance genre. No matter what genre of dance you choose, the body shapes and movement designs are either **symmetrical** (the same on both sides) or **asymmetrical** (one side is in a different design than the other side) (see figure 4.1).

Figure 4.1 Dancers creating designs: symmetrical (a) and asymmetrical (b).

Dancers move in straight lines, zigzags, or in curved or circular **pathway designs** through the space. Adding symmetrical and asymmetrical design elements into movement, you can create various formations and patterns. The speed you move creates the designs and the pathway. These designs and patterns could be performed in several ways:

- *Unison,* where a group moves together and creates a powerful impact on an audience.
- *Sequential movement,* which moves through a dancer's body, or the movement is done in a wave like a pattern through a number of dancers' bodies.
- *Successional movement,* where a number of dancers perform the movement one after another.
- *Oppositional* or *(complementary) movement,* which contrasts or reinforces another dancer's movements.

These dancers are moving in unison, doing the same movements at the same speed in the same direction.

Using these design components in conjunction with the elements of dance, as a choreographer you have a full assortment of movement to select and manipulate to create a dance composition. Similar to a visual artist but using movement as your medium, you can begin to experiment with these materials and design elements to create dance.

Choreographers have a concept that underlies their work and often a message they are communicating to their audience. At the beginning of a choreographic project, the idea for a dance may be clear, but it can also change during the creative process of developing the dance. As an audience member, your background and experience may be from a different place than the choreographer and the dancers. Just like good communication strategies, these ideas may connect or they may not. So, don't expect to always find a choreographer's ideas or message in a work. Rather, you may find your own meaning after viewing, reflecting on, or discussing the work with others.

Music Fundamentals

Dance and music often work together in creating a dance work. The dance is the central focus of the work you are creating, and the music in a dance composition takes the supporting role. Dancers learn to count the music and dance to the beat. So, whether you are dancing or dance making, you are a student of music, too. Therefore, learning the fundamentals of music will enhance your dance experience.

Music is divided into measures. In a measure, each note has a value (figure 4.2). Together the notes in the measure add up to create the measure in a specific time signature, also called *meter*. The concepts of beats, rhythmic awareness, and competency covered in chapter 3 are part of the basics of learning music as it applies to dance.

In 4/4 meter, 4 beats equal 1 measure. In a measure, a whole note equals 4 beats; a half-note equals 2 beats, and a quarter note equals 1 beat. Common 4/4 meter dances include a march, schottische, pavane, and other popular dances.

In 3/4 time meter, 3 beats equal 1 measure. A dotted half equals 3 beats, a half note equals 2 beats, and a quarter note equals 1 beat. Common 3/4 meter dances include a variety of waltzes, the mazurka, and other historical dances.

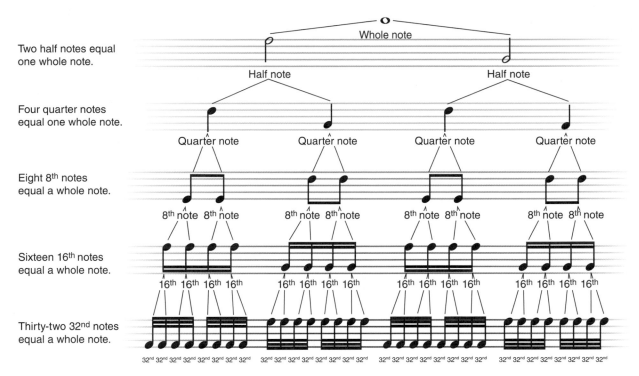

Figure 4.2 Notes and rests.

Other time signatures such as 2/4 meter relate to 4/4 meter while 6/8 relates 3/4 meter.

Common 2/4 meter dances include the march, polka, gallop, and can-can. Common 6/8 meter dances include the jig, the tarantella, and other dances.

Basic musical knowledge includes the following:

- Hearing the beat and distinguishing the notes and their values
- Knowing the rhythmic pattern
- Recognizing the time signature
- Sensing the tempo of the music
- Being able to count the music effectively
- Determining a musical phrase, sections, and the structure of the music

Now that you know these basics of music, practice them in dance class or apply them in creating a dance composition to further your exploration of the relationship between dance and music.

Aesthetic Principles

Like other artistic works, dances have underlying aesthetic principles by which they can be judged and evaluated. **Aesthetic principles** provide standards for determining whether a dance is an art work. Although the aesthetic principles may seem very abstract, keeping them in mind in the choreographic process helps communicate an artistic focus in the dance work. Learning to apply these principles takes time. However, developing an aesthetic awareness of how the principles work separately and together will enhance the development of any dance composition and your viewing of dance choreography too. Aesthetic principles for art works come from a branch of philosophy. Once you see how they work in the realm of dance, you can then shift these same principles to other art forms.

Dancers, choreographers, and dance scholars apply these aesthetic principles to specific dance forms:

- *Unity* of the dance theme, style, or movement choices throughout a dance work gives it wholeness and clarifies the choreographer's statement. See figure 4.3, which groups these principles together.

- *Balance* occurs when the different design and movement aspects of the dance supply an audience with a sense of proportion of a work.

- *Variety* of number of dancers or movements, speed, or dynamics holds both the dancer's and the audience's interest in viewing the dance work.

- *Repetition* of movement or a *variation* of movement or movement themes keeps interest, yet promotes unity by appearing in different places in a dance.

- *Contrast* is a way to stimulate the audience's interest during the dance or helps identify an important moment in the dance.

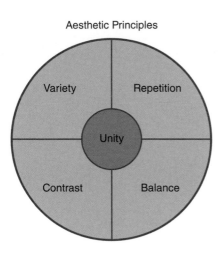

Figure 4.3 Aesthetic principles support dance and other art forms.

Artistry

Dance artists are dancers or choreographers or both. You begin your development as a dance artist the first day you walk into dance class. The first steps are to learn and apply the artistic demands of a dance genre. It takes some time to become familiar with body positions, exercises, steps, formations, and figures. Once you have gained a comfort level in a dance genre, then you can begin to refine your movements and techniques. These early steps in developing as a dance artist take you toward your goal of fluency in a dance language; eventually you are able to express the genre using its vocabulary.

When you learn and perform a dance composition, you focus on your dancing. After you have a solid memory of the movement, you can analyze how

ACTIVITY 4.4   RESEARCH

Viewing Aesthetic Principles

Select a short dance or a major work from a dance genre with which you are familiar from the list provided on the web resource. Before you watch the work, write and discuss the definitions of each aesthetic principle on your own, with a partner, or in a group. View the dance work while keeping in mind the aesthetic principles. Can you identify any of the aesthetic principles being used during the work? Write a sentence or two about what section in the dance contributed to each principle.

Air Mail Dances by Remy Charlip

Remy Charlip was an artist, author, and dancer. In the 1970s he created a series of dances that he mailed to a friend. Charlip created a number of "air mailed" dances with his dance friends around the world. He drew dance figures in poses, then mailed them. The receiver would have to invent movement to connect the poses into a composition. To view some of his contributions to dance, go to http://remycharlip.org/?splash=1. You can see drawings and photos of his air mail dances, read about his dance career, and hear him speak about his dance works. And, your class can re-create these fun dances in the studio. Better yet, draw eight different dance poses, and develop your own air mail dance to mail to a friend.

design, structures, or elements were used in the dance to hone your artistry. Likewise, this practice as a dancer can help you develop your artistry as a choreographer.

Dance artistry is a continuous self-check process. In this process, you determine what will be the next challenge to meet as a dancer and choreographer. These challenges can be technique, creativity, or intellectually based and continue to grow in complexity and subtlety. Your personal layering of these aspects is how you emerge and then evolve as an artist.

Thinking Like a Dancer

When a dance composition is presented, both performers and viewers have responsibilities during the performance. Much of this chapter has been devoted to the dancer understanding the creative process in dance—how to engage in movement invention that leads to designing and developing a dance composition. When viewing a completed dance, performers and viewers analyze the same components.

Viewing Dance Works

When viewing dance works, audience members see dancers moving to music and expressing or communicating a message to the audience. Dance students learn to look deeper into the dance to see how it is composed. They examine dance elements, choreographic structures, and how these components come together with other aspects of the choreography to create the dance.

Before viewing a dance, take a deep breath, clear your mind, and open it along with your other senses to receive the dance performance. After the work, take a little time to absorb it and reflect on what you have seen before you present your ideas. Then, answer these questions:

- Do you have an idea about the choreographer's intent for the work?
- Did the dancers use conviction in their movements and performance to convey movement ideas?
- Did the production elements (costumes, lighting, scenic elements) enhance or detract from the dance?

Using the dance elements, composition, performance, and production information, create a summary statement about the dance you viewed.

If a discussion follows the dance or performance, keep in mind or refresh your memory of the steps for responding to a dance composition presented in chapter 3. Once you have practiced them a few times, these steps for providing positive, respectful feedback will become second nature to you.

Experiencing Dance as Art

The performance of a dance work may contribute to dance performance literature. Not all dances survive or gain the accolade of being called a work of art, a major work of art, or a great work of art. Students in all of the arts study the masters and the great literature of their art form to learn the how artists use design, structures, principles, and elements in their works that have gained a reputation as a work of art. What makes a dance an art work is a question with many answers depending on who you are, what you believe, and what you value.

A work of art should have meaning for you. You should perceive the work through your senses. It may be aesthetically pleasing, it may be thought provoking, it may move you, or it may challenge you. No matter how you react to viewing the dance, the question remains: Is this dance a work of art? You think about it. You discuss. You reflect. You decide.

Summary

Dance composition is moving through the steps of the creative process and the choreographic process using the elements of dance to make dances. Dance works should have an underlying structure and an overall design for a cohesive work. This chapter presented you with design ideas, processes, and structures as well as information about music and other elements that contribute to making a dance.

Dance composition requires experimentation and taking risks, and not all risks are successful. There are no set recipes for success in dance composition; even with the knowledge of the ingredients, an experiment can fail. However, the most important outcome is what you learn from your experience. What do you learn about the work, yourself as a choreographer, and you as a person? These experiments in creating a dance are just like learning in any art form. The elements and possibilities of how these processes work have to become deeply embedded so that you can think and move from a deeply connected place to produce clear movement sequences with meaning. These skills are developed over time, so be patient with your learning curve in developing as a choreographer.

PORTFOLIO ASSIGNMENT

In this portfolio assignment, you can use movement sequences and statements you created earlier or invent new statements. A movement segment organizes a series of movement statements into a cohesive form, similar to when you write a paragraph. A movement paragraph or segment may include contrasting or similar movements, but it concentrates on a single theme or idea. For example, when you did the Movement Invention activity, the primary emphasis was on creating and moving between body shapes at high or low levels. Think back over the movement inventions, phrases, sequences, and statements you created while doing the activities in this chapter. You have collected movement materials to take the next step of composing a movement segment. Like a paragraph, the series of movement statements presented in order should have a structure—a theme for your composition. The movement segments together should be 30 to 45 seconds long.

A theme or structure helps you to compose new movement statements. For example, a theme such as *change* could be stimulated by many subjects such nature, science, or a personal experience. Dance compositions often use musical or narrative structures such as the ones listed earlier in the chapter. For example, using the AB musical structure, you can create a one-movement statement that could represent the A part. The next step is to develop a contrasting movement statement for the B part. Finally, you can put the two statements together to create AB form. Using this form, you could repeat both statements to extend the segment.

After you create your dance paragraph, analyze it. You can run through the movement statements in your mind, or you could video-record or write them and then review them. Using the Movement Statements handout on the web resource, look at the following elements of dance and identify how they were used in the movement section:

Space

Speed or time changes

Energies, efforts, effort actions, and movement qualities

Transitions

Structure

Design

Aesthetic principles

Then, revise and refine your movement paragraph.

Draw diagram of your movement paragraph or segment, or record the final version of it on video to include with your portfolio assignment. Then, write a one- to two-page paper. Dedicate a paragraph to each of the following aspects of your experience:

- Indicate the process you used for developing your movement paragraph.
- Explain the theme or describe the structure you selected for the movement paragraph.
- Identify the elements of dance that were used in the composition.
- Describe your steps in analysis, revision, and refinement of the movement paragraph.

- Outline the challenges and understanding you developed by doing this assignment.
- Summarize your overall experience in composing a movement paragraph.

REVIEW QUESTIONS

Multiple Choice

1. _____Free-form, semi-structured, and structured are components of
    a. choreography
    b. improvisation
    c. musical structures

2. _____The processes for using your body and mind together to tap personal internal creative and movement resources is known as
    a. body storming
    b. choreographic invention
    c. somatic movement awareness

True or False

1. A dance composition focuses on the beginning, the middle, the end, and on the movement between them. _____

2. The source of movement for any dance is external stimuli. _____

3. Dance artistry is a continuous self-check process of technique, creative, or intellectual challenges. _____

Short Answer

1. List the five aesthetic principles that underlie dance composition.

Matching

1. _____choreographer
2. _____dance composition
3. _____4/4 time signature
4. _____symmetrical
5. _____asymmetrical

a. Learning how to make a dance
b. One side of the body is a different design than the other side
c. The same design on both sides of the body
d. Four beats equal one measure
e. The person who creates the dance

 To find supplementary materials for this chapter such as worksheets, extended learning activities, and e-journaling assignments, visit the web resource at www.discoveringdance.org/student.

History of Dance

ENDURING UNDERSTANDING: Dance relates to the political, social, and economic events and the art styles of a specific place and historical era.

ESSENTIAL QUESTION: How have people danced throughout history?

LEARNING OBJECTIVES

After reading this chapter, you should be able to do the following:

- Perform dances from various historical eras.
- Identify dance, dancers, dances, and dance works from various historical eras.
- Analyze historical dances using dance design criteria.
- Connect historical dances to society and the arts during a specific era.

"Dance has been called the oldest of the arts. It is perhaps equally true it is older than the arts. The human body making patterns in time and space is what makes the dance unique among the arts and per-haps explains its antiquity and universality."

Anya Peterson Royce, *The Anthropology of Dance*

"Dancing May Have Helped Early Man to Survive" is the title of an article that appeared in a science publication. A headline like that gets your attention. From what archeologists, anthropologists, and other scientists have found as evidence in various prehistoric sites around the world, the title is possibly true. Scholars of prehistory have established that dance was a communication tool for early man. The headline holds some truth, because man is still dancing today.

Like archeologists and anthropologists, **dance historians** are detectives who seek answers about what happened, why it happened, who was involved, and what role they played in an event or a time period in history.

The history of dance is a collection of stories about people, the dances they performed, and why they performed these dances. Dancers first passed on dances by teaching them to their children, then by writing them or later notating dances using symbols to represent pathways and steps, and, since the 20th

century, recording them in media forms. The collection of dance literature that exists today represents a rich, diverse heritage from all over the world. Some dances represent values of tribal, regional, national, ethnic, or religious groups; they identify their traditions, rituals, and life-event celebrations. Specific dances are those performed in society or in royal courts during various historical eras. Others present dance as an art form with theatrical, entertainment, or recreational categories for specific groups of people.

Historical dance refers to dances performed from centuries since the renaissance through decades in the 20th century. This chapter presents an overview of the history of dance with a focus on historical dance forms. Later chapters each focus on a dance genre, and they include a brief history of that genre and dance artists who contributed to it and the history of dance.

Discovering the History of Dance

Dances come and dances go, but they often influence the next era of dances—even ones that are not similar to them. Dance has a strong link to society in a given time period. It is linked to historical, political, and economic events and to the art styles popular during that era. History and society influence dancers, choreographers, and dances; therefore, they influence dance as a whole. The arts affect dance and dance works, or dance inspires or extends other art styles and aesthetics during a historical era.

As you study any period in dance through its history, keep in mind these three guiding subjects: dancers, dances, and dance works. Awareness of these overarching topics will help you understand the roles and contributions of dance in each era of history.

- *Dancers* include the communities or groups of people who danced and dance professionals or artists who created dance works. Choreographers designed and composed dances, and other personalities such as entrepreneurs, patrons, artists, and writers contributed to dance works.

- *Dances* are the types of dances, dance forms, and their designs that people participated in or professional dancers performed in society or as entertainment during a historical period.

- *Dance works* include dances as part of community participation—what a segment of society does to preserve their heritage or traditions. Dance works also include choreography performed by people who simply enjoy movement and dance or by professional dance artists. Some dance works exist as memories passed down from one generation to the next, written dances preserved by dancing masters, or as notation of dances performed during a particular historical era. Film and video capture live performances by famous dance artists and dance works by choreographers and companies. The collection of dance works recorded in various types of media constitutes the nucleus of dance literature.

Dance is a difficult art to capture. Movement appears and then immediately disappears from sight, only to be retained as a memory in the minds of dancers, choreographers, other artists, and audiences. Having oral, written, and media records of dance allows people access to dances, major dance works, and the people who create these works. These records mean that you can view, restage,

Library of Congress

The Library of Congress has an extensive website. In addition to in-depth overviews of dance since the Middle Ages, it has links to electronic versions of dance manuals, which you can read online. The site also includes a number of video clips so that you can view them, study them, and re-create steps and dances.

ACTIVITY 5.1   RESEARCH

Create a Timeline

Create a dance history timeline from prehistory to the present. The timeline can be a single timeline that focuses on one or more topics such as dancers, dances, and dance works during a historical era or century. Some timelines contain multiple topics, or comparative timelines include in addition to dance topics: other art works that relate to the history of dance, historical events, or technological inventions. For example, the romantic era of the early 19th century began as a literary movement in the last half of the 18th century to focus on humans and their emotions. Romanticism as an art style became popular in novels and poetry, and then was embraced by theater and then dance. Romantic ballets captured the escapism of this art style with dramatic story ballets centered around young women from past historical eras or far-away places. Often the female heroines were caught in love triangles or became fantastic or spiritual beings to resolve their romantic entanglements. Romantic ballets were the 19th century version of today's soap operas.

A simple timeline of a historical era and its time span can feature:

- Dancers, choreographers, and other personalities
- Dances, dance types, or dance forms
- Dance works

These topics provide the information you need for your dance history timeline. Your teacher will guide you as to how much detail to include in your timeline. Later chapters on specific dance genres will provide additional information for the dance history timeline.

You can draw a timeline or find a timeline template for this project on the Internet. In building any timeline, sometimes it is difficult to determine how many pages you will need for one historical era. The first section of the timeline will be dance in the prehistoric period. Beginning with ancient civilizations, you may need to add one or more pages to the timeline as you move from one historical time period to the next. Timelines can contain short pieces of written information, and they may include pictures of famous dancers, choreographers, and dance works.

To create your timeline, first read this chapter. Then using other resources, identify the major time periods such as prehistory, ancient, medieval, renaissance, and so on. You can work with your classmates to compare several sources and verify the date ranges for each time period.

read, analyze, listen, and respond to dance performances and related dance literature about many topics. Awareness of the vast repository of dance works contributes to your dance literacy.

The subjects of dancers, dances, and dance works are the driving forces in the history of dance. Together these subjects work to present an integrated view of the history of dance against the tapestry of history, society, and the arts.

Exploring the History of Dance

This exploration of dance history begins as you learn about dance in each historical period. If you find an era that piques your interest, you can search for more resources to expand your knowledge of the historical time, how dance interacted with society, and other arts during that time.

Prehistory

People danced over millennia of **prehistory** (time before the advent of writing) in order to remember and teach their communal knowledge, tribal traditions, myths, and stories to the next generation. People used dance as a method of communication before they used spoken language and writing (figure 5.1). People danced to teach basic life skills such as hunting, war, and spiritual or religious rituals to ensure continuation of the tribe through fertility dances, and to acknowledge a person's changing role in the community. People danced to acknowledge personal and community achievements, recognize victories or defeats in battles, or celebrate life events such as puberty, courtship, marriage, healing, and death. Dance was the medium of communication in a community or between two tribes or communities.

Outer aspects of the dancer (Relation to environment)

General way of moving = basic subsistence pattern

Specific way of moving = temperature, clothing

Symbolic content of movement Mimetic movements + costume + paraphernalia = environment + basic subsistence + mythic complex

Outer aspects of the dancer (Relation to society)

The event (ritual, rite)

Rites of passage: individual
• birth
• puberty
• marriage
• death

Rites of passage: group
• war
• catastrophe

Rites of passage: seasonal

Secondary aspects of the dancer

As musician
As audience

Inner aspects of the dancer

Stimulation
Transformation
Unification (with group or society)

Figure 5.1 The dancer and the dance in nonliterate societies.

Prehistoric people moved from being nomads to agriculture-based communities who settled in areas where they could grow crops to feed the community. As people developed methods of transportation by land or water, they moved and explored new unsettled areas. They created new communities, which grew into towns and cities. Technology increased the development of tools and goods that in turn increased commerce.

ACTIVITY 5.2 EXPLORE

Create a Prehistoric Dance

Archeologists and anthropologists who study prehistoric eras confirmed the existence of prehistoric dances in various regions of the world through artifacts such as rock art, drawings, and sculptures. Prehistoric dances used everyday movements to celebrate family, community, and life events. A shaman, a spiritual leader or healer in the community, led some dances. Prehistoric communities participated in these types of dances:

- *Life span dances* celebrated birth, coming of age, courtship, marriage rituals, and death.
- *Weapons and war dances* prepared for hunting or war by practicing weapon skills.
- *Agricultural dance events* such as planting or harvesting offered ways to safeguard the tribe or clan's food and survival.
- *Medicine or healing dances* ensured the health of the tribe and healed the sick or wounded. The shaman often performed these dances.
- *Supernatural, spiritual, and religious dances* praised and appeased the gods, ancestors, and elements of nature and the environment such as the sun, the rain, and celestial bodies.
- Other dances included dances that honored tribal leaders or visitors, victory dances after hunting or war, and dances of mourning the dead.

In a group, select a theme from prehistoric life, and create a movement sequence to represent it. The movement sequence could be based on what you know about prehistoric people and their lives or what you imagine a prehistoric dance might be. Create four to eight movements, and put them together as a movement statement that communicates a personal or community event or theme. Practice the movement statement with your group, and repeat it at least four times. As a class, each group can show the movement sequence without telling the audience what the event or theme is. Then the audience can guess each group's theme.

Ancient Civilizations

Throughout the ancient world, cities and states developed across the globe. Dance remained part of life events, religious activities, social celebrations, recreation, and entertainment. Ancient civilizations included people who settled there because of agricultural advantages, war, migrations, or commerce.

In the Egyptian civilization dance was part of religion and entertainment. Professional dancers were trained performers for entertainment hosted by nobility or the rich to celebrate personal or state occasions or they led funeral processions of Egyptian nobility. Male and female dancers are drawn in dance poses on the tomb walls with hieroglyphs to describe the dances (figure 5.2).

In ancient Greece, dance was valued as a part of society. In the golden age of Greece (around 500 BCE), a person was considered educated if he could dance. Ancient Greek citizens celebrated life events, rituals, and religious activities that later transformed into theatrical art.

Weapon and military dances trained young Athenian Greek males as athletes and as warriors for battle. They practiced movements using weapons and participated in mock

Figure 5.2 Hieroglyphs depicting an Egyptian pair dancing.

combat. In Sparta, men and women performed military dances. After battles, warriors reenacted mock battles for the community, and they danced to celebrate their victory or to mourn their dead.

Wedding rituals celebrated the marriage ceremony. In Athens, guests followed the couple in a wedding procession to their new home. The guests sang, leaped, whirled, and stamped in a manner similar to ancient fertility rituals. In Sparta, the wedding couple and their guests danced before the altar.

Funeral dances were processions to the tomb. Following the family and friends, professional mourners performed symbolic gestures such as twisting their hands or beating their chests as they chanted and did processional dances.

Ancient Greeks danced in sacred places to communicate with the gods. Some religious cults danced as part of their rituals. Dionysian cults included women known as *maenads* and men known as *satyrs.* These cults believed that the Greek god Dionysus took control of their minds and actions; as a result, they performed wild dances. Later these activities evolved into a hymn and circular dance around the altar to honor Dionysus.

Stories and myths accompanied by singing, acting, music, and dancing along with hymns to Dionysus developed into three forms of Greek drama presented in huge, outdoor theaters. At the Festival of Dionysus, actors, a chorus, and musicians performed tragedies, comedies, and satyr plays. An onstage chorus supported the actors in these plays. The male chorus members were moving or singing throughout the play. For tragedy the chorus used powerful, symbolic gestures as they moved as a group. In comedies the chorus did quick, light movements, mimed fights, and played games. For the satyr plays, the chorus danced in groups, and they engaged in acrobatics and physical jokes like the slapstick comedy of early 20th-century silent movies.

A Greek dance circa 400 BC from a tomb painting.

In ancient Rome, dance was religious, social, and done for entertainment. Young aristocrats trained in dance as part of their education and to learn social graces. Dancing priests called *salli* worshiped the Roman god Mars and led religious ceremonies with their dances. Male and female professional dancers and acrobats performed in religious and secular events such as festivals. Roman pantomimists wore masks and used movement without words to tell legends, myths, and stories. Accompanied by a flute and a man who tapped out a rhythm, the pantomimists posed like statues, gestured, twirled, and leaped to the music as they told their tales. As centuries passed and the Roman Empire expanded, dance became primarily entertainment at special holidays or events.

From the Dark and Middle Ages to the Renaissance

After Rome fell, hoards of barbarians roamed the known western world. Their destruction led to many centuries in which the civilization of the former Western Roman Empire went into hibernation while civilization flourished in Byzantium, the former capital of the Eastern Roman Empire. In the west, monasteries and isolated feudal landowners survived. Monasteries became religious sanctuaries for people fleeing from war and destruction and where monks copied books to preserve the knowledge of the ancient world. Powerful landowners became feudal lords, who built walled castles and fortresses. People seeking protection farmed a lord's land in exchange for his protection. Armies led by knights fought to increase the lords' property holdings. These isolated feudal communities were self-sustainable cities that could withstand siege. Throughout the Dark Ages and into the Middle Ages, the two most powerful forces were the Catholic church and the growing strength of the nobility. In the Middle Ages dances were associated with the church as sacred or in society as secular.

With the everyday drudgery of hard labor and continued fear of attack, peasants and nobility welcomed events or amusements. For all, dance was an amusement that celebrated the agricultural seasons, life events, religious holidays, and feasts. Throughout the Middle Ages, peasants danced for holidays and feast days. These dances began as pagan practices or rituals from the distant past; over the centuries they were absorbed into religious or other holiday celebrations. In the castle, dance was amusement and entertainment for the nobility where knights and nobles danced with ladies of the court. The nobility danced through the great hall in their lavish attire to present their status in the court. Minstrels and troubadours traveled from castle to castle to entertain; they brought the latest news and songs, taught new dances, and hosted important events in castle life.

The renaissance began in Italy, where the aristocracy loved entertainment. They produced lavish events to welcome traveling royalty, to celebrate marriages, and for political events. Royal houses often had a resident dance master to teach the latest dances along with manners and etiquette expected at court. Dancing was considered an important measure to determine a person's standing in court society. Gentlemen and ladies danced, or they watched talented courtiers perform. Court performances were held either indoors in the great halls or out of doors, such as equestrian ballets, parades, and events with casts of thousands that would rival present-day Olympic opening and closing ceremonies.

During the Middle Ages, dances were classified as **high (haut) dances** with kicking, jumping or hopping movements and **low (basse) dances** that glided smoothly across the floor. In the renaissance, dance suites emerged that strongly related to existing musical forms. First, a **two-part suite** included the pavane and the galliard. Later, a **four-part suite** of dances contained the allemande, courante, sarabande, and gigue. Dance entertainment events at court were often extravagant dance masquerade parties with dancing for the court.

ACTIVITY 5.3　EXPLORE

Dance in the Middle Ages

Society in the Middle Ages was agrarian in nature. Peasants and farmers danced to celebrate life events and seasonal agricultural activities. Feudal courts housed the nobility, knights, and visiting minstrels or troubadours. The aristocracy danced to celebrate life and seasonal events, for court-related occasions, and for amusement. An overview of dances from the Middle Ages will acquaint you with some of the most popular dances. Once you have read this overview, choose a dance you want to learn. Your teacher will guide the class in learning the dances.

Carole

The **carole** was a circular or processional dance accompanied by song. The dance was performed for centuries on church holidays and on festivals such as New Year's Day, May Day, and midsummer. The leader and members of the group held hands in circular or line formations. The dancers walked to the beat of the music and turned their bodies right or left during this walking dance.

Farandole

Peasants and courtiers performed the **farandole** to celebrate the coming of spring. The farandole was a chain dance; people held hands and sang as they ran or skipped to music. The dancers' path wove through the community, moving through houses and around buildings, trees, and wells as they welcomed spring. A choral line dance, the farandole included several figures such as threading the needle, many arches, and the snail.

Basse Danse

A slow dignified walking processional dance from the later middle ages and into the renaissance. Nobles, knights, and ladies of the court performed the **basse danse**. People formed a procession of dancers as trios (two men and one women or vice versa) or groups of four. The dance began with a bow to partners. The gentlemen held the ladies' fingertips loosely or they did not touch. The dancer group glided across the floor gracefully walking, conversing, and displaying their court attire and etiquette.

Branle

Both peasants and nobility performed the **branle**. This group dance of couples was performed in a circle. The dance steps moved counterclockwise to the left and then clockwise using smaller steps. The man's partner stood on his right. The dancers held hands or hooked little fingers. Some dances included short pantomimed sections. Branles were popular dances that varied from region to region.

Once you have chosen a dance to learn, form a group with others who have chosen the same dance. Together select music, then learn and practice this dance with guidance from your teacher.

In 1581, Catherine de' Medici, the queen of France, commissioned what has since become known as the first ballet, *Le Ballet Comique de la Reine*. The ballet made France the recognized leader for future dance developments in the French court. Staged by her court musician, Balthasar de Beaujoyeulx, courtiers danced and sang, and they recited poetry presenting the story of Circe. In reality, the ballet was one of many amusements to distract the court from the political activities of the monarch. A libretto, or written text, of the ballet was sent to courts far and wide, and it inspired other ballet productions. During Catherine's reign she commanded many ballets de cour, or court ballet productions. The production of *Le Ballet Comique de la Reine* is considered a defining moment in dance history—when dance development transferred from Italy to France.

Louis XIV in the role of *Le Roi Soleil*, the Sun King, 1653.

Seventeenth Century

In the 17th century, the French court dominated the dance scene. During this period, a powerful line of French kings danced, staged, and advocated for dance. **Louis XIV** of France built on the work of his forefathers. He is often associated with one of his most famous dancing roles, the Sun King. During his reign, he commissioned over 1,000 ballets and decreed the development of the Académie Royale de Danse (Royal Academy of Dance). The king favored ballets on classical themes with dancers portraying gods and goddesses. In these court ballets, male professional dancers and male and female courtiers performed popular social dances of the day with intricate figures and geometric designs as entertainment for the court. Under the patronage of Louis XIV dance became transformed from an amateur court amusement to providing professional training for dancers and rules of conduct for them through the Royal Academy of Dance.

Eighteenth Century

At the beginning of the 18th century, dancing interludes were interjected into an opera or between acts of drama. Until the death of Louis XIV, ballets continued as entertainment for the court. The Royal Academy evolved into the Paris Opéra and became the center for dance innovation. During the 18th century French dancers migrated to major cities and courts across Western Europe and Russia. These new performance settings provided patronage and financial support for creating new ballets and entertainment. They became places to train the next generation of dancers. The term *choreographer* did not come into use until the 18th century.

Dancers and ballet masters took their works to courts and theaters throughout Europe. Male dancers continued in major dance roles and other artistic roles. Female dancers implemented costume and shoe innovations and took more important roles in the ballets. In 1760, Jean-Georges Noverre authored *Lettres sur la danse et sur les ballet* that identified ballet as an art independent from opera. This new form of ballet, *ballet d'action*, became a self-contained dramatic work with a story told through dance and pantomime.

At the French court, the **minuet** became the major dance of the first part of the 18th century. Hence this period has been called the age of the minuet. The minuet is a couple dance in 3/4 time or other triple meters. The man and woman perform the steps in S or Z figures. In ballrooms, dancers did the minuet and an array of other popular court dances.

During the latter part of the 18th century, **country dances** (contradanses or contradances) from the renaissance became more fashionable as the French king and his court's popularity declined. Some contradances, also known as longways, were performed by couples in two lines facing each other. The dancers chose the order of the steps, and the lead couples changed during the dance. Contradance later became popular in England and in America.

The French Revolution caused dancers and dance masters to relocate across Europe and to America. Other popular dances were lively Scottish reels and jigs. Court dances from the previous century such as gigues, sarabandes, courantes, and other dances continued until the French Revolution. Although many differences were developing between dance performed onstage and dance in society, many similarities remained, too.

An 18th-century dancing master.

ACTIVITY 5.4 EXPLORE

Minuet or Country Dance?

Choose whether you would like to learn the minuet or a country dance, and divide into groups accordingly. With guidance from your teacher, learn, rehearse, and perform one or both of these dances.

As a class, discuss and record these characteristics of each dance:

- The types of movements or steps
- The number of people dancing
- The dance structure and type
- The accompaniment
- Costumes and accessories
- The performing space and the time of the day

Analyze how space, time, energy, and other elements were used within the dance. Finally, answer the continuing questions (who, where, when, and why) in relation to the dance you performed.

Nineteenth Century

The nineteenth century ushered in the Industrial Revolution, followed by numerous wars and continuous economic changes that left uncertain times. During the 19th century, ballet became the art form at the forefront of the short-lived romantic era that began in France. Female dance artists gained star status and took center stage by portraying ethereal spirits who paused fleetingly on the tips of their toes. Later in the century, ballet would move into its classical era in Russia. Under the Czar's patronage and purse, the Russian Imperial Theaters produced entire evenings of ballets such as the *Nutcracker* and *Swan Lake,* which are still performed today. While male dancers took supporting roles onstage, they remained as the choreographers, ballet masters, and artistic drivers. Female dancers attained new technical heights by dancing on the tips of their toes in boxed slippers called pointe shoes.

Most social dances were group dances until in the early 19th-century partner dances emerged and some were considered indecent. In ballrooms, although country dances remained popular, polonaise, cotillions, polkas, mazurkas, waltzes, and quadrilles mirrored a growing sense of nationalism in Europe and the United States. Dance masters taught the latest dances from Europe. Group and couple dances continued throughout the century. The ballroom was an important part of 19th-century social amusements, where proper etiquette and good dancing were expectations of society.

The Grand March

The grand march was the opening dance at a 19th-century ball. In this walking dance, couples moved around the dance floor in a variety of figures that became increasingly intricate.

Dance in America

Since colonial times in America, traveling family troupes and theatrical companies played in theaters. These performers offered varied programs from the big cities on the east and southern coasts to towns on the edge of the frontier. Dancers were versatile artists in these companies. They performed fancy dances or stylized social dances and ballets, along with taking on pantomime, acting, and singing roles in the dramas, operas, and comedies that were part of an evening's entertainment.

Wars and ensuing economic crashes drove audiences to seek entertainment for escape from these life-changing hardships. Throughout the 19th century, most popular entertainment featured dance. In the 1840s, the minstrel show featured songs, dances, and jokes. Later *The Black Crook* took the stage, followed by variety shows, then vaudeville in the last part of the century. The minstrel show began in the 1830s and expanded into a specific form. Lead by Mr. Tambo and Mr. Bones as the masters of ceremonies, the all-male minstrel cast sat on stage. The minstrels told jokes and performed skits, songs, and dances. They wore suits and blackened their faces. Later they whitened their faces. The popularity of the minstrel show expanded as did minstrel companies. Some parts of the minstrel show became absorbed into other American entertainment forms in the 19th and 20th centuries.

In the 1860s *The Black Crook* was a musical extravaganza of dance, song, and recitation. With a thin story line and fantastic scenery, female dancers wearing short costumes and tights held the production together. *The Black Crook* premiered in New York. After its successful run, productions toured cities throughout the world. *The Black Crook* became a milestone in the development of the musical theater form in the 20th century.

Variety halls presented popular entertainment of songs, skits, and fancy dances for male working class audiences. Later in the century, the vaudeville show emerged with songs, dances, skits, juggling, and animal acts as entertainment suitable for women, children, and families. Vaudeville companies boarded trains westward and toured cities and towns on circuits of one-night stands that often lasted for an entire year. Vaudeville acts continued into the 20th century with remnants of the acts in stage musicals, movies, and early television shows.

The 19th century ended with dance having roles in society as art, entertainment, and education. Since colonial times, dance masters had taught fencing and dancing at major Eastern universities. Learning to dance was an established requirement for a gentleman or a lady to hold a place in society. At the end of the 19th century, Melvin Gilbert introduced aesthetic dance for females in physical education.

Sheet music cover from "The Black Crook Waltzes."

Twentieth Century

The 20th century was a period of intense development in many dance forms and in a wide variety of styles because of the dancers, choreographers, entrepreneurs, and educators who contributed to it.

Social and ballroom dances mirrored the society and its trends of different decades throughout the century. The insurgence of Latin dances and their continued popularity added new dimensions to ballroom dance. The 20th century produced a resurgence of folk dances; square, contra, and line dances; and interest in historical social dance forms. Later in the century cities became incubators for urban dance forms and for trendy social dances, breakdancing, hip-hop, and other styles of street dance. For more information about social, folk, or cultural dances, see chapters 6 through 8.

In the early part of the 20th century, dancers and choreographers began to express their ideas about contemporary society. Breaking from classical ballet, choreographers created works known as "new dances," which would evolve to later become modern dance. Throughout the century, modern dancers and choreographers experimented with movement and choreographic forms while some artists created technical styles. These modern dancers and choreographers

Dancers doing the Charleston.

contributed story-based and abstract-themed dance works. During the second half of the century, modern dance moved into its post-modern era. Choreographers concentrated on relating dance to society and everyday living. Dancers experimented with everyday movement, task dances, and site-specific dances among others. Modern dance techniques blended with other dance genres, merging into contemporary dance to become an individual expression of the choreographer.

Twentieth-century ballet underwent stylistic and choreographic changes. At the beginning of the century, Russian-produced avant-garde ballets shocked Paris audiences. Legendary ballet dancers toured far and wide. After the Bolshevik Revolution many Russian dancers settled throughout the world where they continued to perform, teach, and produce ballets. In the United States George Balanchine formed The American Ballet Company, which evolved to become New York City Ballet (NYCB). Lucia Chase and colleagues formed Ballet Theatre Company, which decades later became American Ballet Theatre (ABT). Alongside these major ballet companies in New York, other ballet companies sprung up in the larger cities throughout the United States. Ballet and modern dancers and choreographers performed with companies and in Broadway musicals.

In the second half of the 20th century, American ballet companies toured the world. Their repertories were a mix of romantic and classical ballets from the 19th and early 20th centuries, and contemporary works by 20th-century choreographers. Master choreographer George Balanchine developed his neoclassic style of ballet as the signature of New York City Ballet. Later Jerome Robbins would infuse his ballets with his Broadway work and jazz choreographic styles. Gerald Arpino's cutting edge ballets for the Joffery Ballet reflected visual art styles of the 1960s. During the last half of the 20th century, contemporary ballet gained momentum which continues today. With the many crossovers, confluences, and fusion among modern dance, postmodern dance, ballet, and contemporary ballet the intriguing question for new generations of choreographers to explore is *What is contemporary dance?*

Tap dance and jazz dance emerged as indigenous American dance forms. The roots of these dance forms can be traced to various nationalities and forms of entertainment. During the 20th century, tap dance and jazz dance developed

Fancy Free, choreographed by Jerome Robbins.

because of live entertainment venues, the advent of film, and the development of musical theater productions. Tap dance and jazz dance artists developed styles and presented their work in these productions on stage and screen, which spurred the popularity of these dance genres. These artists and dance educators contributed to jazz and tap classes offered in communities across the country and as university courses. As a result, jazz dance and tap dance moved beyond entertainment into concert dance. In the second half of the 20th century until the present, jazz dance continues to expand its prominence in live entertainment, television, and music videos. Tap dance had a revival during the second half of the 20th century. Another generation of master tap dancers and dance educators built on the previous generations to bring tap dance back to stage and film as a recognized concert dance form.

In the 20th century film and media recording of dance have given students and scholars access to major works in all dance genres. These preserved dances of dance artists and choreographers are a legacy to explore by viewing, performing, restaging, or reconstructing in the classroom.

Viewing dance works by major choreographers from various genres is part of most dance courses. These viewing experiences help you to gain an awareness of many choreographers' major works and develop a memory bank of dance as performance literature. Beyond the pleasure of viewing all kinds of choreography from various historical eras, as a dancer you can begin analyzing and interpreting the dance work. These experiences allow you to compare and contrast dance works within a choreographer's career or among other choreographers producing works during that same time period.

Performing, restaging, or reconstructing a dance work in the classroom requires a great deal of time devoted to learning the dance and learning about the dance and the choreographer who created it. Further research can expand to include the historical, social, and arts context of the period. This dance learning experience can become more manageable when a group or the class learn a short segment of a major work. Then you have the opportunity to feel the movement and be able to reflect and respond about your experience.

America's Irreplaceable Dance Treasures: The First 100

The Dance Heritage Coalition began accepting nominations for American dance artistry, forms, and traditions. The purpose of this project was to make people aware of the richness of America's dance heritage and the imperative to document and preserve it for future generations.

The Dance Heritage Coalition writes on their website, "The irreplaceable dance treasure has made a significant impact on dance as an art form, demonstrated artistic excellence, enriched the nation's cultural heritage, demonstrated the potential to enhance the lives of future generations and shown itself worthy of national and international recognition" (http://danceheritage.org).

Twenty-First Century

In this new millennium, dance is everywhere. Dance in the 21st century has become a global phenomenon produced in theaters, in site-specific settings outdoors and indoors, in education, in recreation, in community, on television, in movies, and on the Internet. The power of dance is in modern society as art, as entertainment, and in all people's lives from toddlers to seniors.

Dance genres are appreciated for their unique characteristics or as a fusion of genres and styles. Television shows and movies have showcased dance forms and performers. Audiences have become more invested in their views and their critiques about dance, dancers, and dance works. The dancers and choreographers considered leaders in dance as art, entertainment, and education are many, and they span the globe. Some of them are moving or maturing from their previous work in the 20th century; others are emerging or are considered rising stars. This continued expansion of dance demonstrates its power as art, education, entertainment, and enjoyment in society today and as a way to continue to build community across diverse cultures.

Thinking Like a Dancer

History can be a mass of people, events, and dates that all seem blended together and not easy to recall. The previous overview of history presented a glimpse of the people and historical events or societies of various time periods and how dance played a role in them. So far in this chapter, you have focused on the three factors of dancers, dance, and dance works in relation to the history of dance. Thinking like a dancer, some additional questions surface for each of the subjects covered in this chapter. The questions apply when you view dances or in later chapters when you experience dance genres in society and on stage. Using these questions repeatedly will help you analyze the dancers, dance, and dance works you encounter in this course and in your future.

Four continuing questions about dancers are:

1. Who danced?
2. Where did they dance?
3. Why did they dance?
4. What did they dance?

These questions lead you toward exploring dance and then dance designs. When looking at dance, several topics emerge that you can investigate in one or more time periods. For example, the 19th-century waltz had its roots in the earlier dance called *the landler* during the renaissance. Sometimes the purpose of a dance changes with society, a setting, or a time period. As you continue to think about dance, these questions arise:

- What was the purpose of the dance?
- What form or forms did the dance have during its existence?
- What supporting arts influenced or were influenced by the dance?

Dance designs are the features of dance forms and dances. Analyzing a dance design begins with looking at how the elements of dance (space, time, and energy) are used within the dance. Refer to chapters 3 and 4, which explore dance elements and dance composition. Comprehending the design elements of a specific dance or dances gives you the means to analyze and then compare dances of a specific dance form or across forms.

Other design elements for you to identify include these:

- Type of movements or steps
- Number of people and their gender
- Relationships and formation
- Dance structure
- Dance genre
- Relationship of the movement or steps to the accompaniment
- Attire, costumes, or street wear, and personal accessories used in the dance such as fans or handkerchiefs
- The performing space and time of performance, if that is important

Some of these items may seem familiar or repeated. They are the same items, but from a different point of view to analyze the dance. This list then returns to some additional repeated items when looking at the dance design in relation to society:

- Does the dance relate to community as a whole or a segment of society?
- How does the dance relate to religious, economic, cultural, or social features of society?
- Is the dance performed as entertainment, amusement, a life event, religion, culture, or art?

All dance design goes beyond the actual dance to include the dance accompaniment, costuming or attire, and the space in which the dance is being performed. You identify these aspects of a dance to understand the dance and how it may have changed over time. Likewise, you learn to analyze dances to gain a deeper understanding of choreography and major dance works that will be presented in later chapters. This experience in dance analysis can connect to using dance notation systems to analyze dances and dance works.

Using the dance design questions provides a model that supplies you with the background and information to apply when executing a historical dance, showing that as a dancer you understand the nuances for performing this dance from a different time period. Furthermore, it prepares you to participate in historical

ACTIVITY 5.5 RESEARCH

Stepping Back Into the Past

You have read about and participated in a wide variety of dances from the beginning of time to the present. In a group, select a time period outlined in this chapter, or find it on the history of dance timeline created during this chapter. Choose a dance from your selected time period, and find music on the Internet to accompany the dance. Rehearse your group dance for performance in class.

After your performance, each person's assignment is to contribute to developing a group summary paper about the dance. The summary should include the following information:

- Describe the dance by answering the who, what, where, when, and why of the dance.
- Research the historical era in a country where the dance was performed. Compose a one-page background paper that outlines the historical and societal events during that century.

Each group member should write a summary page about his or her personal experience of learning and performing the dance. Take on the role of a fictitious character, and write your summary as an entry in your diary. Or write a letter to a relative about doing the dance at a social event.

dancing in theatrical and musical productions, in your community, and in the continuing popular reenactments or pastime of balls from different eras in the past.

Summary

Throughout history dance has been a powerful part of society. As dance moved from communication to amusement to performing art, it separated and expanded in other ways to become entertainment, a health and fitness activity, and a part of education. Learning to perform historical dances and then learning about these dances within contexts of society, the arts, and history helps you gain a sense of this continuum of change that is part of the history of dance—and the history of life.

Select a dance you learned while studying this chapter. In a group perform the dance, and take video to capture the group performance and photos of important formations or movements of the dance. On the appropriate place in your timeline, place pictures of your group performing the dance. You can include your video in your portfolio or on the class webpage. Then write a summary of your analysis of the dance using the dancers and dance questions and the dance design questions model presented earlier in the chapter.

REVIEW QUESTIONS

True or False

1. Dances do not change with society, a setting, or during a time period. _____

2. Louis XIV was known as the Sun King. _____

3. The ballroom was an important part of 19th-century social amusements where proper etiquette and good dancing were expectations of society. _____

4. Dance in the 21st century has become a global phenomenon. _____

Multiple Choice

1. _____Era of history prior to writing is known as
   a. ancient history
   b. Common Era
   c. prehistory

2. _____Professional dancers were trained performers for entertainment hosted by nobility or the rich as early as
   a. the golden age of Greece
   b. Ancient Egypt
   c. the Middle Ages

3. _____*Le Ballet Comique de la Reine,* known as the first ballet, was commissioned by
   a. Louis XIV
   b. Catherine de' Medici
   c. Elizabeth I of England

4. _____Analyzing a dance design begins with first looking at
   a. dancers, community, and time period
   b. music, costuming, and setting of dance
   c. use of space, time, and energy

Matching

1. _____farandole
2. _____basse dance
3. _____minuet
4. _____contradance
5. _____polkas, mazurkas, waltzes

a. Dances of the 19th century

b. A slow, dignified walking processional dance

c. A dance in 3/4 or another triple meter with the pattern of steps in an S or a Z figure

d. A chain dance performed by peasants and courtiers

e. A dance that became popular in 18th-century England and America

Short Answer

1. List the four questions used to study and understand dance through history.

To find supplementary materials for this chapter such as worksheets, extended learning activities, and e-journaling assignments, visit the web resource at www.discoveringdance.org/student.

Social Dance

ENDURING UNDERSTANDING: Social dance represents changes in the times.

ESSENTIAL QUESTION: Why do people do social dance?

LEARNING OBJECTIVES

After reading this chapter, you will be able to do the following:

- Perform one or more social dances with correct footwork, rhythm, and styling.
- Understand social dance history, major dances, and dance artists.
- Comprehend social dance vocabulary and its application in the social dances.
- Practice partner and group work, social dance etiquette, and dance safety.

"Put a little fun into your life. Try dancing."

Kathryn Murray, wife and dance partner of Arthur Murray,
20th-century American social dance instructor and businessman
who developed using footprints to teach dance steps

VOCABULARY

ballroom dances
ballroom exhibitions
cha-cha
closed position
dance sport
foxtrot
merengue
open position
salsa
social dance
swing
waltz

Social trends influence what people wear, what they do for entertainment, and how they dance; in other words, clothes, entertainment, and dances are constantly changing. If you were to compare a list of what is hot and what is not among members of your class and another class in another region of the country, you would probably find some big differences. **Social dances** are a reflection of current trends. While trends change, so do social dances. Yet some historical and traditional dances continue to be popular as basic social dances. Social dance is one gauge of trends in popular culture.

Social dance is a recreational dance form that you usually perform to music with a partner. It often reflects dances from a folk heritage, such as the polka, or

it is linked to various cultures, such as Latin dances from Central and South America. A wide variety of social dances exist, spanning from today's most popular and trendy dances, to retro dances such as swing dancing, to enduring traditional dances such as the foxtrot or cha-cha from the 20th century, to dances that have been popular for centuries such as the polka or the waltz. Social dance also includes group dances from childhood, such as the bunny hop, or ever popular dances that are staples of weddings and parties, such as the chicken dance and the Macarena.

If you become a serious social dancer, then you can explore **ballroom dancing**. On television or the Internet you can view **ballroom exhibitions** in which highly trained dancers perform choreographed social dances. Competitive amateur and professional ballroom dancers can participate in competition dance festivals around the world. Ballroom dancing at high level of competition is considered **dance sport**, and it has been recognized as an Olympic sport.

This chapter explores social dance and its influence on other dance genres, and it provides ways to look at social dance to support your dancing in the classroom.

! ACTIVITY 6.1   DISCOVER

What's Hot?

Conducting a survey about "What's Hot?" is as easy as texting or e-mailing several people of your age in another place. Using this survey the class can collect these responses and get a barometer on current trends. After deciding what the current trends are in fashion, sports, dance, entertainment, and other activities, what do you predict will be the next *What is hot*?

Discovering Social Dance

Think about some occasions in the past when you have done social dancing. You might have gone to a school dance, or perhaps in a physical education unit your class danced in the gym. Maybe at a family wedding you danced at the reception with a relative, or you danced with friends at a party. Perhaps you were invited to attend a formal ball at the civic center to support a charity drive, or in last year's musical you and your partner danced the lindy hop. These examples are just a few of the many for why, where, and when you do social dance.

Social dance has deep ties to society and hence changes with the times. It displays trends and responds to historical, political, societal, and arts happenings in a specific era of time. Social dance has been called a mirror of society. A mirror can be a true reflection, or it can be a distorted view.

DID YOU KNOW?

Dance Marathons

Dance marathons were popular beginning in the 1920s. The record for the longest dance goes back to 1930 when Mike Ritof and Edith Boudreau started the marathon on August 29th in a Chicago ballroom. They stopped on April 1, 1931 after 5,152 hours of dancing. The couple claimed the dance marathon record and $2,000 each. The exact rules for the dance marathon are unknown, but certainly the couple had breaks.

ACTIVITY 6.2 JOURNAL
Your Social Dance

Develop a list of where you have done social dance. In a paragraph, explain why you do social dance. What social dances do you do—the latest dances, traditional dances, retro dances, or historical social dances? Whom do you dance with?

Exploring Social Dance

Social dance has deep historical roots in communities of common people and in royal courts. Villagers hopped, skipped, and ran as they celebrated seasonal agricultural events such as planting and harvest as part of outdoor festivals and fairs. In the renaissance royal courts, nobility glided around great halls to display their elaborate rich clothing and their graceful movements. Dancing masters taught the dances and social etiquette, which were important measures of social status in the court. Some dances began centuries ago and are still performed today but often in different forms. Other dances came and went as a result of war, political events, or society changes. Most social dances were group dances until in the early 19th century when partner dances emerged. Dance masters wrote guides to the ballroom and social etiquette for men and women as well as how to perform the current dances. Today many groups re-create these dances at period balls or as entertainment to accompany reenactments of historical or military events.

The 20th century went through many social changes with as many different social dance periods as there were decades. In the early years of the 20th century, Vernon and Irene Castle introduced animal dances such as the turkey trot, the bunny hug, and the grizzly bear, in which dancers held each other in close embraces that were considered risqué. The Castles created the Castle walk and also codified many of the new dances that were popular before World War I.

In the 1920s the jazz era was in full force as were women's rights and Prohibition. Almost everywhere flappers danced the Charleston. Actor Rudolph Valentino took the tango mania from clubs to the silver screen. Beginning in the 1920s, around-the-clock dance marathons expanded across the nation.

In the 1930s, radios brought music into people's homes. In the clubs, big dance bands of Cab Calloway, Benny Goodman, Tommy Dorsey, and Count Basie helped in the development of swing dancing and the Lindy hop. These band leaders, their music, and the dances that emerged during this period became known and the Big Band Era. Fred Astaire and Ginger Rogers glided and whirled across the movie screen in their elegant and sophisticated social dances.

When the United States entered World War II, ballroom dance became an important social and recreational activity. Dance teacher Arthur Murray (1895-1991) taught people to dance in six easy lessons. After World War II, social and social historical dance migrated to the Broadway musical stage. During the 1940s big dance bands infused Latin American rhythms, songs, and dances into social dancing.

In the 1950s, the Latin style took over dance clubs. First the mambo of Afro-Cuban heritage was followed by the Cuban cha-cha-cha (which became the cha-cha) and the merengue (also a Caribbean dance). During the 1950s the record industry expanded as they moved to vinyl. By the end of the decade, rock and roll changed social dance so that partners no longer danced together, but each person gyrated freestyle to the beat. From the 1950s into the 1960s fad dances came and went; the bossa nova, the swim, the mashed potato, and others made the music charts. Popular social dances moved to the Broadway musical theater stage in stylized versions. On television, the show *American Bandstand popularized the music and dances of the times* from the 1950s through the 1970s.

At the end of the 1970s, John Travolta ignited the disco era with his performance of the hustle in the film *Saturday Night Fever* (1977). The movie spurred the 1980s disco explosion, and disco became popular all over the world. While breakdancing took over the streets, people did the Electric Slide as a group dance at weddings, and at the end of the decade people were moving to a South American dance, the Lambada. During the 1970s, country-western dances resurfaced with the growth of the country music industry. Country-western dance and music continues to gain popularity in the United States and across the world.

From the 1990s and into the 21st century, the salsa, another Cuban and Afro-Caribbean dance form that had been around since early in the 20th century, took over the dance floor and swept into dance entertainment shows.

Since the 1970s, street dancing such as break dancing, hip-hop, and other later forms evolved through improvisation to music. Street dancing allows a dancer to create a personal identity and style, or a group to portray its attitude toward culture and society. Street dance can take the form of social, cultural, entertainment, and concert dance.

As you can see, there is a wide range of social dance to sample and enjoy. Now, it's time to dance.

ACTIVITY 6.3   RESEARCH

Social Dances and Society

List two or three examples of social dances and determine how they either mirrored or did not mirror what was going on in society at the time. You can use this chapter and chapter 5 as a starting place for some dances to consider. Explain why you concluded that the dance did or did not mirror society at the time. After doing some web research about each of the dances you selected, now what do you think?

Learning Social Dance

You can do social dance on your own—just dancing to music and improvising movement, expressing yourself in your personal space. Or, you can dance with a partner—holding hands, joining fingers, or simply dancing together without touching.

At parties or similar occasions, groups participate in social dance. These **group social dances** include formations such as lines, circles, or dancers scattered around the dance floor. Often group line dances act as icebreakers to get everyone in the group out on the floor and moving for fun. Some well-known dances popular at weddings, parties, and other social gatherings include the chicken dance, the conga line, or dances from childhood.

In **partner dances** you and a partner learn the same steps but move in different directions. If you are new to social dance, there are a variety of basic dances to try. If you have had social or ballroom experience, then you could either review basic dances or challenge yourself to try a new dance.

Social Dance Etiquette

Inviting someone to dance with you requires practicing social dance etiquette. In some settings the invitation can be casual. In formal settings, social dance etiquette is required.

The etiquette of asking a female partner to dance is steeped in historical social dance tradition that was part of the gentleman or lady's expected manners in the ballroom. How you conducted yourself in the ballroom and your performance of the popular dances of the times related to social standing in society.

These days, when you are meeting someone new, good etiquette is to introduce yourself. In traditional settings, generally a male asks a female to dance, but either partner may ask the other. Asking someone to dance is as easy as saying, "Would you like to dance?" Accepting the invitation is as easy as saying, "Yes, I would like to." On some occasions, the person invited to dance may decline an invitation by saying, "No, thank you." This answer may be given because of personal reasons. The person may or may not share the reason, but it should be respected. Then the leader escorts the partner onto the dance floor and back to the side of the dance floor once the dance is finished. Both partners thank each other for the dance.

Attire for a social dance depends upon the informality or formality of the social event. In general female attire spans from casual skirts and blouses or dresses to formal attire, and footwear they can comfortably dance in. Men wear shirts and slacks for informal occasions or suits for formal attire, with appropriate shoes they can dance in.

Once you begin to dance, etiquette applies on the dance floor, too. Similar to driving on different lanes on a highway, on the dance floor, lanes exist for dances performed at different speeds. The outside lane is for faster dances, while the inside lane is for slower dances. You dance the cha-cha, swing, and some other dances in a contained space that does not interfere with other couples. Following these simple rules of dance floor etiquette can help you navigate the dance floor and enjoy your dancing more.

Partner Positions

Social and ballroom dance partners move together within a frame. One person leads and the other follows. In traditional ballroom dance, a male leads and a female follows. Partner positions have a variety of handholds: hands not joined, one hand joined, **closed position,** and **open position** (see figures 6.1 to 6.4).

Basics of Social Dance

The following basic concepts include social dance vocabulary to help you learn how to perform social dances.

- *Step patterns* are the patterns of steps you perform, and they relate to the beat of the music.
- *Line of direction* is the path in which you or you and your partner are moving on the floor. It is either determined by the leader, or all dancers or couples move in the same direction.
- *Footwork* is the length of the step, foot placement, and weight distribution in the direction you are traveling or when you are changing direction.
- *Rhythm* is an even or uneven pattern of the steps or the music. Learning the rhythm of the steps helps combine the movement to the music.

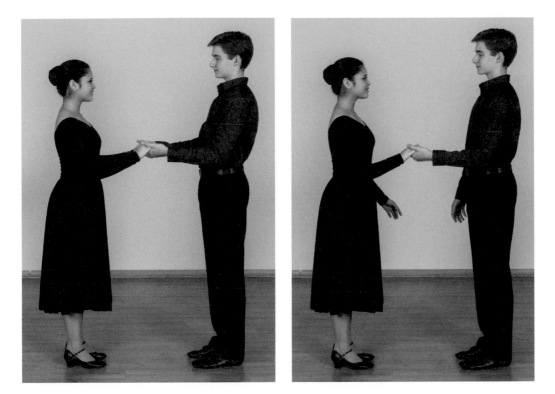

Figure 6.1 Hands joined: couple faces each other, in their personal space; elbows close to their bodies, hands are joined.

Figure 6.2 One hand joined: couples facing with one hand joined.

Figure 6.3 Closed position: partners face each other with shoulders and hips square. The leader places the right hand on the follower's center back below the shoulder blades. When the leader's right hand presses on the follower's back, it indicates the direction they will move. The follower's left hand rests on the leader's upper arm. The leader holds the follower's right hand in his left hand.

Figure 6.4 Open position: the leader and follower stand side by side.

- *Tempo* is the timing of the steps, which are slow or quick in relation to the meter of the music.

When you learn a social dance, first listen to the music to learn the rhythm. You should determine the beat, the number of beats to the measure, and then how the footwork corresponds to the music. As you listen, hear and count the music (in 2/4 or 4/4 or 3/4 time signatures), then relate the counts to the footwork of the dance.

Then, begin to do the steps of the dance to the rhythm you heard in the music. You might need to start slowly without the music, gradually building to the tempo of the music. Eventually, you can do it with the music. It takes practice, but once you can execute the steps of simple dances with ease, you can progress to more complex dance steps or dances to challenge yourself and have fun.

Traditional Social Dances

From the 19th to the 20th century a number of traditional social dances gained and maintained popularity on the dance floor. Each dance presented in this section offers basic exercises to learn the rhythm and movements of the dance. These dance exercises are just starting places for you to continue your learning of each dance. You may already know the steps and progressions of some or all of these dances from previous dance experiences, or the dances may be new to you. Either way, these exercises help you get a sense of the dance rhythms and movements on which you can then extend your vocabulary of steps to create your dance. If one dancer is male and the other female, the man becomes the leader. If both dancers are the same gender, then one person takes the role of leader and the other person the role of the follower.

Foxtrot

The **foxtrot** is an American social dance named for Henry Fox, who "trotted" to ragtime music. The Castles contributed the smooth, sophisticated style which the foxtrot is known for. Performed in 4/4 time, the basic steps move forward and back at a quick or slow tempo and progress to turns and combinations.

The foxtrot is a couple dance. The couple uses the closed position for this dance.

Learning the foxtrot begins with simple steps of walking forward and then backward to a one step (quick tempo) and then a dance walk (slow tempo).

ONE STEP   The leader begins stepping forward with the left foot; the follower begins stepping back with the right foot.

Count(s)	Footwork	Cue
1	Step left foot forward.	Quick
2	Step right foot forward.	Quick
3	Step left foot forward.	Quick
4	Step right foot forward.	Quick
1-4	Repeat one step backward, beginning with the left foot.	

DANCE WALK   For the slow rhythm, each dance walk takes two counts.

Count(s)	Footwork	Cue
1-2	Step left foot forward.	Slow
3-4	Step right foot forward.	Slow
5-6	Step left foot forward.	Slow
7-8	Step right foot forward.	Slow
1-8	Repeat dance walk backward, beginning with the left foot.	

FOXTROT COMBINATION: TURNING BASIC STEP   You can do the turning basic step forward, backward, or diagonally. The turning step is presented using quick steps on each count. You can also perform it slow, using two counts for each step.

Count(s)	Footwork for leader	Cue
1	Step left foot forward (no turn).	Quick
2	Step right foot back (transfer weight to the right). Start turn left. Complete an eighth to a quarter turn to the left between this step and the next.	Quick
3	Step side with left foot.	Quick
4	Step right foot to left (transfer to the right).	Quick
1-4	Repeat the turning basic step forward, beginning again with the left foot stepping forward to continue the turn.	

(continued)

Turning Basic Step *(continued)*

Count(s)	Footwork for follower	Cue
1	Step right foot backward (no turn).	Quick
2	Step left foot forward (transfer weight to the left). Start turn left. Complete an eighth to a quarter turn to the left between this step and the next.	Quick
3	Step right foot to the side.	Quick
4	Step left foot to right, and transfer weight to the left.	Quick
1-4	Repeat the turning basic step backward beginning with the right foot to continue the turn.	

Waltz

During the 19th century the **waltz** gained and maintained popularity in the ballroom. It is danced in 3/4 time with a swinging quality to a slow, medium, or fast tempo (such as the Viennese waltz of the later 19th century). In this dance, both dancers are in the closed position and should focus on footwork.

DANCE WALK   The dance walk for the waltz is a combination of full-foot (flat) and lift (on the balls of the feet) positions in 3/4 time. This combination takes 6 counts.

Count(s)	Footwork	Cue
1-2	Step full feet (leader uses left foot, follower uses right foot).	Slow, down
3-4	Step on ball of foot (leader uses right; follower uses left).	Slow, up
5-6	Step on ball of foot (leader uses left; follower uses right).	Slow, up
1-6	Repeat moving forward. The leader begins with the right foot; follower uses left foot.	
1-6	Practice moving backward.	

BOX TURN   Turning can be counterclockwise or clockwise. In closed dance position, a turn is an eighth or a quarter rotation. The turn is initiated on the forward or the back steps.

Count(s)	Footwork	Cue
1	Step forward (left foot flat).	Slow or down
2	Step side (right foot, up).	Slow, up, or lift
3	Step together (left foot, up).	Slow, up, or lift
4	Step back (right foot flat).	Slow or down
5	Step side (left foot, up).	Slow, up, or lift
6	Step together (right foot, up).	Slow, up, or lift

Swing

Swing dance has had many variations, including the lindy hop, the jitterbug, the West Coast swing, the East Coast swing, and others. The dance is in 4/4 time and can have simple to complicated footwork, different couple positions and many handholds with your partner, swing outs and ins, turns, and other stylistic movements.

SINGLE OR BASIC STEP   For this dance, partners join hands. The basic swing can be done forward, backward, to the side, or turning. This basic step, called a single, can become a double or even a triple by adding additional steps to it.

If you are unfamiliar with swing dancing, start by doing the single, and then move up to trying the double. The double begins with a dig (toes of a foot before the first full foot step).

Count(s)	Footwork
1	Step side with left foot.
2	Step in place with right foot.
3	Step backward with left foot on ball of foot.
4	Step in place with right foot.

When you are ready, try the triple basic step. In the triple, there are three quick steps for each of the first two steps in the pattern The counts for the first triple step is 1 followed by the second triple counted 2, and the back step 3, and step in place is count 4.

ARCH OUT   In semiopen position, the leader does the foot pattern, and the follower turns under his left arm. The follower ends facing the leader, still holding his hand.

DISHRAG   The leader and follower join hands. The follower moves to the leader's left (follower's right). They turn back to back, arching and return to face each other, followed by a basic step.

Merengue

The **merengue** is a Caribbean dance performed in two styles. Haitian style has a smooth quality. Dominican Republic style uses a shift of weight between one bent and one straight leg. The basic steps move to the side, forward, or back. This easy, fun dance is in 2/4 or 4/4 time and has a quick tempo. Couples can use closed or open dance positions.

Count(s)	Footwork
1	Step side with left foot.
2	Step right foot to left (transfer weight to the right).
3-4	Step side with left foot; step right foot to left (transfer weight to the right).
1-4	Repeat 1-4, and then change sides.

Cha-Cha

The **cha-cha** originated in Cuba as the "cha-cha-cha" and became popular in the 1950s. It is a combination of the mambo and swing styles. Danced in 4/4 time, couples are in closed or shine (partners face each other but do not hold hands) positions.

BASIC STEP   The rhythm of the cha-cha crosses over measures in the music. In the basic footwork, the couple holds the first count of the measure and moves on the second count. This beginning hold or pause on the first beat of the music is what the couple should focus on before stepping on count 2 of the measure.

Count(s)	Footwork
1	Hold
2	Slow
3	Slow
4	Quick
&	Quick
1	Slow

BACK BASIC   This step is used only at the beginning of a dance. As basic footwork, moving back the couple holds the first count of the measure and moves on the second count. This beginning hold or pause on the first beat of the music is what the couple should focus on before stepping on count 2 of the measure.

Count(s)	Footwork	Cue
2	Left foot steps side.	Slow
3	Right foot steps back.	Slow
4	Left foot steps forward.	Quick
	Right foot steps together (next to left foot).	Quick
&	Left foot steps in place.	Quick
1	Right foot steps in place.	Quick

FORWARD BASIC   Partners have hands joined or in the shine position. The forward basic follows the same rhythmic and step pattern as the cha-cha back basic step.

Count(s)	Footwork	Cue
2	Step left foot forward.	Slow
3	Step right foot back.	Slow
4	Step left foot in place.	Quick
&	Step right foot in place.	Quick
1	Step left foot in place.	Quick

The cha-cha can progress to include a crossover step with partners in the side to side position while doing a cha-cha step and half turn.

Salsa

Salsa is a newer version of the mambo. The Mambo developed in the mid-1940s and became known as the "King of Latin Dances." Newer versions of the mambo are primarily known as *salsa*. Salsa continues to be a popular dance form. The time signature is 4/4. The rhythm is quick, quick, and slow. While doing the salsa steps, bend and straighten the knees to develop the hip movement known as the Cuban motion (Bennett 2006). Other salsa steps include side steps, back or front breaks, and underarm turns.

BASIC STEP

Counts(s)	Footwork	Cue
1	Step left foot forward.	Quick
2	Change weight to right foot.	Quick
3-4	Step close left beside right.	Slow
1	Step right foot back.	Quick
2	Change weight to left foot.	Quick
3-4	Step close right beside left.	Slow

Social Dance Safety

When you learn and practice social dances with a partner, you both need to work together with kinesthetic awareness of your own space and your space as a couple. With this awareness, you can move safely around the floor doing the dance steps in time with the music. When dancing with a partner becomes familiar, you and your partner can enjoy the social aspects of moving to the music while talking to each other.

Respecting your space, your partner's space, and the space of others while moving slowly or quickly requires perception, kinesthetic awareness, and continued attention to your steps in a pattern to the music.

EXPLORE MORE

Visit the web resource's Explore More section to learn more about country-western and line dances. These dances have a long history in the United States. Country-western and line dances regained their popularity because they were featured in movies and because of the growth of the country music industry. These dances continue to be popular throughout the United States and the world.

Creating Social Dances

To do a social dance with a partner, you both need a grasp of the basic steps, the rhythm, and the timing for the dance. Then the leader and the follower can move

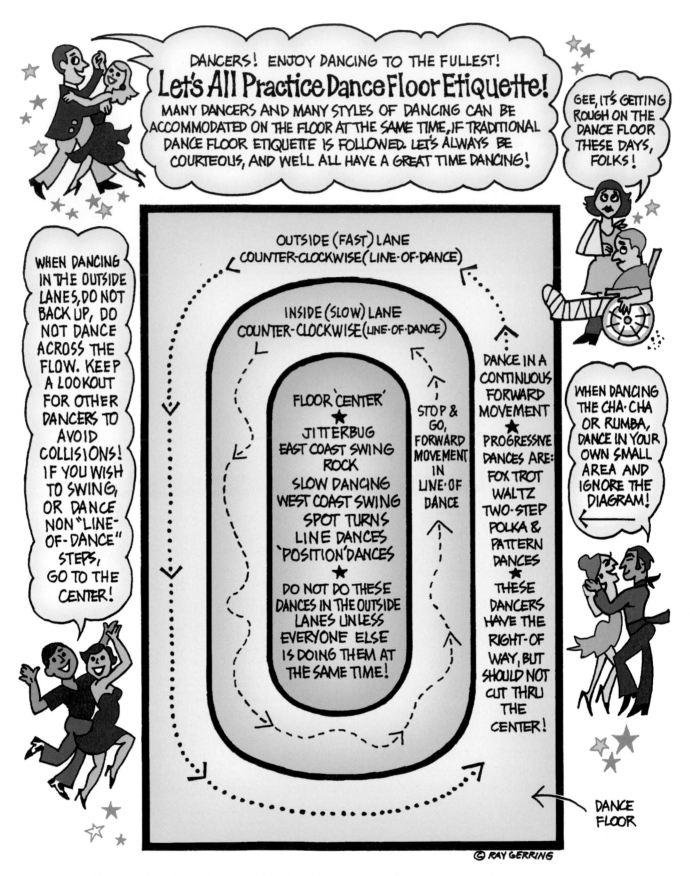

Knowing the fast and slow dance lanes on the dance floor is part of practicing social dance etiquette.

Fred Astaire and Ginger Rogers

Fred Astaire and Ginger Rogers were social dance stars of the early 20th century. Their style and grace got America out of the theater seats and dancing. Viewing one or two of their movies gives you a sense of the times, the society, and the roles of men and women on the dance floor and in life. After viewing two of their dances in a movie, do some research and write a paragraph to capture the historical era in which the movie was produced. Include information about the dances, the dancers in relation to the times, and their movies.

through the dance for an enjoyable experience. Your teacher will teach you the basic steps to guide you in learning a social dance. Then you and your partner can practice one or more of these basic steps along with other couples to experience social dancing in a group setting.

Dancing in a social situation is quite different from the sophisticated choreography for exhibition or competition ballroom dance events. In a social situation, the leader selects the steps and their sequence. In exhibition or competitive dance events, these highly trained dancers have to execute a series of required steps and movements to qualify or compete.

Thinking Like a Dancer

Couples social dance depends on the interaction of two people, thus it requires subtle communication. The leader establishes the rhythm, the steps, and the direction. The follower uses the cues from the leader's hands. This kinesthetic awareness and communication takes moving together as a couple to a new level of awareness of the dance and the dance experience.

When dancing with a partner, the leader is responsible for the choreography and focusing on doing the basic steps to the music. If you are the follower, then try moving in unison; do not try to lead. The leader and the follower should have patience and consideration for each other. Focus on dancing as a couple and using dance floor etiquette. Thinking like a social dancer before you move onto the floor may require reviewing the illustration on dance floor etiquette or keeping it as a checklist in your mind so that you and your partner can enjoy your dancing.

Summary

Social dances are recreational dance styles that have a rich history and can be fun, lifelong dance activities. This chapter reviewed the basics of some popular social dances, including etiquette and safety. Learning social dance contributes to your dance literacy and your personal life. It adds a new dimension to your dance experiences and complements other dance genres.

Recent reality dance shows on television and on the Internet take social and ballroom dance to a new level of complexity, including athletic and artistic requirements that are well beyond what is usually performed on the dance floor.

To begin, do some research by watching several of the shows. If you are a committed viewer of one show, then choose one or more other shows to give you a broader view of the shows. Then write a response paper and answer the following questions:

- What do you think are the positive and negative effects of one of these reality TV dance competitions?
- Would you like to be a contestant on one of the shows? Why or why not?
- What would you dance? And with whom? What would you title your dance?

REVIEW QUESTIONS

True or False

1. The cha-cha has been named the "King of Latin Dances." _____

2. The line of direction refers to you and your partner moving around the floor and is determined by either the leader or all couples moving in the same direction. _____

3. Social dance safety relies on respecting your space and that of others while moving to the music. _____

Multiple Choice

1. _____The bossa nova, the swim, the mashed potato, and others made the music charts as Fad dances in the
   a. 1930s into the 1940s
   b. 1950s into the 1960s
   c. 1980s into the 1990s

2. _____Animal dances such as the turkey trot were created by
   a. Arthur Murray
   b. John Travolta
   c. Vernon and Irene Castle

3. _____During the 1970s, country-western dances resurfaced because of
   a. the country music industry
   b. dance stars on television
   c. national heritage values

Short Answer

1. List three ways to social dance.

Matching

1. _____cha-cha

2. _____foxtrot

3. _____salsa

4. _____swing

5. _____waltz

6. _____closed position

7. _____open position

a. 1950s popular dance that originated in Cuba

b. Partners face each other and the leader places his right hand on the follower's center back below the shoulder blades

c. Cuban or Afro-Caribbean dance form early in the 20th century

d. Early 20th-century American social dance named for Henry Fox

e. A dance in 3/4 time that gained and maintained popularity in the 19th-century ballroom

f. Dance with a variety of forms and styles that has simple to complicated footwork and many handholds with your partner

g. The leader and follower stand side by side

 To find supplementary materials for this chapter such as worksheets, extended learning activities, and e-journaling assignments, visit the web resource at www.discoveringdance.org/student.

Folk Dance

ENDURING UNDERSTANDING: A folk dance is passed on from generation to generation.

ESSENTIAL QUESTION: What is a folk dance?

LEARNING OBJECTIVES

After reading this chapter, you will be able to do the following:

- Perform one or more folk dances with correct footwork, rhythm, and styling.
- Interpret folk dance vocabulary and its application in folk dances.
- Understand folk dances from various nations, cultures, and geographic regions.
- Practice partner and group work, folk dance etiquette, and dance safety.

VOCABULARY
contradance
folk culture
folk dance
folklore
square dance

Folk dance is the dance of the people (the *folks*). Participating in folk dance verifies your identity with a nationality or cultural group with a similar background and history. It gives you a way to connect to your heritage—your national or ethnic origin, cultural values, or traditions—and to that of others. Folk dances can be regional, national, and international.

Like social dance, folk dance began in centuries past, and some dances are still part of society today. Folk dances are traditional dances passed from generation to generation within a heritage to carry on dance and other traditions. Some folk dances are centuries old, while others have been developed more

recently. For example, during the 20th century, countries in Africa emerged and continue to evolve with new generations creating dances. These contemporary folk dances celebrate or remind people of historical events, triumphs, and sorrow that is part of their heritage.

Folk dance is one area of folk arts, which include music, visual arts, and crafts. **Folklore** is a collection of myths, stories, jokes, tall tales, and dramas that are part of a folk culture. **Folk culture** is the heritage of a group through stories, ceremonies, and cultural practices that include music, dance, food, and language. These and other cultural practices link the past of a particular group or tribe to the present.

Throughout the world folk festivals celebrate people's heritage through music, dance, food, and more. People attend them to renew their connection with their heritage or to learn about another culture. Preserving folk arts is a global phenomenon.

Discovering Folk Dance

In your community or town, it is likely that your friends and neighbors come from different backgrounds than you do. The United States, like many countries across the world, has become home to people with roots in many cultures. Do you know your family's heritage? If you don't already know this information, talk to your relatives to learn about your family's past. If it is not an option or your family doesn't know, make your best guess based on information you have.

Once you have information about your heritage, you can try to link it to a folk dance or dances. Folk dances can either be linked to your family's country of origin, or they can be dances from the country you live in now. Just as people travel and immigrate, so do folk dances.

ACTIVITY 7.1 JOURNAL

Folk Dancing

For the first part of this activity, your teacher will lead you in learning one or more folk dances, giving you a sense of the fun of participating in folk dancing.

As you respond to these questions in your journal, provide examples from your experience with folk dances you tried in class:

- What did you like about a folk dance you learned in class?
- Where there some challenging parts of learning the folk dance?
- What was your overall impression about doing the folk dance?

Using this activity as a starting place, you can investigate more about folk dances as part of your heritage. Do you know a folk dance from your family's country or from the region you live in? To answer this question you can ask a family member about folk dances they remember, or you can research folk dances from your family's country or a folk dance from the region where you live now.

Based on the information you found, select a folk dance that you believe represents you and your cultural heritage. Write a paragraph about the dance. Do a web search on the dance to learn its country of origin and who, where, and why people perform the dance.

Exploring Folk Dance

Folk dances are products of the people who danced them. A folk dance could celebrate life events such as courtship or marriage, special calendar events such as May Day, historical or religious days such as feast days, or seasonal dances such as a harvest dance. Folk dances include a number of dance categories, types, forms, and styles.

Types of Folk Dances

Some folk dances are historical, traditional, or contemporary. Folk dance movements have strong connections to geography, climate, and the indigenous cultural values of the people in a region or country. In general, geography and climate heavily influence folk dance types and styles (see table 7.1).

Folk dances are indigenous to a country, region, or culture. People take their folk dances with them when they move to new places. Depending on the occasion, folk dancers may wear street clothes, or often they wear costumes that represent traditional or national pride associated with the dance. Folk music and dance movements match each other. The music reinforces the dance; songs can be sung a cappella (without music) or with music. Instruments and musical arrangements are unique to the dance and the people. Folk dances can be categorized into types that cover everyday life and events (Lawson 1955).

Table 7.1   Categories of Folk Dances

Work dances Hunter dances Fisherman or sailor dances	Courtship dances Wedding dances Fertility dances	Ritual dances Sun dances Moon-worshipping dances	War dances Sword dances

Today, popular folk dances include square dancing, clogging, **contradancing**, highland dancing, and Irish jigs. Other American dance favorites include country-western, **round dances,** and line dances.

Partner Positions

In folk dance, partner positions are shared with social dance and a variety of folk dance styles. Closed position in folk dance is the same as in social dance. Partners face each other. The leader places the right hand around the follower's center back below the shoulder blades (figure 7.1). With this hand position, the leader directs the movement. The follower's left hand rests on the leader's upper arm. The leader extends the left arm to the side at above shoulder height. The follower extends the right arm to the side at above shoulder height. The follower places the right hand in the leader's left hand. Here are some additional partner positions in folk dance:

Semiopen position is a variation of the closed position. Partners open their bodies slightly while facing in the line of direction (figure 7.2).

Open position presents the leader and the follower standing side by side (figure 7.3).

Side position is when each partner faces opposite directions. Side positions include two variations:

Banjo position is where the partners have their right sides together (figure 7.4).

Sidecar position is where the partners have their left sides together (figure 7.5).

Promenade position means both partners face front, then join right hands and left hands (figure 7.6).

Shoulder–waist position is done with the couple facing each other. The leader holds the follower's waist, and the follower places a hand on each of the leader's shoulders (figure 7.7).

Inside-hands-joined position means dancers stand side by side facing the same direction and hold inside hands (figure 7.8).

Varsovienne position means the leader stands slightly behind on the left side of the follower. The dancers' left arms are shoulder level. The dancers clasp right hands and left hands (figure 7.9).

Figure 7.1 Closed position.

Figure 7.2 Semiopen position.

Figure 7.3 Open position.

Figure 7.4 Banjo position.

Figure 7.5 Sidecar position.

Figure 7.6 Promenade position.

Figure 7.7 Shoulder–waist position.

Figure 7.8 Inside-hands-joined position.

Figure 7.9 Varsovienne position.

Formations

Basic folk dance formations use a *single circle* formation, which has these two variations:

- All leaders and followers face the center of the circle (figure 7.10*a*).
- Couples face one another and as a group create a circle (figure 7.10*b*).

Double circle has these three variations:

- Couples stand next to each other so that they can move counterclockwise. Leaders stand on the inside circle and followers on the outside circle (figure 7.10*c*).
- In the inside circle, leaders stand side by side. Followers face their partners, creating the second circle (figure 7.10*d*).
- Partners face each other and create a double circle (figure 7.10*e*).

Set of three people has two variations.

- Three people stand side by side (figure 7.10*f*).
- Three couples stand side by side (figure 7.10*g*).

Other formations are chain, circular formations, serpentine, processional, square, and double lines.

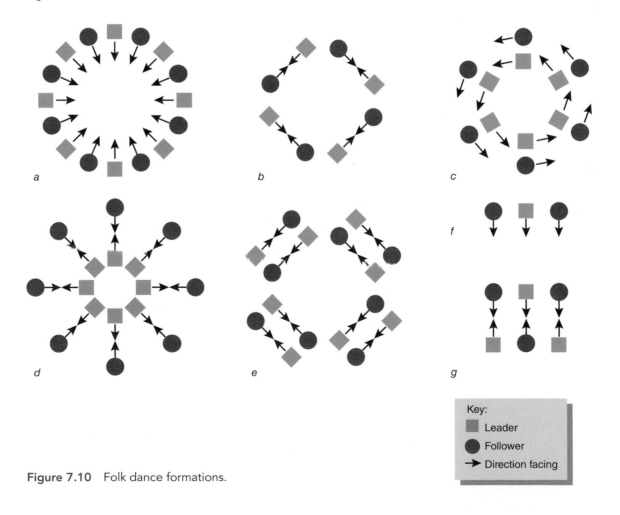

Figure 7.10 Folk dance formations.

119

Structure

A folk dance is a synergy of both movement and music. The sections of a folk dance directly relate to the sections of the music. If the music includes lyrics either sung for or to accompany the dancers, then the sections conform to musical structure. Often the structure can be separated as A, B, C, and so on. Sometimes these sections are repeated in the dance, or the entire dance is repeated several times in succession.

Basic Folk Dance Steps

Folk dances use simple, repetitive steps performed in various formations. These steps may alternate by starting with one foot and then the other. Basic folk dance steps are combinations of walk, run, leap, hop, skip, slide, and gallop.

Two-Step

This step alternates feet. It is performed forward, backward, and to the side in 2/4 time.

Count	Footwork
1	Step right.
2	Step together (left foot).
3	Step left.
4	Step together (right foot) or hold; if the dancer holds, the weight remains on the left foot.

This step alternates feet. It is performed forward, back, and to the side in 2/4 time.

Polka

The polka step is a combination of a hop and three steps performed in 2/4 time.

Count	Footwork
&	Hop left foot.
1	Step right.
&	Step left.
2	Step right.

The polka step is a combination of a hop and three steps performed in 2/4 time.

Schottische

Three steps and a hop alternate feet done to 4/4 or 2/4 time. The step moves forward, backward, or to the side. The following example is in 4/4 time.

Count	Footwork
1	Step left.
2	Close right foot.
3	Step left.
4	Hop left.

Three steps and a hop alternate feet done to 4/4 or 2/4 time. The step moves forward, back, or to the side. This example is in 4/4 time. Step-hop can be combined with the schottische.

Grapevine

The grapevine step is done in 4/4 time and uses four movements with crosses either front or back while moving to the side.

Count	Footwork
1	Cross right foot over left, and step on right.
2	Step on left to the side.
3	Cross right foot behind left, and step on right.
4	Step on left to the side.

The grapevine step done in 4/4 time uses four movements with crosses either front or back while moving to the side.

Often folk dance steps cross various dance forms, such as the basic waltz step used in social dance. Other steps may be unique to a specific folk dance. The puzzling question is whether a folk dance is a social dance. The answer to this question is that it depends on the dance and the historical era. Some folk dances moved into the ballroom to become social historical dances, and some dances continue to be folk dances.

ACTIVITY 7.2   EXPLORE

Comparing Folk Dances

Select a folk dance with which you identify as part of your personal or family heritage. Take a poll of the class to find the most popular folk dances. List the dances in groups that reflect different types of cultural heritage. Then, your teacher can guide the class in selecting a dance from the list that is described in the section titled Basic Folk Dances. Dance books or the web can provide you with directions on how to perform the dances. With some basic research you can determine what country the dance represents, who dances it, and where and why people dance it. You may even find a video on the Internet so that you can see a performance to actual musical accompaniment and perhaps with the dancers in traditional costumes or attire. Although folk dance is primarily preserved through oral tradition, written resources do exist.

Learning to *read* a dance requires some translation from written terms into movement. This skill comes in handy for dancers. You might find several Internet videos that can enhance your understanding of the dance, its formations, and style. First, learn the folk dance and practice it several times until you can perform it without checking your resources for the dance. Once you fully understand the movement, the music, the formations, and the positions through all the sections of the dance, you are ready for the next step. Analyze the dance formations, partner positions, steps, structure, and music. Then respond by writing a summary of what you learned about the dance. First, list the title of the folk dance and its country or region of origin. Then identify the dance design components (formations, partner positions, steps, structure, and music) in the folk dance you performed.

With your teacher's guidance, you can extend this experience: View a folk dance by another group, and mentally compare and contrast the elements and structure used in the dance (formations, partner positions, steps, structure, and music). At the end of your folk dance analysis write a summary paragraph about the folk dance you viewed. List the name of the folk dance you viewed and include at least three similarities and differences you noticed between the dances.

Learning Folk Dance

You learn a folk dance by first performing steps and then sections in sequence. Pick a dance to learn. Once you have learned the complete dance, take a breath and check your personal space, your partner, and the group space to ensure that when the group gets moving everyone is dancing safely.

To begin learning, you first learn step 1, and practice it until you, your partner, or the group feel comfortable without the music. This will help everyone focus on the step pattern, direction, rhythm, and counts. Then do step 1 with the music.

Learn step 2, and practice it to where you feel comfortable. Then, do step 2 with the music.

EXPLORE MORE

The list of basic folk dances presents a selection of dances and styles that represent people and their heritage. This tour of folk dancing would not be complete without learning about folk dances in America. In the Explore More section on this chapter's web resource, you will learn about the history of American folk dance. You'll learn a longways dance, **square dance**, and a circle dance from various regions of the United States.

Go back and do step 1, and add on step 2. Practice the steps with the music.

Continue this process until you have completed learning the dance. Now, you are ready to practice and refine the steps, partner holds, figures, and formations. Once you have memorized the dance sections and style, you can move to the next level—having fun and enjoying the dance.

After doing the dance several times, write the dance using folk dance vocabulary. Write or draw formations, partner positions (if applicable), pathways, and steps for each section of the dance. Folk dances repeat steps and sections, so indicate the number of repetitions of a step or the repeat of an entire section. Your teacher will determine if you should include some background or historical information about the folk dance, the music used, and attire worn for the dance you performed.

Basic Folk Dances

You may remember some of the following dances from your past experiences in folk dance. They come from all over the world. This list is a place to start to learn more, but you can also expand your knowledge by researching other folk dances on your own. Simply do an Internet search on the words "folk dance," and see where it takes you.

Troika (the three horses) is a Russian folk line dance for two females with a male in the middle.

Misirlou is a Greek line dance that moves in a serpentine path.

Doudlebska polka is a dance from the village of Doudlebska, in South Bohemia, from the former Czechoslovakia (now Czech Republic). Couples form a circle in closed dance position. The men or leaders are nearest the center of the circle.

Journeyman's blacksmith is a Bavarian dance for two couples who form a square. In this dance, dancers slap their thighs and clap.

Yole is a traditional western African dance from the Temne people of Sierra Leone. This group dance is done by the entire community as part of festive occasions.

Maypole dance is done to celebrate May Day, or May 1. In this dance, people dance around a maypole. In England it has been popular for centuries and is part of May Day celebrations in other parts of the world. The popularity of the maypole dance continues in many countries.

Mexican waltz is a partner dance performed in a double circle. This dance combines aspects of folk dance and social dance. For some of the dance, the group

John Bennett

Dr. John Bennett is a professor, a surfer, an author, and a dancer who teaches folk dances from America and around the world to students preparing to teach in K-12 schools and at professional conferences. Bennett got hooked on folk dance when he was required to take it in college. This led him to study with some of the great teachers of the 20th century who had an amazing amount of knowledge about folk dances and their styling as well as tremendous background information about folk art and folklore, which contribute to learning and appreciating folk dances. Bennett's work has kept this important dance genre alive through the students he has prepared to teach others about folk dance.

moves in the circle. In other sections of the dance, partners dance together in the circle and waltz in closed dance position.

Tarantella is an Italian historical dance that remains a popular folk dance in the Italian community.

The *flower drum lantern dance* is a popular Chinese folk dance performed as a seasonal or festival dance. The group dance incorporates dance, song, and music from gong and drum. Martial arts and acrobatics may be part of the dance depending upon the talents of the group.

Varsovienne has been popular in many countries and is part of many folk, social, and square dances.

ACTIVITY 7.3 EXPLORE

Analyzing Folk Dances

In a group, find a rendition of a folk dance you select from the list of basic folk dances or a dance you researched on the Internet. View a couple of versions performed by different groups. Observe the formations, partner positions, basic steps and step sequences, and arm movement to the music. Determine the sections of the dance, then identify the differences between the two versions you viewed.

Thinking Like a Dancer

Performing folk dance gives you an opportunity to experience and think about the relationship of dance to society. It also allows you to put the dance in context of a particular time in history. Before you learn to perform a folk dance, you can view authentic folk dance groups performing it and use your observation skills and knowledge of dance to appreciate and learn about it. When re-creating a folk dance, you should do the dance with the appropriate energy and efforts that create the style of movement. Stylistic information adds authenticity to your performance of the dance and appreciation of the people who perform it as part of their heritage.

ACTIVITY 7.4   RESEARCH

Present Your Folk Dance

After you have rehearsed and performed your folk dance for the class, present steps of the dance to the class and then tell them about the dance. To prepare for this presentation, research and write about the following:

- Who performed the dance?
- Where do people perform this dance (country or region of origin)?
- Do people in other countries perform this dance?
- When is the dance performed?
- When and by whom is the dance performed today and for what reason?

For your group performance you can either find or create costumes. Or, you can find photographs of traditional costumes on the web. Determine whether they are historical costumes. Do people who perform this dance wear these same costumes today?

After the dances are performed, all the dancers in the class can take turns sharing one or more things about the dance and how it relates to them or their background.

Summary

Folk dancing has a long history. Like people, dances move from one place to another, creating many variations and styles of one dance. Beginning in the 20th century, folk dance became a dance form taught in schools and colleges. Over past decades international folk dance has gained popularity on college campuses and community centers as a way for people to learn or keep their dance heritage alive, to explore new dances, or simply for the social experience of folk dancing. Folk dance clubs, camps, organizations, and festivals formed to celebrate and preserve folk dance heritage. Folk dance companies throughout the world continue to perform dances of people across the world. Folk dance is for everyone. It is a way to experience the joy of dancing as part of your heritage or sharing a dance with someone with a different heritage. Doing your folk dances is continuing the tradition.

Folk dance offers a variety of options for a portfolio activity. You and your teacher can decide on one of the following activities.

- Restage a folk dance you know to a contemporary song. Explain your choice for the contemporary song and how you adapted the original folk dance.
- Compare and contrast two folk dances of the same type but different countries. How do geography, climate, folk values, music, and other folk arts change or not change the dance? Through a web search find photos of the original dance and different versions from several countries.
- Research and then perform a folk dance, and explain how the dance is part of the folk art of the country. Then, create a poster or media presentation to accompany your presentation.
- Chart your identity and heritage. Do some research, and find a dance that you believe represents your cultural heritage. Write an autobiography that connects your nationality and heritage.

REVIEW QUESTIONS

True or False

1. Folk dances can be regional, national, and international. _____

2. Musical instruments and arrangements are standard for all folk dances. _____

3. The sections of a folk dance relate to the sections of the music that can be repeated. _____

4. Folk dance uses partner positions, formations, and steps that are unique to its dances. _____

Multiple Choice

1. _____A collection of myths, stories, jokes, tall tales, and dramas are considered to be
    a. folk culture
    b. folk heritage
    c. folklore

2. _____Two factors that influence the development of a folk dance are
    a. climate and geography
    b. people's lifestyles
    c. music and vocal abilities

3. _____Contemporary folk dances celebrate or remind people of
    a. current movements
    b. historical or heritage events
    c. popular arts styles

Short Answer

1. List four different folk dance formations.

Matching

1. _____troika (the three horses)
2. _____misirlou
3. _____Doudlebska Polka
4. _____journeyman's blacksmith
5. _____tarantella
6. _____two-step
7. _____schottische
8. _____polka
9. _____grapevine

a. A Bavarian couples dance featuring thigh slaps and claps

b. A Russian folk line dance for two females with a male in the middle

c. A circle dance for couples from South Bohemia

d. The step done in 4/4 time uses four movements with crosses either front or back while moving to the side

e. A Greek line dance that moves in a serpentine path

f. An Italian historical dance and a popular folk dance

g. The step is a combination of a hop and three steps performed in 2/4 time

h. Three steps and a hop alternate feet, done to 4/4 or 2/4 time

i. A step that alternates feet and is performed forward, backward, and side in 2/4 time

To find supplementary materials for this chapter such as worksheets, extended learning activities, and e-journaling assignments, visit the web resource at www.discoveringdance.org/student.

Cultural Dance

ENDURING UNDERSTANDING: People dance all over the world.

ESSENTIAL QUESTION: How does a cultural dance represent the values and beliefs of a culture?

LEARNING OBJECTIVES

After reading this chapter you will be able to do the following:

- Understand the cultural geographic regions, cultures, and major dance forms.
- Participate in one or more cultural dances using correct footwork, rhythm, and styling.
- Translate cultural dance vocabulary into re-creating one or more cultural dances from different parts of the world.
- Evaluate and respond to cultural dance performances.

> "Any problem in the world can be solved by dancing."
>
> James Brown, 20th-century African American musician, dancer, and activist

If you had a ticket to travel anywhere in the world, where would you go? What if you wanted to learn about the world without leaving school or home? Just jump on the Internet, pick a country you have been curious about, and take a tour. A country's website is an electronic travelogue providing links to travel opportunities, photos of the natural and physical attractions in the country, tours of cities, and other special points of interest. These websites present the country's customs, food, arts, and the cultures of ethnic groups that are indigenous to the country and that region of the world.

All over the world, dance has been a part of cultures from prehistory. Within geographic regions are distinct differences in dances because of the people's ethnic and cultural diversity. In any region dance can be ritual or religious, traditional, historical, or contemporary dance performed as custom, recreation, entertainment, or art.

From earliest times, dances in all regions of the world celebrated life events of people or important happenings in communities. Throughout history because of war, migration, and political changes, dances changed as did dance's role within a culture as a whole or in communities. These changes extended to the people, their values and beliefs, their languages, their ways of life, and their arts. Appreciating a people's culture, their arts, and recognizing their artists makes us global citizens.

This chapter presents an overview of cultural dance, which will not only expand your knowledge of dance but enhance your knowledge of the deep complexity of culture and of cultural change throughout the world.

Discovering Cultural Dance

Dance has been called the universal language; you live in a world that dances. Take a look at the map of the world and its continents (figure 8.1). Geographers have identified distinct natural and physical features (ecosystems) in regions throughout the world. Studying a geographic region that supports human culture is also known as **cultural geography**. Within these geographic regions are specific cultural regions of the world.

In each of these cultural regions are countries, people of various racial and ethnic groups, and their cultural values. Their arts include dances from aboriginals or **first people (**the original people who inhabited the land since millennia ago) who migrated to these regions because of war, famine, economic hardship, or other reasons. The common elements of culture include the following (Blankenship in press):

- It is a way of life, learned and shared with future generations.
- It changes with time and is symbolic.
- The economy drives a culture.

Culture is a community or society's knowledge, beliefs, values, customs, and common heritage. If you were to look at the cultural geographic areas of the world, you would encounter commonalities and differences that make each country or

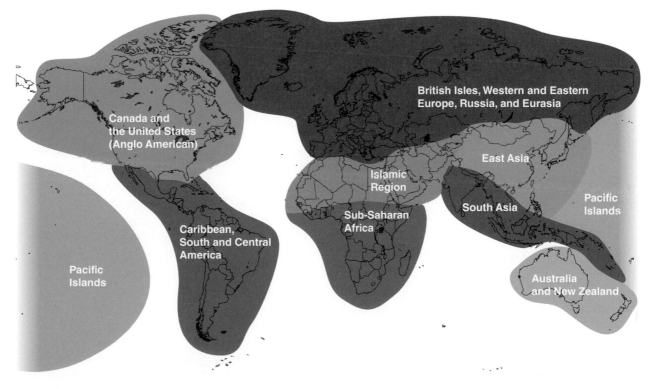

Figure 8.1 Regions of the world.

People Like Me

People Like Me is the arts education program of the San Francisco Ethnic Dance Festival and World Arts West. For 15 seasons this organization has presented an extraordinary festival featuring dancers and dance companies that represent cultures around the world. On their website, the festival provides their Online Encyclopedia of World Dance, which includes performers, information about selected dances and dance styles, musical instruments, and history of the dance style. Attending the festival to view cultural dance performances by artists from across the world would be an awesome experience. Visiting the San Francisco Ethnic Dance Festival and World Arts West website provides easy access to a virtual tour of dance around the world.

ACTIVITY 8.1   EXPLORE

Dance Around the World

Using a map of the world, survey the geographic region that your teacher assigns to your group. Search a region's or country's website, then describe the physical features of each region or country. Next, research and describe the people of that area and their culture, and find examples of a traditional dance they perform. If you can locate a video performance of the dance, write a brief descriptive summary about it. In your summary include the following information:

- Background or history of the dance
- Who dances
- When and where the dance is performed

Describe the music that accompanies the dance and the dancers' clothing. Add a photo of the dancers performing, and list references or web links to your online sources.

region unique. People have many different views about defining and describing dance from geographic or cultural regions of the world. Some people consider dances from across these regions to be examples of *world dance*, while others might call these dances *cultural dance*. Regardless of where you live in the world, you participate in dances that reflect a lot or a little of the culture.

Exploring Cultural Dance

Specific countries have dances that identify with a region and its culture immediately. For example, African dances or Indian dances have styles that make them readily identifiable, as do other cultural dances from across the globe.

When you study dances as part of a culture, you are using different lenses to see each dance in its cultural context. Earlier in this chapter, you discovered that culture is a concept in human geography. It also has deep connections to the fields of cultural anthropology, ethnology, and ethnomusicology. **Cultural anthropology** is the study of humans and their culture, which includes social structures, languages, laws, religion, arts, and technology. **Ethnology** is the study of the cultural life of a community. An **ethnologist** lives in a community for several years to record the everyday life of the people and their culture. **Ethnomusicology** is the study of a people's music in relation to its culture or society. **Ethnomusicologists** may extend their study to dances performed to the music of the culture.

Countries all over the world have traditional dances, but they are actually evolving products of history, migration, wars, and political and societal changes of the people who perform them. Today, in one country you can encounter many cultural dances, including the following:

- Dances of aboriginals or first people.
- Dances of early settlers who migrated to the area and brought their culture to their new home. In various historical eras, the dances may have colonial or postcolonial versions.
- Blended dances created after wars changed a people and their culture. These dances are not created overnight. In an invaded country, the original people and the new arrivals may or may not embrace each other's cultures or dances. A **cultural clash** may occur, and the two groups may resist each other's influence. Blending outside influences into existing traditions takes place over time.
- Newer variations of traditional dances that evolve from generation to generation. These dances absorb and blend personal, group, and societal trends that can change a dance and its performance.
- Dances of tribes, first people, and ethnic groups who strive to keep their ancestral traditions alive in contemporary society. People preserve these dances to share their heritage with the young people of their community.

All cultural dances presented in the overview of dance types connect to the three common elements of a culture (see Discovering Cultural Dance).

If you add all these elements together, you get two deep understandings:

1. Culture is about participating as a community; it can be related to ritual, spiritual, and life events and celebrations.
2. Culture can be defined as a way of life that is learned, shared with future generations, and changes with time.

Participating, viewing, and learning about cultural dance and the roles it plays in societies leads to awareness and appreciation of other people and their cultural values.

Experiencing a cultural dance means taking a look at the movement from the perspectives of both the cultural dancer and the requirements of the dance. The ideas you have learned about other dance forms so far or will encounter in this book may not apply to cultural dances. So, discard your preconception of cultural dances, and involve yourself in perceiving and experiencing the movement. Then you will be poised to find the meaning or essence of the dance and gain some insights about the dancers who perform it. Experiencing cultural dance requires you to observe through a different kind of dance lens; you must see as an ethnologist would, paying attention to the dance in the context of its home culture.

EXPLORE MORE

Take a virtual dance tour! On the web resource, you will visit a variety of countries across the globe. Each country provides an overview of its geography, history, and some of its most important dances. Key search terms in some of the dance genres provide ways to view and learn a dance or movement sequence. The dance tour provides an overview from which you can explore more through researching the countries and their wealth of dances.

Mexico

Mexico has a wealth of natural and cultural resources, with diverse landscapes from mountains to jungles, and historic traditions reaching back more than 3,000 years. Mexican dance captures the rhythm, emotion, and movement of a vibrant society with a heritage rich in tradition.

America

The United States is a country of vast natural and cultural resources and is populated by people from a vast variety of cultural heritage. Since prehistoric times, Native Americans have danced to express their traditions and cultural values. Contemporary urban dance forms began to express social changes in the United States during the latter 20th century.

Europe

Europe is a huge continent with many nationalities and their dances. Chapter 7 (Folk Dance) contains a variety of folk dances from countries throughout Europe, Russia, and other countries.

Africa

Africa is the second largest continent in the world with 54 countries. African people and cultures represent a diversity of economic and social structures with various beliefs, religions, and arts. For centuries African cultural dance has captured the spirit of life events, community and spiritual beliefs, and identities of tribes and clans of various regions.

In Africa, dance is an integral part of ceremonies, festivals, and rites. African dances are done in many countries throughout the world.

India

India is the seventh largest country in the world. For nearly 3,000 years, dance art has existed in India and is a significant aspect in Indian culture. Classical Indian dance includes a wide range of forms and styles that reflect various geographic centers, history, and traditions.

Japan

Japan is a group of islands off the east coast of Asia. According to legend, Japan was founded in the 7th century BCE. Japanese cultural dances relate to religions and social eras in Japanese history. Japanese cultural dance forms and styles span historical court dances, religious dances, and traditional folk dances. In Japan, dance remains an integral part of historical theatrical entertainment.

Japanese dances are passed from generation to generation.

Exploring these countries is just the starting place for learning about cultural dance. You may want to continue your virtual travels to other countries. These countries may connect to your family heritage, a place where a friend came from, or a country you hope to visit in the future. Whatever the reason, you can go there today and share what you learned with the class.

SPOTLIGHT

Dance Diplomacy

In early 2010 modern and contemporary dance makers from the groups Urban Bush Women, ODC, and Evidence, a dance company, took part in the first U.S. pilot program to tour internationally as the gateway of cultural exchange among nations. The purpose of this "dance diplomacy" was to create a model cultural exchange initiative. The international tour, supported by the U.S. Department of State, reached global audiences of more than 15,000 in 16 cities of 9 countries in Southeast Asia, South America, and Africa. The second season in 2012 reached global audiences of 25,000 in 24 cities in 13 countries in Africa, the Middle East, Central Asia, and Southeast Asia.

U.S. embassies and the U.S. Department of State Bureau of Educational and Cultural Affairs partner with dance companies, leading cultural and community-based organizations, and educational institutions to host unique residencies that create opportunities for engagement and exchange. One of these cultural exchanges is DanceMotionUSA, which sends American dance companies overseas to connect with audiences through workshops, lecture demonstrations, and public performances.

ACTIVITY 8.2 EXPLORE

Learn a Cultural Dance

In a small group, find a dance from the country you visited on the web in the exploration activity Dance Around the World. The cultural dance you select could be

- a traditional dance,
- a folk dance,
- a social dance,
- a dance that provides entertainment for visitors, or
- a dance that is considered an art form or part of another art such as drama or theater.

Find two videos of the dance. After watching the videos, learn several movements, poses, a movement sequence, or the entire dance. Through your reading and research about this dance can you discover

- who dances,
- when and where they dance, and
- why they dance.

Identify a list of unique characteristics of the dance (review dance designs in chapter 5). Then, further explore the background and history of the dance to answer this question: How does the dance relate to or represent the people, their culture, and society?

Thinking Like a Dancer

While dance may be your central focus, thinking like a dancer about cultural dance includes analyzing dance as part of the broader cultural context of a country or a region. A dance could have historical significance and connect to myths, legends, or literature. The dance may be a celebration of a holiday, a certain group of people, or a life event.

ACTIVITY 8.3   RESEARCH

Analyze a Cultural Dance

In your group, practice the cultural dance learned in the previous activity. After you have learned the dance, analyze it using dance elements. Review your dance element handout from the web resource to identify how space, time, energy, efforts, relationships, and their subcomponents are used in the dance. Then, answer these questions:

- How do the dance and the music relate to each other?
- Does the dance have a structure?
- What are three major features that make the dance unique?

Using your analysis, create a group composite report to record these characteristics of the dance. Share your group report with the class.

Summary

Cultural dance is the enduring memory of humanity that passes from one generation to the next. Just like many memories, people sometimes contribute their uniqueness to the dance as a result of their experiences or desire to share in the continuation of the dance. This chapter introduced you to some cultural dances from around the world and encouraged you to take your own Internet tour of the world to discover cultural dances. Deepening your understanding of cultural dance is key to understanding your friends, your neighbors, and yourself.

Select and view a complete dance from a cultural geographic region that is different from the one your group was assigned in the first activity. When viewing this cultural dance, put your ethnologist hat on to answer these questions:

- How do the dancers use space, time, energy, efforts, and associated elements in the dance?
- How do the dancers relate to each other during the dance?
- What is the relationship of each dance to the music or song that accompanies it?

View the dance again, and determine the choreographic design and structure. Then, answer these questions:

- Do the dancers' clothes and accessories relate to the dance?
- What is the purpose for the dance performance (traditional, community, life event, religious, entertainment, or art)?
- Does the dance express specific aspects or values in the culture?
- Have any prominent dance artists contributed to the development of this dance as art and then extended its presence in other parts of the world to make it more popular?

Summarize your analysis of this cultural dance as representative of a cultural region. Take your findings to the next level: Repeat the process to compare a traditional cultural dance to contemporary renditions of the dance form or a fusion of traditional and contemporary dance forms. Is it possible to identify two or three traditional elements or parts of the dance? How about two or three contemporary elements or parts of the dance? Did the traditional and the contemporary create a unified choreographic work?

Write your report, and create a poster or a media slide presentation to share with the class. Then post your research process and report in your portfolio.

REVIEW QUESTIONS

True or False

1. Dance has been a part of the world's cultures from prehistory to today. _____
2. Dance has been called the universal language. _____
3. Appreciating a people's cultures and their arts and recognizing their artists makes us global citizens. _____
4. Traditional dances remain unchanged as they pass from generation to generation. _____
5. Dances of any region can be ritual or religious, traditional, historical, or contemporary, and they can be performed as entertainment or art. _____

Multiple Choice

1. _____Within a geographic region a variety of dances exist because of
   a. topography and climate
   b. people's heritage and economics
   c. race, ethnicity, and rituals

2. _____A dance of historical significance, a celebration, or a life event best describes a
   a. cultural dance
   b. community dance
   c. traditional dance

3. _____The value of a cultural dance form uses
   a. a Western definition and lens for description
   b. the unique characteristics and style for each dance
   c. the people's culture and their heritage

4. _____Studying a geographic region that supports human geography is also known as
   a. physical geography
   b. personal geography
   c. cultural geography

5. _____In cultural dance you study the who, where, when, and why of a dance to study
   a. how the dance represents the people, culture, and society
   b. the history of the dance and its characteristics
   c. the people who performed the dance and their lifestyle

Matching

1. _____first people
2. _____culture
3. _____cultural anthropology
4. _____cultural clash
5. _____ethnology
6. _____ethnologists
7. _____ethnomusicology
8. _____ethnomusicologist

a. The study of a people's music in relation to its culture or society

b. Original people who inhabited the land since millennia ago

c. The study of humans and their culture which includes social structures, languages, laws, religion, arts, and technology

d. May extend their study to dances performed to the music of the culture

e. A cultural disruption and challenge to the existing traditions in an environment

f. The study of cultural life of a community

g. A community or society's knowledge, beliefs, values, customs, and common heritage

h. Lives in a community to record the everyday life of the people and their culture

 To find supplementary materials for this chapter such as worksheets, extended learning activities, and e-journaling assignments, visit the web resource at www.discoveringdance.org/student.

Ballet

ENDURING UNDERSTANDING: Ballet is a classic, Western dance genre and a performing art.

ESSENTIAL QUESTION: How does ballet help me express myself as a dancer?

LEARNING OBJECTIVES

After reading this chapter, you should be able to do the following:

- Recognize major ballet works, styles, and ballet artists in history.
- Execute basic ballet technique, use ballet vocabulary, and perform barre exercises and center combinations.
- Apply ballet etiquette and dance safety while dancing.
- Evaluate and respond to classical and contemporary ballet performances.

"Learning to walk sets you free. Learning to dance gives you the greatest freedom of all: to express with your whole self the person you are."

Melissa Hayden, former New York City Ballet soloist

VOCABULARY

adagio
à la seconde
à terre
allegro
ballet
ballet technique
barre
center
dancer directions
derrière
devant
en l'air
turnout

At the ballet, male dancers perform leaps that seem to suspend in the air. Female dancers balance poised on the tips of their toes with the other leg extended perpendicular to the floor. Ballet dancers spin, jump, and glide across the stage at incredible speeds or extend their legs and arms slowly to create beautiful poses. Ballet is a dance genre that focuses on dancers acquiring a strong technique to execute steps and poses flawlessly. Beyond the technique, the dancer adds quality, style, and expression.

Ballet began as a Western classical dance genre over 400 years ago and has evolved into an international performing art. Performers who learn ballet today are not only ballet dancers; they are dancers of modern, contemporary, jazz, and other dance forms, too. Football players, gymnasts, ice skaters, and other athletes use ballet technique as part of their athletic training. In addition, ballet has become a popular fitness workout. Throughout the world, ballet is studied in schools, universities, conservatories, and studios.

This chapter provides ways to look at ballet as a dance genre to support your dancing in the classroom. You will learn about ballet, its movement vocabulary and terminology, its history, its dancers, and the choreographic artists who create ballet dance works. Also, you will view selected works from ballet performance literature and respond to them.

Discovering Ballet

Watching video clips from famous ballets is like viewing art works that showcase **ballet styles** from various historical eras (see Viewing Ballet Choreographic Styles activity on the web resource). Watching ballet can be a kinesthetic experience and therefore helps develop your kinesthetic sense. As you watch dancers move, you perceive the ballet through the senses of sight and sound, connecting them to your own sense of movement.

❗ ACTIVITY 9.1   DISCOVER

Ballet Styles

After looking at the different ballet styles posted in your classroom, select a ballet style that appeals to you. Then imagine dancing your version of that ballet style. Plan in your mind, then create a movement statement or sequence that captures your interpretation of the ballet movements in that style. Compare how dance elements (patterns in the space, time, energy, effort, and qualities of movement; see chapter 3) apply to your movement statement or sequence. Share your movement sequence with another classmate or in a small group. Summarize your findings for your movement sequence.

Exploring Ballet

In the renaissance French kings and their court dancers danced in ballets. Later, professional dancers moved ballet from the court to the theater. During the 19th century, ballet became a performing art with romantic and classical style ballet works. In the 20th century, ballet spread across the world through touring companies, dancers, and choreographic artists. Over the last several decades, contemporary ballet has blended modern and other dance genres to express contemporary themes in ballet works. Likewise, ballet has contributed technique and style to the development of other concert and entertainment dance genres. Your first step in exploring ballet is to take several steps back in history to understand its development.

History of Ballet

Ballet began in the Italian courts during the renaissance. Dance was an amusement and an entertainment. Dance masters taught courtiers popular dancers and proper etiquette for many social occasions that were part of court life. Court entertainments of dance, music, song, and pantomime were included in masked balls, as part of interludes between acts of plays, and between courses at banquets. The term *ballet* comes from the Italian term *ballare,* meaning "to dance;" *ballo* refers to a dance in the ballroom.

Ballet moved from Italy to France when Catherine de' Medici married the heir to the French throne, King Henry II. She produced what is now known as the first ballet, *Le Ballet Comique de la Reine,* in 1581. The extravagant performance lasted from 10:00 p.m. to 4:00 a.m. This lavish court entertainment was copied at courts throughout Europe. The ballet made France the recognized leader for future dance developments. In the French court King Louis XIII was a dancer,

DID YOU KNOW?

Cross-Training

Ballet has become popular as cross-training for more and more athletes. Gymnasts and figure skaters have incorporated ballet steps into their sports for many years. Later 20th-century athletes such as Olympic swimmers, NFL football players, and British soccer players used ballet training as a way to enhance their sport skills, making the dance studio their secondary training center.

Several years ago, two British researchers compared the fitness of ballet dancers from the English National Ballet with the British Olympic Swimming team. The ballet dancers scored 25 percent stronger than the swimmers in a range of fitness tests. In 7 of the 10 tests, the ballet dancers scored higher than the swimmers. This test is just one of many that have led athletic programs and sports teams to take ballet classes.

Athletes who perform ballet have found it the most rigorous training. The professional ballet dancer uses the entire body to build strength and power for performances that last sometimes 3 hours or more. In addition to acquiring physical stamina, dancers must have strong concentration and endurance to meet the physical and mental athletic challenges of dance as a performance art.

and with his court he performed many ballets as amusements and entertainment. Louis XIV performed as a dancer and gained the title the "Sun King," the name of one of his most famous dancing roles. Pierre Beauchamp, the king's dancing master, is credited with clarifying the five positions of the feet. At the French court during Louis XIV's reign, ballet was serious entertainment and amusement for the courtiers. He produced over 1,000 extravagant ballets performed by court dancers and by all-male professional dancers, who enacted the female roles in his ballets. He preferred classically themed ballets based on Greek myths.

Court ballets were more akin to a musical theater production. The performance space was in the great hall. The King had the best seat in the audience, while courtiers by their rank sat or stood around the performance space. The production had a story line or theme. Dances were based on the social dances of the day. Music for the dances used popular dance tunes or may have been composed especially for the ballet. Costumes displayed the latest fashion worn at court but with elaborate decorations and accessories to symbolize the dancer's role. Scenery included set pieces, painted backgrounds, and wagons that moved dancers or musicians around the space. Torch bearers were stationed around the great hall to provide lighting for the performance.

Ballets continued to be dance interludes between dramatic or vocal performances or entire performances. Sometimes ballets were part of themed balls such as pastoral or masquerade balls.

An ardent patron of the arts, Louis XIV established the Académie Royale de Danse (Royal Academy of Dance). Jean-Baptiste Lully, a court musician and dance supervisor, became the administrator for the academy. He instituted the requirement that professional dancers had to attend classes and rehearsals. In the next century the academy would become the Paris Opéra.

Eighteenth-Century Ballet

In the 18th century, ballet moved from the court to the theater, where music, costumes, and dance changed. With new choreographers and composers came fresh ideas about what was ballet. Dancers and choreographers developed new artistic visions and expanded ballet technique in the opera houses and theaters in London, Milan, and Vienna that began to rival the Paris Opéra. At the Paris Opéra male dancers continued to dominate the stage. During the century, female dancers began to take on more central roles, developed their technique to compete with male dancers, and introduced costume and shoe innovations. Some of the French ballet masters visited or relocated in Russia. Their influence over time was the foundation for the development of Russian ballet. Major dancers and choreographers of the 18th century are included in the sections that follow.

GAETAN VESTRIS Gaetan Vestris was the premier dancer at the Paris Opéra and leading dancer in Europe. His leaps and newly developed pirouette justified his claim for the title "God of the Dance."

MARIE SALLÉ   Marie Sallé was a French dancer who was popular at the Paris Opéra and at London theaters. She abandoned the elaborate hairstyles, corsets, and wide panniers that were fashionable; instead, she danced in soft gowns and with her hair down.

MARIE CAMARGO   French dancer and rival of Marie Sallé, Camargo had a brilliant technique that included beaten steps and petit allegro combinations. She instituted costume reforms, which included shortening her skirts so that her jumps and beats could be seen. She removed the heels from her shoes to dance in flat-soled slippers, which were a forerunner of the ballet slipper.

JEAN-GEORGES NOVERRE   Jean-Georges Noverre was a French dancer, teacher, and choreographer who served as dance master in many European courts and theaters. In 1760, Jean-Georges Noverre wrote *Lettres sur la danse et sur les ballets*, about a new form of ballet called *ballet d'action*, a form of art that was independent from opera. The ideas for ballet d'action summarized various choreographers' experiments during this era. Ballet d'action presented a story told in dance and mime. His ballet *Médée et Jason* exemplified the concepts of ballet d'action.

The precepts of Noverre's *Letters* stated the following:

- Ballet should be technically brilliant but dramatic and emotionally expressive.
- In all dances, plots should contribute to a unified ballet work.
- Scenery, music, and plot should appropriately support the ballet theme.
- Pantomime should be simple and realistic to convey its message.

The 18th-century ballet began with *opéra ballets,* in which gods and goddesses danced. Later in the second half of the century, ballet d'action told stories through dance and mime about humans in pastoral or country settings.

During the 18th century, dancers, choreographers, and ballet masters took their works to courts and theaters throughout Europe. Some of the French ballet masters visited or relocated in Russia. Their influence over time was the foundation for the development of Russian ballet in the 19th century.

Romantic Ballet

Romantic ballet provided escapism from the drudgery of work that escalated because of the Industrial Revolution. In romantic ballets, female dancers took central roles that often contrasted realism with fantasy, while male dancers moved into supporting roles and remained the artistic directors. Female roles captured the romantic ideal of women as delicate beings. In contrast, some female roles represented the roles of independent women emerging during that historical era.

Romantic ballets were dramatic action stories told through dancing and pantomime. Romantic ballets most often told stories about love triangles. The romantic ballet form was two acts. In Act I, female dancers usually portrayed villagers. In Act II the dancers were transformed into spirits or similar ethereal beings.

The following sections introduce some ballet dancers, choreographers, and ballets of the romantic period.

MARIE TAGLIONI (1804-1884)   Marie Taglioni was Italian dancer trained by her father. She became a star at the Paris Opéra in the ballet *La Sylphide*. Her dance style epitomized the romantic dancer. She wore the romantic style tutu, a long white tutu with tight bodice that inspired female fashion of the period. Taglioni was one of the first dancers to pose for an instant on the tip of her dance slipper. Pointe dance technique was to develop throughout the century to create new technical requirements for the female dancer. Later in her career she danced the lead role in *Pas de Quatre* (for more information, see Jules Perrot).

CARLOTTA GRISI (1819-1899) Carlotta Grisi was an Italian dancer who studied with and became the partner of Jules Perrot. She performed the lead dance role in the ballet *Giselle* with Perrot's choreography. Grisi was considered a technically strong dancer. In her career she danced many other leading roles in romantic ballets and was one of the four stars in the *Pas de Quatre*.

FANNY ELSSLER (1810-1884) An Austrian dancer trained in Vienna, Fanny Elssler became a star at the Paris Opéra. She toured the United States with her troupe and with American dancers she picked up in major cities along the East Coast. Elssler had strong technique. Her signature dance was *La Cachucha*, a sensuous, earthy solo.

JULES PERROT (1810-1892) Considered the greatest male dancer of the romantic period, Jules Perrot was a French dancer and choreographer. He danced and staged his ballets in theaters across Europe before going to Russia, where he restaged his ballets. His works extended the ideas of ballet d'action; they integrated believable characters and mime into the plots of these story ballets. In contrast, he choreographed *Pas de Quatre*, an abstract ballet, for the four female stars of romantic ballet (Marie Taglioni, Carlotta Grisi, Fanny Cerrito, and Lucile Grahn).

Classical Ballet

Russian ballet had been importing French ballet masters since the 18th century to train Russian dancers and produce state-supported ballets. Russian ballet developed and flourished in the Russian Imperial Theatres, which offered opera, ballet, and drama. In the 19th century, dancers and choreographers brought romantic ballets to Russia and created new works, transforming ballet into its classical style of a performing art.

Classical ballets told stories through ballet, character dance, and pantomime. These ballets were entire theatrical evenings of entertainment. The ballets' stories combined themes of fantasy and realism. The ballet productions transported the audience to earlier times, exotic places, or fantastic settings for an entire evening. Classical ballets contained two or more acts; for example, the *The Nutcracker* ballet has two acts, while *Swan Lake* has four acts. These story ballets included a plot, dances by an entire company of dancers, and mime sequences. The climax of a classical ballet is a *grand pas de deux* danced by the *premier danseur* (leading male dancer) and the *ballerina* (leading female dancer). *Pas de deux* translated means "a dance for two." The pas de deux form began in the romantic era but acquired its form in classical ballets. The pas de deux in classical ballet has several sections.

The first variation is an *adagio*, a slow duet that showcases the ballerina in supported poses, multiple turns, and lifts. The second variation is the male solo. The next variation is a female solo. The final variation is a series of short dance sections by both dancers to present their technical virtuosity.

The following sections describe some of the dancers and choreographers who were instrumental in the development of classical ballet.

MARIUS PETIPA (1819-1910) Marius Petipa was a French principal dancer at the Paris Opéra before moving to St. Petersburg, Russia. Petipa created over 50 ballets. He choreographed lavish evenings of ballets. These extravaganzas included ballet, mime, and character dances (a blend of ballet and folk dance styles). Petipa collaborated with composer Pyotr Ilyich Tchaikovsky and with choreographer Lev Ivanov. Some of Petipa's ballets or pas de deux sequences from full ballets are still performed today, such as *Swan Lake* (choreographed with Lev Ivanov) and the *Don Quixote* pas de deux from the ballet by the same name.

LEV IVANOV (1834-1901) Russian native Lev Ivanov worked in Petipa's shadow for many years. Ivanov's claims to fame include *The Nutcracker* and *Swan Lake*, acts II and IV. Both ballets continue to be performed today.

PIERINA LEGNANI (1863-1923) Italian-trained ballerina Pierina Legnani first became famous in London for performing 32 fouetté pirouettes, or continuous, fast, whipping turns. The next year she repeated her 32 fouettés on the Russian stage in the ballet *Swan Lake*. In Russia, Legnani brought a new level of technique and dancing en pointe that challenged and motivated Russian dancers.

ENRICO CECCHETTI (1850-1928) Behind the scenes, Italian dancer, ballet master, and ballet theoretician Enrico Cecchetti trained Russian and Italian dancers who performed in ballets of this era. (See Methods and Schools of Ballet, later in this chapter.)

Ballet in the United States Before 1900

Beginning in colonial times, major cities established theaters on the East Coast. English theatrical companies toured these cities performing operas, ballets, and dramas as entertainment. The first ballet produced in America was *La Forêt Noire*, which was imported from France near the end of the 18th century. Colonial American dancer John Durang (1786-1822) was a circus performer and dancer. He performed ballet pantomimes (popular dramatic presentations with ballet and mime interludes) in colonial theaters.

In the 19th century, the following notable American ballet dancers emerged.

AUGUSTA MAYWOOD (1825-1876) American-trained dancer Augusta Maywood performed in the American version of *La Sylphide* in New York. In Europe, she was the first American ballerina to perform at the Paris Opéra; in Italy, she became a prima ballerina (a leading female dancer) at La Scala Opera House Theater.

MARY ANN LEE (1823-1899) An American-trained dancer who studied in Paris, Mary Ann Lee returned to form a company that toured U.S. cities. She was the first American to play the role of Giselle in the ballet of the same name.

GEORGE WASHINGTON SMITH (1820-1899) American-born George Washington Smith was a dancer and choreographer who joined Fanny Elssler's company when it toured the United States. He partnered with Mary Ann Lee on tour and became the first American to dance the role of Albrecht in *Giselle*.

During the 19th century many European dancers toured the United States as members of family troupes performing in circus acts and ballets. In the second half of the century while the states were preparing for war, the Italian Ronzani Ballet Troupe toured the United States. Some of the Italian dancers remained in the United States and continued to perform ballet in stage shows such as *The Black Crook* and other popular forms of entertainment.

Twentieth-Century Ballet

Twentieth-century ballet began when a Russian theater director and entrepreneur named Serge Diaghilev brought his company, Diaghilev's Ballets Russes to Paris in 1909. He selected an all-star cast from the Russian Imperial Theatres to present new choreography in his company's premier Paris performance. For the next two decades, Diaghilev's company traveled throughout Europe, the United States, and South America presenting works by new choreographers and dancers. The company presented a variety of styles from the classical repertory as well as avant-garde works that shocked audiences. The dancers' technical virtuosity and artistry would astound the world and usher in a new era of ballet.

The following sections describe some of the dancers and choreographers who were instrumental in the development of 20th-century ballet.

MICHEL FOKINE (1880-1942)   Russian native Michel Fokine trained and performed in Russia before joining Diaghilev's Ballets Russes company as dancer and choreographer. In the early years of the Ballets Russes, Fokine's choreography made the transition from classical to 20th-century choreography and contributed to the company's success. Later he immigrated to the United States to teach and continued to choreograph. His works were based on five precepts (rules), which he published in *The London Times*, a further extension of ideas presented in ballet d'action that Perrot had developed in Russia in the 19th century. Fokine choreographed mainly story ballets, but his signature work was an abstract ballet. These are his best-known works:

- *Les Sylphides* (1909): Fokine's signature work, this abstract ballet captures the essence of romantic style ballets.
- *Petrouchka* (1911): The story of a sad clown puppet at a 19th-century Russian carnival.
- *Firebird* (1910): A fairy tale in which a prince meets a magical firebird.

ANNA PAVLOVA (1881-1931)   Anna Pavlova was a Russian prima ballerina at the Russian Imperial Theatres. She joined Diaghilev's Ballets Russes for a year, then she left to create her own company and tour the world. Her works included classical ballet and her experimental works. Her signature work as a dancer was the *Dying Swan* solo, which Michel Fokine choreographed for her.

VASLAV NIJINSKY (1890-1950)   A Russian-trained dancer, Nijinsky joined Diaghilev's Ballets Russes as a dancer and later emerged as a choreographer. His soaring leaps impressed audiences. Nijinsky choreographed cutting edge ballets that were sometimes shocking to audiences. In 1917 Nijinsky became mentally ill and left the company. His work as a dancer raised the bar for male dancers. His major choreographic contributions include these:

- *Le Après-midi-d'un faune* (*The Afternoon of a Faun,* 1912): In this controversial ballet, Nijinsky used the music of French composer Claude Debussy and Greek sculpture as inspiration.
- *Le Sacre du Printemps* (*The Rite of Spring,* 1913): This avant-garde ballet used rhythm and movement to re-create an ancient ritual to music by Russian-born composer Igor Stravinsky.

In the decades that followed the Bolshevik Revolution in Russia and World War I, Russian dancers and choreographers settled across Europe, the United States, and South America. They brought their artistry to new places and new students to develop ballet in countries all over the world. Some of these dancers-turned-choreographers produced ballets from the first decades of the 20th century.

Neoclassic Ballet

Neoclassic (meaning "new classic") ballet is a style that was built on classical ballet technique but overlaid with contemporary ballet style to create a new classic style. The following sections discuss George Balanchine, who made major contributions in this style, and other choreographers whose works went on to influence the evolution of 20th-century ballet.

GEORGE BALANCHINE (1904-1983) Dancer and choreographer George Balanchine was born and trained in Russia. In 1933, he emigrated after wealthy American entrepreneurs invited him to the United States to establish and direct the company and the school of The American Ballet. The company closed, but the school survived. By the end of the 1940s, the New York City Ballet emerged, and Balanchine became its artistic director and choreographer. He is known as the father of American ballet. During his career he created over 400 ballets. Most of his works were abstract ballets in the neoclassic style.

Balanchine wanted to express modern 20th-century life and ideas in contrast to classical ballet. His intention was to capture the spirit and athleticism of American dancers. The abstract ballets (ballets without a story) he choreographed focused on the dancers and his manipulation of ballet into contemporary messages. Some of his major ballets include:

- *Serenade* (1935): This ballet is an early Balanchine abstract work in neoclassic style.
- *The Four Temperaments* (1946): This neoclassic ballet presents the clean, athletic lines that are recognized as Balanchine's signature style.
- *Agon* (1957): A series of abstract dances performed to the music of Igor Stravinsky, the ballet is a contest between different groups of dancers.

JEROME ROBBINS (1918-1998) Jerome Robbins was an American-born dancer, choreographer, and director who contributed modern ballets to the New York City Ballet (NYCB) repertory. Before joining NYCB, Robbins had danced and choreographed with Ballet Theatre (later known as American Ballet Theatre, also located in New York). Robbins joined NYCB in 1950 as a dancer, and two years later he became the associate artistic director of the company. In his ballets, real people danced on stage moving in ways that reflected what was happening in society at the time. Robbins' works provided a complimentary vision to Balanchine's work. These works are among the many he created:

- *Fancy Free* (1944): This story ballet is about three sailors on leave in New York.
- *Dances at a Gathering* (1969): An abstract, contemporary ballet for 10 dancers to the music of Frédéric Chopin that celebrates dance and dancers.

By the end of the 1930s, Ballet Theatre formed as a second New York company. The company's number of dancers, choreographers, and its repertory of dances included both classical and modern ballets. During the 1940s, British choreographer Anthony Tudor created works that ensured the company's success. His choreographic approach created ballets with story lines guided by emotions. These ballets included works such as *Lilac Garden* and *Pillar of Fire*. They were termed *psychological ballets.*

With this strong repertory, Ballet Theatre continued to evolve. In the 1960s the company became American Ballet Theatre (ABT). Both ABT and NYCB toured nationally and became recognized as international companies.

In the second half of the 20th century, ballet took new directions. New York City Ballet and ABT toured internationally. New ballet companies in New York and cities around the nation emerged with new artistic directions that were to absorb the contemporary society and arts styles. The defection of dancers from then Soviet Union brought a new infusion of classical training that would blend into the rapidly developing contemporary ballet styles of choreography.

ROBERT JOFFREY (1930-1988)   Originally from Seattle, Robert Joffrey studied at the School of American Ballet and studied modern dance in New York. In the 1960s after a dance career in various ballet companies, he formed the Joffrey Ballet with Gerald Arpino in New York. The Joffrey Ballet repertory was a combination of revived 20th-century ballets and new contemporary ballets. The company toured, and in the 1990s it resettled in Chicago. Robert Joffrey's choreography includes contemporary ballets such as *Viva Vivaldi* and *Astarte*.

GERALD ARPINO (1928-)   A dancer and company director of the Joffrey Ballet, Gerald Arpino choreographed contemporary, topical ballets. In the 1960s and 1970s, his works incorporated movements from many sources. He created ballets based on contemporary art styles such as pop art that attracted new audiences to ballet. A signature work of Arpino's is *Trinity*, a rock ballet.

ARTHUR MITCHELL (1934-)   Arthur Mitchell is from Harlem, a large neighborhood in the city of New York. He attended the school of The American Ballet and then joined the NYCB as the first African American dancer in the company. In the 1960s, Mitchell retuned to Harlem to form a ballet school as the foundation of Dance Theatre of Harlem. The company's repertory is a mix of Balanchine's works, Mitchell's works such as *John Henry*, and works of a host of other new choreographers with a wide range of styles. The Dance Theatre of Harlem produced reinterpretations of classics; one of those works was a Creole version of *Giselle*.

SUZANNE FARRELL (1945-)   Cincinnati-born dancer Suzanne Farrell studied and performed with NYCB. She created many leading roles in the Balanchine repertory. In the 1960s she left NYCB to perform in Europe and then returned to the United States restaging Balanchine works and teaching.

During the 1960s and 1970s Russian dancers defected or disowned their country then known as the Soviet Union, now known as the Russian Federation to live and contribute to American ballet. The following sections discuss some of them.

RUDOLF NUREYEV (1938-1993)   Russian-born and -trained Rudolf Nureyev left the Soviet Union to continue his dance career. On tour in Europe with the Kirov Ballet, he defected in Paris in 1961. After performing with the Royal Ballet, he came to the United States. Considered one of the foremost male dancers of the 20th century, he danced, partnered, choreographed, and restaged works in Europe and the United States. He appeared in films and in 1983 became the director of the Paris Opéra Ballet.

MIKHAIL BARYSHNIKOV (1948-)   Baryshnikov trained in Russia at the Imperial Ballet School (now the Vaganova Ballet Academy) and joined the Kirov Ballet. On a tour with the Stars of the Bolshoi Ballet, he defected in Canada and came to the United States. Baryshnikov performed with ABT and NYCB. He expanded his dance career even further by doing works of modern dance choreographer Twyla Tharp. Later he had a short-lived acting career before working on the White Oaks Project, experimenting in contemporary dance choreography. His impressive dancing talents, technical virtuosity, and his extensive repertory from classical ballet to contemporary ballet inspired the next generation of dancers.

NATALIA MAKAROVA (1940-)   A Russian-born ballerina, Natalia Makarova came to the West in the 1970s. She re-created and staged many classical ballet roles and performed contemporary ballets. She went on to restage ballets for companies in the United States and Europe.

ELLIOT FELD (1943-)   American-born Elliot Feld performed ballet, modern dance, and on Broadway before starting his first of several generations of the Feld Ballet. His company members taught New York City school children. Some of these young dancers would later join Feld's company. His contemporary ballets have a fresh, eclectic style. An earlier work called *Harbinger* is a dance about games, while his *Grand Cannon*, a work for two men and six women, is a ballet that radiates Feld's style.

ALONZO KING   American-born choreographer Alonzo King is from Georgia and choreographs contemporary ballet works. His company, LINES Ballet, performs his extensive repertory. He studied with ABT and the school of The American Ballet, and he danced with Alvin Ailey among others. He danced with Dance Theatre of Harlem before starting his school and founding his company in California. King's extensive choreography and his company have gained him an international reputation. Here are two of his works:

- *Soothing the Enemy* (2000): In this contemporary ballet, the characters face their fears.
- *Dust and Light* (2009): In this ballet, King brings together exquisite movement in changing landscapes to beautiful music.

By the end of the 20th century, ballet had morphed into contemporary ballet. Underlying this style was the traditional ballet technique. Contemporary ballet demanded that dancers train in ballet and other genres such as modern and jazz dance to interpret the ballets being created. The proportions in the mix of dance genres and styles depended on the choreographer's idea of how to balance them to express the work. Contemporary works are as eclectic as the choreographers who create them. Most contemporary works are abstract ballets, some works contain social statements, and lately portraying human emotions has been a trend.

Ballet companies want to preserve classical repertory, yet they must appeal to current audiences' interests and continue to produce works that appeal to a wide audience. These two contrasting needs contribute to the complex history of this dance genre.

Methods and Schools of Ballet

Several methods (systems) of ballet evolved as a way to teach technique and styles of performance. Sometimes teachers choose to blend these methods.

Enrico Cecchetti developed the Cecchetti method while teaching his dancers in the Russian Imperial Theatres. In the early 20th century he lived in London, and he recorded his ballet curriculum in the 1920s. His method continues to inspire today's dancers through several international organizations that teach it.

The Russian method, (also called the *Russian school*) refers to a number of ballet methods of which the Vaganova method is one of the best known. Russian dancer, choreographer, and teacher Agrippina Vaganova developed her method for teaching ballet while she taught the advanced classes in ballet at the Leningrad Choreographic Academy, now known as the Vaganova Academy of Russian Ballet. In 1934 she published her ballet method, *Basic Principles of Ballet*, which is used widely today.

During the 19th and 20th centuries other ballet training systems evolved in Europe and the United States. In England, the Royal Academy of Dance (RAD) developed a graded ballet curriculum that evolved over several decades through the work of many devoted dance educators. The RAD curriculum is taught around the world. In the latter 20th century, the Balanchine method of training emerged. The ABT school has developed a training curriculum that is reaching into academic and community settings.

Basics of Ballet Class

The ballet class is made up of two sections, the barre and the center. At the barre, dancers execute exercises to gain strength and practice technique in preparation for dancing in the center. The second part of the class, or center, is exercises, steps, and combinations done in the middle of the dance space or across the floor. Ballet exercises or steps are performed as adagio (slow) movements or allegro (fast) movements to musical accompaniment.

Because ballet had a long history as part of the French court, ballet terminology uses French language terms. Like any other dance genre, learning ballet requires creating a movement–language connection. Knowing both the term and the movement helps you communicate the language of dance with others. Spoken languages and written terms can sound and appear differently. In ballet, you have the added feature of translating the written or spoken term into movement. Knowing the literal translation of the ballet term in your spoken language, sometimes called an *action word*, can be helpful in remembering the step or the ballet term.

Characteristics of **ballet technique** include classical alignment of the body, the outward rotation of the legs from the hip sockets known as **turnout**, positions of the feet and arms, and pointed feet. Alignment, turnout, stance, weight transfer, and balance are basic movement principles you use when you learn ballet technique. They are part of learning positions of the feet, arms, and body; poses; exercises; and steps.

Ballet Class Safety

To ensure your safety, follow the dance class rules that your teacher sets. In addition, pay attention to your clothing and accessories and to your space. Shoes should fit well with elastic straps and ties tucked in. Be sure your hair is pulled away from your face and secured so that you can see and it doesn't hit you or another dancer in the face. When dancing as a group at the barre or in the center or when moving across the floor, you need to practice awareness of personal space and group space. Following the teacher's instructions for entering or leaving the space will help to avoid traffic jams or personal collisions. When moving across the floor, you should move without stopping and keep aware of other dancers moving across the floor.

Ballet Dance Wear

As in any dance class, you teacher will tell you the dress code for the class. In classes where you wear leotards or other dance wear, the dance wear information presented here will apply or be similar.

In a traditional ballet class, women wear a black leotard with pink or beige tights. Ballet slippers are pink or beige to coordinate with the tights. For the classical ballet hairstyle, all hair (including bangs and wisps) is pulled off the face and secured in a bun at the back of the head. Wearing jewelry in ballet class such as dangling earrings, necklaces, bracelets, watches, and rings is not encouraged, mainly for safety reasons.

Men traditionally wear black tights with a black leotard or a white tee-shirt. The tee-shirt should snugly fit the body. Men's tights stretch long enough so that dancers can wear a belt or elastic band around the waist. Dancers fold the tights over the belt for a smooth look. Male dancers wear an undergarment called a dance belt (similar to athletic support) under their tights. Men wear white or black socks over their tights, and shoes are white or black. Hair is kept off the face.

Positions of the Feet

Classical ballet has five basic positions of the feet. In these positions, the weight of the body is vertically centered over the feet and the entire foot rests on the floor (full-foot position).

first position: The heels of the feet touch, and both legs are equally turned out (figure 9.1).

second position: The feet are separated about the distance of one and one half of your foot length up to shoulder-width apart. Both big toes are on a straight line to ensure equal turnout (figure 9.2).

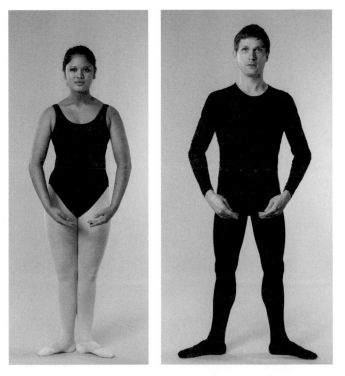

Figure 9.1 First position. **Figure 9.2** Second position.

third position: The heel of the front foot touches the middle of the arch of the back foot (figure 9.3).

fourth position: The distance between the back and front foot is the length of one of your feet. For the beginning dancer, fourth position can be forward of first position or third position (figure 9.4).

fifth position: The heel of the front foot touches the back foot (figure 9.5).

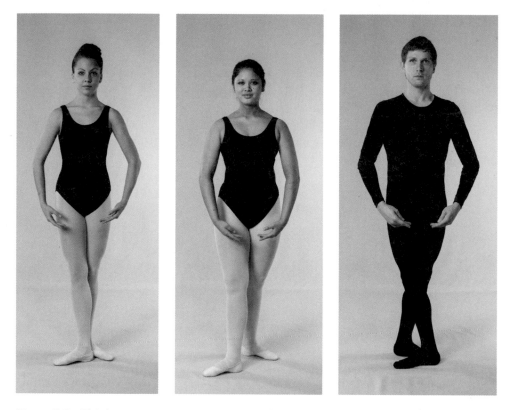

Figure 9.3 Third position.   **Figure 9.4** Fourth position.   **Figure 9.5** Fifth position.

Active-foot positions are positions where the working foot is resting on or off the floor or it is positioned somewhere on the supporting leg. These foot positions all use turnout of the supporting and the working legs:

B+ (also called attitude à terre derrière): The working leg is bent. The knees may be apart or together. The working foot is pointed with the big toe resting on the floor behind the supporting foot.

sur le cou-de-pied (on the neck of the foot): The working leg is bent with the foot positioned in front or behind the ankle.

retiré (withdrawn): The working leg is turned out and bent in à la seconde. The working foot is positioned under the knee of the supporting leg. For retiré devant (withdrawn front), the little toe touches the supporting leg under the knee. For retiré derrière (withdrawn back), the heel of the working foot touches behind the knee. Another common retiré position is in the middle; the pointed foot touches the side of the supporting knee.

Positions of the Arms

Classical ballet has five basic positions of the arms. They are numbered similar to the positions of the feet. In these long, curved lines your arms slightly flex at the elbows and the wrists, and your hands extend the lines created by the arms.

preparatory position (sometimes referred to as fifth position en bas): The arms stretch down in front of the body with the sides of the little fingers almost but not touching the body (figure 9.6).

first position: The arms stretch in front of the body parallel to the bottom of the sternum or higher, forming an oval shape. The hands are slightly separated (figure 9.7).

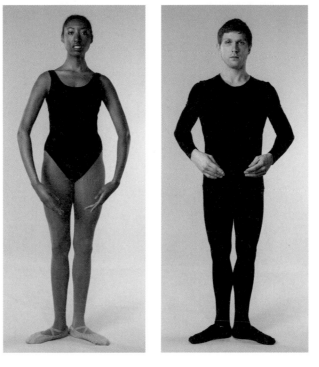

Figure 9.6 Preparatory position. **Figure 9.7** First position.

second position: Arms stretch à la seconde (immediately in front of the sides of the body) just below shoulder height (figure 9.8). In the Cecchetti method and some other styles, the arms slope downward and are slightly rounded.

Figure 9.8 Second position.

153

demi-seconde (half-second) position: The arms stretch at half the height between second position and fifth position en bas (figure 9.9).

third position: One arm is high overhead, while the other arm stretches in second position (figure 9.10).

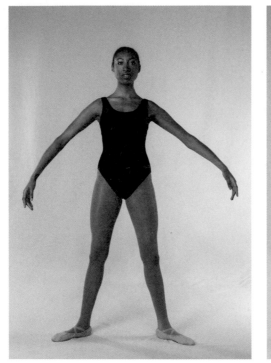

Figure 9.9   Demi-seconde position.

Figure 9.10   Third position.

fourth position: One arm is high overhead, while the other arm curves in front of the waistline (figure 9.11).

fifth position en haut (high): Both arms raise high overhead (figure 9.12).

Figure 9.11   Fourth position.   Figure 9.12   Fifth position.

ACTIVITY 9.2   EXPLORE

Practicing Positions

Learning positions of the feet and arms is essential to learning ballet. Moving through parts of an exercise, pose, or step, you pass through one or more of these positions. If these positions are new to you, then practice each one. Begin with the photo or the written description to construct each position. First, do a position of the feet, and do a self-check. If you read the description to execute the position, then self-check your position with the photo. If you started with the photo, then self-check your position with a written description. Learn all of the positions of the feet, then repeat this process for positions of the arms. Finally, put the positions of the feet and the arms together.

If you are already familiar with the positions of the feet, then do a self-check using the description or the photo. Then go through all the positions, connecting them in order from first to fifth.

Your teacher will guide you in learning the sequence of foot positions. Following the foot sequence, practice the positions of the arms in sequence. Then put them together in sequence.

Dancer Directions

In the studio or onstage, **dancer directions** are similar to stage directions, but they use numbering systems instead. The Cecchetti and Russian methods of ballet use different numbering systems for dancer directions (figure 9.13).

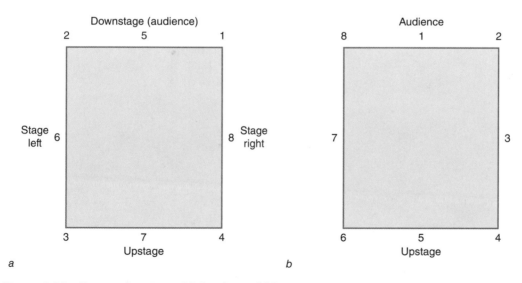

Figure 9.13   Dancer directions: *(a)* Cecchetti; *(b)* Russian.

Dancers use body and working leg directions in relation to the studio or performance space. Basic body directions face the audience and the downstage corners. Facing the audience, your working leg extends and foot points **à terre** (on the floor) or **en l'air** (in the air), **devant** (to the front), **à la seconde** (to the side or second position), or **derrière** (to the back of the body).

The Barre

The first part of the ballet class is called the barre. Often before the traditional barre exercises, dancers do a pre-barre warm-up. This warm-up can be a set of general warm-up exercises to warm the body, or it can be a personal pre-barre warm-up that targets specific parts of your body or includes specific exercises to prepare you for the barre exercises.

The **barre** is a series of exercises that prepare you for dancing in the center. A traditional barre is a set sequence of ballet exercises; a less traditional barre is modified because of time, purpose, or other requirements. As you learn ballet, the barre exercises include more components that add to the challenge of performing them. A second definition of the term *barre* is the actual bar—a rail that helps you to increase or test your balance while doing the barre exercises.

The barre portion of class begins with pre-barre warm-up exercises. As a beginning dancer, you face the barre and place both hands on it. As you get more experience and balance improves, you place one hand on the barre. With one hand on the barre, you can move the other arm through positions in preparation or during exercises.

All exercises at the barre use turnout. To begin the exercises at the barre, you stand in first, third, or fifth position. You teacher will determine which position is most appropriate for you to start and end a barre exercise. Following are the basic barre exercises. Your teacher may add more exercises and ballet vocabulary in class.

demi-plié (half bend of the legs): Executed in all foot positions, the full foot remains on the floor.

grand plié (big bend of the legs): Continuing from the demi-plié, you release the full-foot position (your heels lift) as you descend. The heels return to the floor, followed by the legs straightening as you ascend. In second position, your heels stay on the floor the whole time.

battement tendu (stretched beating): From the starting position the working leg and foot slide from the full-foot position along the floor to a pointed-foot

The ballet barre prepares dancers for the center section of class.

position on the floor. The pointed foot reverses its path to full-foot position in the ending position.

en croix (in the shape of a cross): A combination of front, side, back, and repeat of the side as a pattern for the working leg. Your teacher may demonstrate or say, "Do four battement tendu en croix." This means that you will do four battement tendu to the front, then four to the side, then four to the back, and four to the side. Battement jeté (dégagé), frappé, développé, and grand battement use the en croix pattern.

battement jeté or dégagé (battement thrown—or disengaged—from the floor): From the beginning position the working leg is in a full-foot position and stretches along the floor to a pointed position off the floor. On the return, the working foot points on the floor and continues sliding back into the beginning position. The height of the leg off the floor determines the term; a higher position is jeté, and a lower position is dégagé.

rond de jambe à terre (circular movement of the leg on the floor): From the starting position, the working leg does a preparation. The simplest preparation is to stretch the working leg and pointed foot à la seconde and either close in first position, or do a first port de bras while you remain standing in first position. The ronds de jambe exercises can be learned as separate parts; the rond de jambe à terre en dehors and the rond de jambe à terre en dedans can follow one another as parts of the exercise.

Starting with the rond de jambe a terre en dehors in first position, the working leg and pointed foot in pointe tendue stretches devant. The working leg rotates while the pointed foot traces a half circle on the floor through à la seconde to derrière (or outward away from the supporting foot). Then the working foot sweeps from the pointed position derrière, through full-foot first position to pointe tendue devant and continues the number of ronds specified for the exercise and ends in first position.

For ronds de jambe en dedans, the working foot sweeps from first position to the pointe tendue derrière position, tracing a half circle on the floor through à la seconde to devant (or inward toward the supporting foot). The working foot sweeps through first position to pointe tendue derrière and continues the number of ronds in the exercise and finishes in first position. Usually the dancer practices eight ronds in both directions.

battement frappé (struck beating): On the preparation, point the working foot à la seconde and then place the foot on the front or back of the ankle in sur le cou-de-pied position. The working foot may be flexed or pointed depending on the ballet method or school selected by your teacher. Keeping the working leg turned out, strike either the floor or near the floor while straightening the lower leg and point the working foot. Then sharply return to the position on the ankle. Throughout the frappé, the upper leg remains quiet as the lower leg strikes and stretches before it returns.

battement développé (battement developed): From the starting position, bend the working knee as the working foot slides up the front or back of the supporting leg. The working foot stops under the calf muscle at a low passé (mid-lower-leg height) or retiré (under the front, back, or side of the supporting knee). Keeping the working leg turned out, extend the lower leg to a straight leg devant, à la seconde, or derrière at approximately 45 degrees for the beginning dancer. On the return, the working leg lowers to a point on the floor before sliding into the beginning position.

grand battement (big kick): From the starting position, brush the working leg off the floor to a straight pointed position in the air. On the return, lower the working leg to a pointe tendue before sliding back into the beginning position. The height of the grand battement depends on your experience, control, and balance.

The Center

The **center** is a series of exercises, steps, and combinations of steps. You have to concentrate on the movements, directions, and timing while integrating technique and movement principles to create a solid presentation of each combination. The center part of class has several sections.

CENTER BARRE EXERCISES   Your teacher may have you do barre exercises in the center (without the barre), such as battement tendu en croix and battement tendu or passés en promenade en avant or en arrière. Other center barre exercises are listed next.

port de bras (carriage of the arms): These exercises move through the classic arm positions.

first port de bras: Beginning with the arms in fifth position en bas (preparatory position), raise both arms to first position across from the rib cage, open to second position, and return to fifth en bas. When first port de bras is used as a preparation for an exercise or combination, the arms may remain in second position until the end of the combination when they return to fifth position en bas.

second port de bras: Beginning with the arms in fifth position en bas, raise the arms through first position to fifth position en haut. Then stretch the arms outward through second position, and return to fifth position en bas.

Ballet steps can be categorized as introduction or transition steps, adagio steps or poses, or small or large allegro steps that make up combinations and dances. Introduction or transition steps are steps that begin or connect steps in a combination.

pas de bourrée (stuffed steps): From the starting position and moving right, step the working (left) foot behind the supporting (right) foot. Step on the right foot to the side, and close the left foot in the beginning position. The back and side steps are done on three-quarter relevé with both feet finishing in demi-plié.

glissade (gliding step): In the starting position, do a demi-plié. Remain in demi-plié as the working leg and foot do a low battement jeté à la seconde. Push off the supporting leg to straighten both legs barely off the floor. Transfer the weight to the first leg, and quickly close the other leg in the starting position.

chassé (chasing step): In the starting position, demi-plié. Remain in demi-plié and shift the weight so the front leg slides along the floor to fourth or second position. Pull both legs together in the air in the chassé to the side. In the chassé devant, the back leg initiates chasing the front leg. Both feet land together in the starting position, demi-plié.

ADAGIO POSES AND STEPS   Adagio poses and steps are often learned at the barre and then practiced in the center. Doing adagio combinations requires the dancer to hold poses for a certain number of counts or execute slow, fluid movements drawn out over a number of measures. Adagio movements require strength, control, and balance, attributes gained with practice and over time. Adagio steps and combinations present challenges in completing the movement to its fullest in relation to the music.

adagio (slow movements): Adagio is the section of the center where dancers practice slow sequences of movements.

arabesque: The name *arabesque* comes from a Moorish ornament that has similar lines. The arabesque can be a pose, a step in adagio, or a step in an allegro combination. It has many variations depending on the school or method. For example, the Cecchetti method uses five arabeques. The Russian school has four arabesques. Other ballet methods and styles include a similar numbers of arabesques. Figure 9.14 shows the basic first and second arabesque poses from the Russian and Cecchetti methods. Your teacher will present in class additional arabesques as they are introduced.

Figure 9.14   First arabesque, Russian *(a)*; second arabesque, Russian *(b)*; first arabesque, Cecchetti *(c)*; second arabesque, Cecchetti *(d)*.

battement développé (battement developed): This movement is learned at the barre as an exercise. In the center, battement développé is performed en croix as a combination or as a step performed as part of adagio combinations.

Classical positions of the body include eight basic positions. In beginning ballet class, some or all of these positions are learned and practiced in a sequence as an adagio combination.

In some of the classical positions, you extend the working leg forward, to à la seconde, and backward. In all of these positions, the body faces front or to the audience. Your arms are in second position. These positions are the same directions used in practicing exercises at the barre.

Croisé devant and effacé devant are two classical positions of the body that apply in a number of poses used in the center section of the ballet class.

croisé devant (crossed in the front; figure 9.15): Your body faces a downstage corner. Extend the downstage working leg and pointed foot to the same corner. The upstage arm is overhead and the other arm is in second position. Your head turns; your eyes are focusing on the audience.

effacé devant (shaded in the front; figure 9.16): Your body faces a downstage corner. Extend the upstage working leg and pointed foot in front of the body. The downstage arm is in fifth position en haut. The upstage arm is in second position. Your head turns and may tilt; your eyes are focusing on the audience.

Figure 9.15 Croisé devant.   **Figure 9.16** Effacé devant, Russian method.

ALLEGRO STEPS Allegro steps are fast, brisk movements. In the center, you do two types of allegro: petit (small) allegro steps and grand (large) allegro steps. Petit allegro steps start in third or fifth position and include the following:

pas de chat (step of the cat): With the back leg, do a passé derrière and then leap to the side. Quickly with the other leg do a passé and close the leg front and into the starting position.

jeté (thrown): Brush your back leg off the floor at dégagé height. Push off the other leg, and leap to the other leg. The pushing leg ends in coupé derrière. This sets up the back leg to repeat the initial brush of the jeté to the other side.

assemblé (assembled): Brush your back leg to dégagé height. Hop vertically off the other leg, and assemblé (close the legs in the air before landing or on the floor as you land).

Grand allegro includes large jumps, hops, and leaps that move across the floor.

ballet walks: Starting in first or third position, walk through the toes, ball, and then heel of one foot and then the other. The body is aligned and moves with grace and ease.

arabesque sauté (arabesque hop): Step into the arabesque position and do a complete hop, hold the pose in demi-plié, then repeat on the other side.

grand jeté (big leap): Using runs as the approach, brush the front foot forward, push off the back leg for the air moment, and land in demi-plié on the other foot. Hold the landing briefly, and then begin the runs for repeating the leap on the other side.

sautés (jumps): Beginning sautés are performed in first or second positions. Demi-plié, and do a vertical jump into the air ending in your starting position. Practice a series of four or eight sautés in first position. Then repeat the series in second position. Combine sautés using both positions. Begin the sautés from first position and then land in second position. Repeat the sautés, beginning in second position and ending in first position demi-plié. Practice a series of eight sautés changing foot positions, beginning in first position and changing to second position and continuing to alternate these two positions. Then repeat the combination beginning in second position.

changement (changing): Starting in third or fifth position, jump vertically into the air with your legs straight and feet pointed; change your feet in the air so that the front leg changes to the back, and land in the same position with the opposite foot in front.

SPOTLIGHT

Fernando Bujones (1955-2005)

Born in Miami, Fernando and his mother returned to Cuba. At seven years of age he was selected for the Professional School of Dance and was put in the first all-boys class in Cuba. He trained under teachers from Alicia Alonzo's Ballet Nacional de Cuba. At age nine he escaped Cuba and became a scholarship student at School of American Ballet in New York City. He joined the American Ballet Theatre and became the company's youngest principal dancer. In 1974, he became the first American dancer to win a medal at the International Ballet Competition in Varna, Bulgaria. At 19 years old, Bujones, representing American Ballet Theatre and the United States, won the gold medal at the ballet Olympics-type competition. In addition to the gold medal, he won a certificate for highest technical achievement. His classical style, meticulous technique, and athletic approach were the ingredients for his line, power, and elegance in performance. His artistry propelled him to superstar status internationally.

ACTIVITY 9.3 EXPLORE

Translation, Please

All dance genres have a term for an exercise, step, formation, or pose that you learn in order to communicate using the vocabulary of that genre. Most often you become acquainted with the dance step or movement and then connect the term. Because ballet terms use the French language, you have to stretch your vocabulary skills a bit; as a bonus, you get to learn some terms in French. Similar to other dance genres, in ballet you begin by learning exercises or steps. This chapter presents photographs or descriptions of ballet vocabulary. Each description includes the ballet term in the French language followed by its English translation. The translation is most often the clue to remembering the movements of the step and the name of the ballet term in the French language. For example, the ballet step *pas de chat* translates into *step of the cat*. When you do the step, say the words *step of the cat* and then *pas de chat* to yourself. Soon you will be able to repeat *pas de chat* and know it means *step of the cat*. Or, visualize *pas de chat* as a step in your mind. This visual connection with the term will help you recall the step and the ballet term, too.

Using this strategy you can practice translating dance terms into movement or from the French language into English. Your teacher may add other ballet terms to the vocabulary list for this chapter and will decide whether you do this activity by yourself or in a group.

Write each ballet vocabulary term on a separate index card. Turn them facedown. Select a card, and test yourself. On a sheet of paper copy the ballet term, write its English translation, and then get up and dance the term. If this is a group activity, everyone participates in translating the terms. While you are doing this activity, you can note on your paper any terms you think you might want to review. This activity prepares you for class and for the chapter vocabulary test, too.

révérence (thank you): You perform this choreographed bow or curtsy at the end of a traditional ballet class to thank the teacher and musician for dance if he or she accompanies your class. After the *révérence*, traditionally, students applaud the teacher and the musician for dance.

When you perform the barre and center movements, focus on your technique. Using correct ballet technique helps develop graceful, smooth movements; gravity-defying jumps with soft, soundless landings; turns, and leg extensions. These are some of the goals ballet dancers seek to attain.

Thinking Like a Dancer

Beyond knowing the movements and the counts, you need to think about other things to develop as an artist. First steps include being a responsible dancer. This means learning the movement and practicing the parts of an exercise or step that you are unsure of so that you are prepared for the next class. It may seem challenging, but some strategies are available to help you tackle the task.

Using the *watch, listen, do* strategy helps you learn the movement. When the teacher presents the movement, stand and observe to see the whole picture—what the legs and feet are doing, what are the body directions, if there are arm movements, and how the movement relates to the music. While the movement is performed, you need to listen to the music. Then you can determine the rhythm of the step and the counts in relation to executing the exercise or step to the music. Your teacher may say the action words or French terms while demonstrating the movement; or, your teacher may say the counts while executing the movement to the music. Then it is your turn to dance. Practicing the *watch, listen, do* strategy helps you make this connection a part of your routine.

While doing the dance steps, you have to think of a lot of things at once. To tackle this multitasking in your mind, break down each task. First, learn the parts of the step and their relationship to the music. The next level is applying the technique requirements and movement principles. The last is filling out the musical phrase, expressing the movement and the music. Breathe through movement phrases. Presenting the movement as a dancer means gaining confidence in movement, which takes time and patience.

Becoming a dancer requires continuous development. It takes time and patience to put all of the moving and thinking parts of doing ballet technique or other dance genres into a seamless integrated performance. In any dance genre, there is always something more to explore through your movement, expand through practicing, or understand both in mind and body. These continued refinements to your execution of movements, use of transitions, and sculpting of body line will one day transform you from a student to an artist.

✔ ACTIVITY 9.4 ASSESS

Evaluate Your Development

Performance attitude is part of becoming a responsible dancer. This activity is just an introduction to reflection and application of what all dancers do every day. Dancers do this self-check in their minds. To gain this habit of evaluating your development to continue toward present goals or to set new goals, answer the following questions. To begin with, you could do this evaluation after every class until you memorize the list of questions and do the self-check mentally. Then repeat the self-check several times each week after class, and before and after each performance testing. Developing a performance attitude crosses all dance genres and dance activities, so this activity can be applied to dance genres and activities you engage in in the future.

- Awareness of personal space
- Observing, listening, and learning exercises or combinations presented in class
- Memorizing the exercises and steps so you can present them accurately in time to the music and with appropriate quality or style
- Applying technique to movement
- Becoming aware of how movement principles interact with exercises and steps

These processes take place all the time. So, take a moment and reflect on the items in this list and your self-assessment of your development as a dancer. After you have completed the rubric on the web resource, write a summary paragraph about what you believe are your next goals.

Your teacher will guide you as to how often to do this evaluation or may change the items in the assessment tool depending upon the activity or class goals. A copy of this assessment tool is available on the web resource for you to print and use.

Summary

Ballet is a dance genre with a history beginning in the renaissance. Over the centuries, dancers, choreographers, and personalities developed a codified technique of distinct vocabulary of exercises, positions, poses, and steps recognized as ballet. The traditional ballet class contains two parts. You begin class at the barre. The barre provides support to help you acquire the strength while learning and practicing the exercises. Barre exercises present a wide variety of ballet techniques the dancer learns in preparation for the second part of class. The center section of ballet class is where you learn to dance. First, adagio or slow movement combinations provide challenges in moving body parts in coordination to the music while balancing on one or both feet without a barre. In contrast to adagio, next sections of the class are a petit allegro or quick steps followed by grand allegro or large leaps and jumping movements. Other sections of the center include learning introductory or transitional steps and turning steps. Learning a basic ballet vocabulary of different exercises, steps, positions, and poses is the foundation for additional study in ballet and knowledge to transfer or combine with other dance genres and styles you learn.

PORTFOLIO ASSIGNMENT

Your teacher will assign you to a group in order to construct a barre exercise, an adagio combination, or a petit or grand allegro combination. Your group will be assigned to construct a one-, two-, or three-step combination. Refer to the text in this chapter to determine what exercises or steps are appropriate to select from for the adagio or allegro type of combination your group will develop.

One-step exercises or combinations:

At the barre or in the center portion of class, one-exercise or one-step combinations are performed a specific number of times. At the barre a one-step combination can have variations to the following:

- The directions in which the exercise is performed (if applicable) or if the exercise is performed in a pattern such as front, side, back, side, or en croix
- The number of repetitions of the exercise
- The number of repetitions of the exercise done on one foot

In the center, one-step combinations are good ways to practice a step to memorize all the movements in the correct sequence for a step, to get the rhythm and timing of the parts of the step in your body, and to practice your transfers of weight and balance as you learn the step.

Two-step exercises or combinations:

At the barre, an exercise is performed a specific number of times such as four times, sometimes followed by another exercise for the same or similar number of times. In the center portion of ballet class, a step may be performed a number of times followed another step. The second step can be

- an equal number of repetitions of the first step in the combination,
- a way to transfer from performing the first step to the other working leg or alternate side, or
- a way to finish the combination.

A two-step combination should generally end on two feet.

Three-step exercises or combinations:

In a beginning ballet barre exercise, the third step in an exercise is often holding the final foot position for a few seconds to indicate you have completed the exercise.

Another option (which your teacher will decide on based on whether it is appropriate for each person) is finishing a beginning exercise with a full-foot position or a balance en relevé facing the barre.

In the center a three-step combination is similar to a movement statement. It has a beginning step, a middle, and an ending step. Since the three-step combination is performed to a musical phrase of 4 counts, the middle step is repeated to complete the phrase.

1. Select a beginning step by looking through the list of introductory steps listed in the chapter.

2. Add two steps. The second step could be a step moving in the same direction, or you could repeat the first step in the same direction or to the other side.

3. Finish the combination with one step or so that both feet end on the floor. If you repeat the combination, determine whether you will repeat it on the same side or if the combination then alternates to begin to the other side.

Your teacher will help your group to determine the length of the combination and the number of repetitions in the combination. After the group develops its combination, learn it and perform it for another group or the class.

As a group, write out your combination on a sheet of paper, and give it a title. Then post the combinations around the studio.

Take a ballet class by reading and learning the exercises and combinations posted. Read the written exercise with a partner or in your group to learn to perform it. Practice the combination several times. In your journal identify the exercise by its title, and indicate and number the steps in the combination. Write a response about what you learned from performing this combination.

REVIEW QUESTIONS

True or False

1. Ballet shoe strings should be tied and tucked into the shoe. _____

2. Dancers perform a révérence at the end of a traditional ballet class. _____

3. Ballet comes from a Russian term meaning "to dance." _____

4. In a traditional ballet class the center is followed by the barre. _____

5. The father of American Ballet is George Balanchine. _____

Multiple Choice

1. _____A romantic ballet can be described best by one of the following phrases:
   a. features a male dancer
   b. tells a story in two acts
   c. uses classical music

2. _____Neoclassic ballet is defined best as
   a. a contemporary ballet about a classic myth or story line
   b. ballet done in a contemporary style on modern topics
   c. classical ballet with contemporary costumes and music

3. _____Which of the following are classical ballets?
   a. *Les Sylphides, Petrouchka, Giselle*
   b. *Pas de Quatre, Dances at a Gathering, Agon*
   c. *Swan Lake, The Nutcracker,* and *Sleeping Beauty*

4. _____Rond de jambe à terre moves in two directions
    a. tracing a half circle outward or inward in relation to the supporting foot
    b. from front to back and back to front
    c. front, side, back, side

5. _____Contemporary ballet can best be described as
    a. ballet performed to today's pop and urban music
    b. blended ballet, modern dance, and other dance genres
    c. traditional ballet performed in contemporary costume

Opposites

Define each term, and then find its opposite.

1.	_____adagio	a.	relevé
2.	_____à terre	b.	en l'air
3.	_____demi-plié	c.	derrière
4.	_____devant	d.	allegro

Short Answer

1. Using the following diagram to represent the stage, insert the correct dancer directions. Write in the blank provided whether the dance directions are from the Cecchetti or Russian method. _____

 To find supplementary materials for this chapter such as worksheets, extended learning activities, and e-journaling assignments, visit the web resource at www.discoveringdance.org/student.

Modern Dance

ENDURING UNDERSTANDING: Modern dance is a classic and contemporary dance genre.

ESSENTIAL QUESTION: How does modern dance help me express myself as a dancer?

LEARNING OBJECTIVES

After reading this chapter, you will be able to do the following:

- Recognize major modern dance works, styles, and dance artists in history.
- Execute basic modern dance technique, use modern dance vocabulary, and perform memorized movement exercises, combinations, and created movement sequences or studies.
- Apply modern dance etiquette and dance safety while dancing.
- Evaluate and respond to traditional and contemporary modern dance performances.

"The Dancer believes that his art has something to say which cannot be expressed in words or in any other way than by dancing . . . there are times when the simple dignity of movement can fulfill the function of a volume of words."

Doris Humphrey, 20th-century American modern dancer, choreographer, and author

VOCABULARY
chance dance
improvisation
modern dance

If you asked five different modern dancers or choreographers the question *What is modern dance?* you would get five different answers. The answers would be personal, relating to the person's point of view of society, politics, or life. So, one definition of **modern dance** and its contemporary directions would be *a dance genre that enables a choreographer to present a personal point of view.* Modern dance developed to express the choreographer's, the choreographer-dancer's, or dancers' points of view through movement. Given this broad set of definitions, it is no surprise that modern dance is constantly changing.

Modern dance is a form of concert dance. Early modern dancers and choreographers presented their dance works in theaters to establish the modern dance genre as a performing art. Contemporary modern dance choreographers may seek other performance spaces beyond theatrical spaces, such as museums, parks, and a variety of buildings, structures, or outdoor settings, to show their work.

This chapter provides ways to look at this dance genre to support your dancing in the classroom. You will learn about modern dance and its terminology, its history, its dancers and choreographic artists, and the major styles and works of this genre, and you will view selected works from the modern dance literature.

Discovering Modern Dance

Modern dance has many facets—creative, educational, and artistic processes and experiences—that contribute to the languages of dance. On the creative side, the dancer and the choreographer use their deep, unique perceptions of body and mind as sources for exploring, creating, and expressing movement. On the educational side, modern dance provides an opportunity for the dancer, the choreographer, and the audience to learn about the human body, the human condition, and social and societal themes through movement. Dancers and choreographers of modern dance make use of the creative process to expand their ways of thinking about movement. This process includes personal discovery of a vast movement vocabulary for artistic expression and creation. Just as other arts may use materials for various purposes, modern dance uses movement in many ways—realistically, abstractly, and symbolically—to artistically communicate meaning.

To begin your exploration of modern dance, recall the elements of dance from chapter 3. You will use these elements as tools for discovering your point of view in modern dance.

! ACTIVITY 10.1 DISCOVER

Express Your Point of View

On a sheet of paper write some of the passionate ideas or topics that drive your interests. Select one, and create a movement sequence about it. On the back of an index card, write you name. On the front of the card write a word or phrase to identify your passion. The class can collect everyone's driving passions and separate them into groups. Working together in your group, share your topics and movement sequences.

Before each person creates a movement sequence, your group should decide the length of the sequence (such as 4 or 8 counts). Then, you each work on your own to create your sequence. Collectively or individually select music or create a sound background (it could be a recording of the words at various intervals or it could be a soundscape you and your group creates) to accompany your work. Your teacher will guide you in the length of time for this activity and selections from which to choose for the music or soundscape. Practice your work together. Collectively select a title for the work. Designate one of the dancers to collect your ideas about the group work and write a brief introduction about it. This information can be presented either before or after you have done your dance.

DID YOU KNOW?

Dance and Technology

Many modern dance choreographers since the beginning of the 20th century have experimented with dance and technology. Over the 20th century these pioneers explored theater technology and computer generated dance technology that spurred modern contemporary dance into multimedia dance. Some choreographic examples are listed here:

- Bill T. Jones created a work titled *Ghostcatching*, in which his dance movements appear as a series of interwoven colored chalklike drawings. He accompanies the performance with his singing of gospel hymns.

- Trisha Brown collaborated with interactive artist Marc Downie and other artists at Arizona State University to develop a live motion capture of dancers' movements projected by computer. The interactive performance was translated into lines and shapes with dynamics that formed and reformed as the dancers moved.

- Today a number of choreographers use telematics performances, which involve the use of video with live performance; they are simultaneously presented at two or more remote locations.

Exploring Modern Dance

Modern dance includes many possibilities for expression. The combination of dance elements the dancer or choreographer chooses and how they express the movement makes this genre challenging for those creating it and intriguing for those watching it. The movement expressions may be the movement itself or deeply felt emotions, ideas, concepts, or personal statements the choreographer wants to share with others—dancers and audiences.

When creating modern dance choreography, you must have a choreographic concept for the work that you can communicate to the dancers so that they can understand and interpret the movement. Some choreographers provide large amounts of movements and expect dancers to figure out how to make the movement into an integrated whole. Other choreographers provide a framework and have dancers create the detailed movements in the infrastructure.

Before you begin to create or perform modern dance choreography, you need to know what type of choreographic structure you are working with. Modern dance works can be categorized into these types:

- Story-based or dramatic work: Modern dances can retell myths, stories, literature, or dramatic works. This type of dance may present events in sequence, or the choreographer can use literary devices to change, compress, or extend some of the story events within a dramatic structure. Early modern dance choreographers created works of this type.

- Abstract forms: Modern dances can use ideas, themes and emotions, and personal or social statements as the basis for a choreographic work. Many postmodern and contemporary modern dances are abstract works.

- Eclectic themes: Some abstract dances focus on movement in relation to the music or movement as the message in the dance, and audience members interpret their own meaning of the dance work.

- Improvisational forms: In its simplest form, improvisation is spontaneous movement. Some improvisational works begin with a framework, a concept, or a problem to which the dancers respond; they create movement and relationships to explore the concept or solve the problem. The semistructured improvisation begins with dancers doing improvisational movement explorations. Then the choreographer chooses certain movement sequences or compositional poses to include in the work.

- Chance: A series of random movements selected by chance contribute to a type of modern dance called **chance dance**. Movements are selected from an extensive modern dance vocabulary or from a choreographer's style. The choreographer or the dancers determine the movement sequence. Then, dancers perform their movements beginning at various times, and end their movement sequences at different times to create an event.

These choreographic structures have evolved as modern dance has developed through history. The following section guides you through that history.

History of Modern Dance

Modern dance is a 20th-century performing art, but its sources began in the 19th century as societal changes surfaced through wars and economic turmoil. During the 19th century, the arts went through radical changes from romanticism, such as the poetry of Byron, to realism, such as the drama of Ibsen. Throughout the century, social dancing remained popular in ballrooms. Onstage fancy versions of social dances were part of many theatrical entertainment forms. Beginning in the 1830s, female educational institutions emerged with academic curricula that encouraged women to do exercise and become physically active. In the second half of the century on and off the stage, the popular Delsarte system of poses and gestures grew in popularity to express emotions in poetry and dramatic recitations. Nearer the end of the century while men focused on gymnastics and calisthenics, women practiced aesthetic dancing as part of physical education. At the Chicago World's Fair in 1893, exotic dancers from across the world performed for fair-goers, inspiring future dancers and choreographers.

Early Twentieth Century

During the first three decades of the 20th century, many social and political changes occurred both in the United States and Europe. This changing landscape resulted in new styles of art that influenced dancers and choreographers who sought ways to express contemporary society through their so-called *new dance*. These forerunners of modern dance created groundbreaking dance works that distinguished them as separate from classical ballet. Some of them are discussed next.

LOIE FULLER (1862-1928)   An American dancer, singer, and actress, Fuller gained her fame as a dancer in Europe. She used color, fabric, movement, sound, and light to create her innovative dances as a complete theatrical experience. Her movements used natural body motion to express emotion and spontaneously interpret the music. Major works in her repertory included *Serpentine Dance* (1891), *The Butterfly* (1892), and *Fire Dance* (1895).

ISADORA DUNCAN (1872-1927)   Born in California, Duncan began her career as a show dancer in Chicago. Her dancing career took off in Europe, where her work was more accepted than in the United States. Duncan created a personal style as a dance artist. She performed to classical music of 19th-century composers. Her dances were simple but heroic abstract dances often inspired by ancient Greek art. Duncan's movement was motivated by emotion expressed through the entire body. She wore free-flowing costumes and danced barefoot. Although she started schools in Europe to train dancers, she did not leave a codified technique. Six of her students became known as the *Isadorables;* three students would continue Duncan's work in the United States. Major works in her repertory included *Marseillaise* (1915), a successful solo dance that Duncan performed, and *Marche Slave* (1917). The theme of this dance was Russian peasants' struggle for freedom.

RUTH ST. DENIS (CA.1877-1968)   Born Ruth Denis, she grew up in New Jersey. Her mother taught her Delsarte movement. She studied ballet before becoming a dancer in vaudeville and concert halls, where she assumed the more exotic name of Ruth St. Denis. Beginning in 1904 she created a series of solos based on Oriental deities, and she performed them throughout Europe. St. Denis provided audiences with popular entertainment while presenting a glimpse of Eastern traditions and her spiritual values of her art. Later, she would experiment with abstract dances. St. Denis is known as the *First Lady of American modern dance*. Major works from her repertory include:

- *Radha* (1906): This solo masterpiece featured the goddess of the five senses. This work became the design for later solos.

- *Incense* (1906): St. Denis replicated the movements of smoke from burning incense.

- *Soaring* (1920): Choreographed with her student, Doris Humphrey, four girls dance and pose using a large square of silk as a prop.

TED SHAWN (1891-1972)   A native of Kansas City, Missouri, Ted Shawn became interested in dance during college. In 1910 he saw Ruth St. Denis perform *Incense*. By 1914, St. Denis and Shawn married, and the following year they established the Denishawn School of Dancing and Related Arts in Los Angeles. Shawn's technique and choreography used ballet (done barefoot), Native American dances, and dances from around the world. During the 1920s the Denishawn company of dancers toured the United States and the Far East. In 1933, he established an all-male dance company, Ted Shawn and His Men, which toured until it disbanded in the 1940s. He established Jacob's Pillow as a summer institute for studying modern dance. Shawn's contributions as a dancer, a choreographer, a teacher, and a writer laid significant foundations for the development of modern dance. Major works from his repertory include:

- *Xochital* (1921): Based on an Aztec legend, Shawn created a solo for Denishawn student Martha Graham.

- *Kinetic Molpai* (1935): This dance featured eight male dancers and a leader from Shawn's all-male company.

First Generation of Modern Dance

In the early 20th century dance artists began a dance revolution that was to evolve into a new performing art. In the 1930s, John Martin, a newspaper critic and author, coined the term *modern dance*. Denishawn had been an incubator for future dancers and choreographers. Four pioneers emerged as leaders: Martha Graham, Doris Humphrey, and Charles Weidman represented American-based dance directions; Hanya Holm came from the German expressionist dance tradition.

Through the 1930s, 1940s, and 1950s Martha Graham, Doris Humphrey, Charles Weidman, Hanya Holm, Katherine Dunham, José Limón, and other modern dancers began to define and establish modern dance as a performing art form through their dancing, choreography, and development of techniques. These artists often assumed both roles of dancer and choreographer in creating new dances. Their work created the foundations from which modern dance would move in the following decades. Teaching summer sessions at Bennington College, Graham, Humphrey, Weidman, Limón, and Holm created a strong connection to physical educators who took these courses and returned to teach modern dance in colleges across the nation. This artist–educator exchange was critical for developing modern dance as an artistic and an educational dance genre.

MARTHA GRAHAM (CA. 1894-1991)   Originally from Pennsylvania, Graham attended the Denishawn School of Dancing and Related Arts and joined the company. In 1923, she headed for New York, opened her own studio, and began creating solos. Her dances became the source of her movement vocabulary and later her technique. Graham's early dances were stark, angular, and expressed the inner conflicts within man. During the 1930s, Graham's fascination with the American Southwest and the frontier became a theme that lasted over a decade. Over the next several decades, Graham's interests changed; she developed dance works about female characters from literary sources or history, psychological themes, the telling of Greek myths, and then later, cosmic themes. Graham's movement theory and technique were based on contraction and release. Her movement requires a centered body using breath and oppositional forces. Graham collaborated with composers, artists, and a sculptor to make her modern dance works a theatrical art form. Major works from her repertory of the first era of her dances include:

- *Lamentations* (1930): In this early signature solo, a female dancer sits on a bench encased in fabric. Her sculptural shapes are an emotional dance portraying grief.
- *Appalachian Spring* (1944): In this work, a young pioneer couple celebrates the building of their new home and envisions their future life together.
- *Seraphic Dialogue* (1955): This work tells the story of Joan of Arc as maid, warrior, and martyr.

DORIS HUMPHREY (1895-1958)   Born near Chicago, Humphrey auditioned for the Denishawn School of Dancing and Related Arts and immediately became a member of the company. St. Denis and Humphrey collaborated on the concept of *music visualizations* and created abstract dances during the 1920s. In 1927 she and Charles Weidman went to establish a school and company in New York. Her choreography explored the conflict of man with his environment and included strong social content. Humphrey's technique is based on the theory of *fall and recovery*. Her book *The Art of Making Dances* was published in 1959. It has become a classic in the field of dance choreography. Major works from her repertory include:

- *Air for the G String* (1928): A baroque, choral dance.
- *The Shakers* (1931): This piece captures religious practices in Shaker society.
- *New Dance* (1935-1936): A trilogy of dances, they focus on various situations of an individual and society. The dances include *New Dance, With My Red Fires, and Theatre Piece.*

CHARLES WEIDMAN (1901-1975)   Born in Lincoln, Nebraska, Weidman went to Denishawn to study, and there he met Doris Humphrey. Together they established a company and school in New York, which became known as the Humphrey-Weidman studio and company that dissolved in 1945. Then, Weidman created his own company and produced his dances. His choreography was predominantly a mix of dance, mime, and comedy, but he created some pure movement works as well. Some of his works were autobiographical or celebrated the incongruities of humans. Here is a sampling of his work:

- *Flickers* (1941): A dance about early films.
- *Fables of our Times* (1947): A dance based on the stories of James Thurber.

- *Brahms Waltzes, Opus 39* (1967): A work to honor Doris Humphrey, his partner.

HANYA HOLM (1893-1992)   Born in Germany, Holm attended the Mary Wigman School in Dresden, Germany, and became a member of the company. Wigman, a German expressionistic dancer, attracted students from across Europe. Holm came to New York to start a Wigman school, later renamed the Hanya Holm School. In her later career, she directed and taught modern dance in universities. Holm's choreography focused on space and emotion. She blended Wigman's and Rudolf Laban's work (see Modern Dance Technique, later in the chapter) into her movement. Her technique avoided personal stylization which made it attractive to many modern dancers and teachers. On Broadway she choreographed many musicals. Her work influenced choreographers and companies such as Alwin Nikolais and Pilobolus later in the 20th century.

From the 1940s through the postwar era and the 1950s contributions from Katherine Dunham, José Limón, Lester Horton, Anna Sokolow, Eric Hawkins, and other modern dance artists established a broader base for modern dance as a performing art. During this period the work of the four pioneers continued to strengthen modern dance as it became a mature art form.

KATHERINE DUNHAM (1909-2006)   Born in Chicago, Katherine Dunham was a dancer, choreographer, anthropologist, teacher, and writer. In the 1930s she founded Negro Dance Group and created her *Haitian Suite,* based on her earlier anthropology studies. Dunham continued to explore blending African, European, Afro-Caribbean, and American dance. These dance forms became the foundation for Dunham technique. She choreographed on Broadway and performed in films during the 1940s. Dunham made many contributions to 20th-century American dance as a dancer, choreographer, and social activist. She influenced the next generation of modern dance artists, and her technique continues as one of her legacies.

JOSÉ LIMÓN (1908-1972)   Born in Mexico, José Limón moved to California as a child. He studied dance with Doris Humphrey and Charles Weidman for 10 years before creating his own choreography in 1937. In 1946, Limón collaborated with Doris Humphrey as co-choreographers to form the José Limón Dance Company. His choreography used strong literary themes as a basis for his powerful, dramatic, narrative dances. His works ranged from narrative to abstract. *The Moore's Pavane* (1949) is one of his significant works. Limón's technique builds upon Humphrey's movement principles. His technique molds the body to express emotions and ideas.

LESTER HORTON (1909-1953)   Born in Indianapolis, Lester Horton moved to the Los Angeles area in the late 1920s. He performed in concert settings, in nightclub revues, and later in movie musicals. Hence, his choreography connects to the development of jazz dance too. His works had a wide audience appeal using African American, Haitian, Mexican, and Native American cultural themes. In 1942 he formed the Lester Horton Dance Theater and School. His technique influenced West Coast jazz dance through the strong, versatile dancers that were to carry on his legacy. Horton technique expands the dancer's movement scope and builds a versatile dancer.

⬥ ACTIVITY 10.2 EXPLORE

Learn From Early Modern Dance Choreographers

Your teacher will guide you through this group activity. The teacher may teach a modern dance section from an existing dance of a choreographer or create a short movement sequence for the class that is based on a style of one of the early choreographers.

After you learn the modern dance sequence, take a few minutes to reflect on how you would describe the use of dance elements—space, time, energy, effort, relationships, effort actions, qualities, and dynamics—that characterize the movement sequence. For a class discussion, summarize your findings, and be ready to share your reflections about the use of dance elements and what you think about this style of movement.

ERIC HAWKINS (1909-1994)   Born in Colorado, Hawkins began his dance career in ballet. As the first male dancer in Martha Graham's company, she created many roles for him. Hawkins began creating solos, which led to the later establishment of his company. His technique stressed natural movements based on his philosophy from Native American, ancient Greek, and Asian sources. His works used the stage as a two-dimensional canvas, creating a unique modern dance style. He was a champion for the role of the male dancer in modern dance.

From the 1960s through the end of the 20th century, modern dancers and choreographers such as Alvin Ailey, Alwin Nikolais, Merce Cunningham, Paul Taylor, Trisha Brown, Twyla Tharp, Bill T. Jones, and many others explored, extended, expanded, and changed the landscape of modern dance into its postmodern era. The Judson Theatre was a laboratory for some of these artists and for the directions modern dance would take in the second half of the century.

In the last half of the 20th century, choreographers experimented with everyday movement, multimedia tools, and technology to stretch personal and aesthetic boundaries of modern dance as a contemporary art form. Many of the choreographers sent messages about social and gender issues and political topics.

ALVIN AILEY (1931-1989)   Born in Texas, Ailey and his family moved to California. He studied and performed with Lester Horton. Taking Horton's teachings, Ailey went to New York, where he studied Graham and Dunham techniques. In 1958, Ailey founded the Alvin Ailey American Dance Theater. His choreographic style used Horton technique, African overtones, and social jazz dance components. His work contributed to the development of jazz dance, too. Ailey used blues, spirituals, and gospel music to accompany his high-energy choreography. His many works include:

- *Revelations* (1960): Ailey's signature work, this group of dances represents a response to adversity and celebrates life's joys.
- *Cry* (1971): A solo work that Ailey created for Judith Jameson, this dance represents African-American women and their struggles.

ALWIN NIKOLAIS (1910-1993)   Born in Connecticut, Nikolais was trained as a musician but was drawn to dance when he saw Mary Wigman perform. He studied with Wigman, Hanya Holm, and other modern dancers. In the 1950s he wrote his first electronic score and started the Nikolais Dance Theatre. His works used motion, color, light, and sound to construct an imaginary microcosm for audiences to experience. Among these abstract works, Nikolais' *Imago* (1963) shows an imaginary civilization and people who inhabit it.

By the 1960s, modern dance had become well established. Dancers from the major modern dance companies were seeking new ways to express their choreography. During the 1960s the Judson Dance Theater provided a laboratory for these choreographic innovators and a testing ground for the directions these artists would take in future decades.

MERCE CUNNINGHAM (1909-2009)   Born in the state of Washington, Cunningham joined the Martha Graham Dance Company in the 1940s. In 1953 he started his own company. In the 1960s he experimented with dances created by using chance and immediacy. In 1964, Cunningham began staging what he termed *events* in museums, gymnasiums, studios, and outdoors. He moved on to creating dance events in which dancers memorized a number of movement sections from various Cunningham works. They were not told the order in which they would perform these sections until the event was about to begin.

For many years, Cunningham collaborated with musician John Cage and visual artists on groundbreaking dance works. Cunningham's dances focused on space and time. He believed that music and dance coexist as separate elements. Cunningham developed a technique that uses leg gestures and directional movements so that the dancers glide across the floor resisting gravity. His early works include:

- *Variations V* (1965): Dancer movements trigger photoelectric cells placed around the stage, creating the music for the dance.
- *Canfield* (1969): This piece was made up of a series of dances based on chance movements that changed with each performance.

ACTIVITY 10.3   EXPLORE

Study in Abstract Modern Dance

Abstract modern paintings and sculptures can inspire movement. Modern dance choreography often expresses a choreographer's abstract theme or idea. (See the description of abstract dance at the beginning of the chapter.) Your teacher will decide if you work alone or in groups for this activity. Begin by trying several ordinary or everyday movements and gestures as you normally do them. Then repeat these movements and gestures, but do them bigger, smaller, then at a different speed or energy, to find how they change until they become what you consider an abstract version. Now, select an emotion or an idea. Using dance elements, make two or more movement statements to express the emotion or idea. Play with the movements you have selected to transfer them into an abstracted style.

Your teacher will give you a list of music to choose from. Choose a piece to accompany your movement study or serve as a background to your movement. Then, title your abstract modern dance study. Rehearse and refine your movement study to present to another group or to the class. If a work of art inspired your movement study, share a copy of it after you have performed the study.

PAUL TAYLOR (1930-)   From Pittsburg, Pennsylvania, Paul Taylor went to New York and danced in the Martha Graham Dance Company. He formed a small company and began choreographing in the 1950s. In the 1960s the Paul Taylor Company went on its first international tour. Taylor's choreographic works extend from abstract to dramatic, humor to satire. He often uses classical music to accompany his works. His choreographic style encompasses a light, almost balletic style with some shading of Graham technique. His choreography includes:

- *Aureole* (1962): This work is an abstract, lyrical dance for two men and three women.
- *Big Bertha* (1970): This piece presents an ironic view of the all-American family.

Late Twentieth Century

In the 1970s and 1980s the postmodern movement brought choreographers and their experimental works to the attention of more audiences. Works by Laura Dean, Steve Paxton, Trisha Brown, and Twyla Tharp took different directions.

LAURA DEAN (1945-)   A New York native, Laura Dean danced with Paul Taylor's company. Her early dance experiments combined movement, song, and music. In the 1970s she formed the Laura Dean Company and used minimalist movement. Her work *Spinning* (1970) was focused entirely on the idea of spinning and done to the minimalist music of Steve Reich.

STEVE PAXTON (1939-)   Originally from Arizona, Steve Paxton went to New York, where he danced with the Limón and Cunningham companies. A founder of an improvisation company, The Grand Union, he went on to develop contact improvisation as a dance medium. His exploration of games, improvisation, and gravity expanded dance invention for large groups of trained and untrained dancers. Contract improvisation fused Eastern philosophies into the searching for new movement, which was to expand the influence of postmodern dance and choreography.

TWYLA THARP (1941-)   Originally from Indiana, Twyla Tharp had diverse dance training in many genres before studying modern dance and jazz in New York and performing with Paul Taylor's company. During the 1960s, she experimented with movement and started her own company. In the 1970s her work became recognized when she choreographed for the Joffrey Ballet. Her choreography of *Push Comes to Shove* for Baryshnikov at American Ballet Theatre (ABT) was a huge success. She went on to choreograph for Broadway productions and movies, and to direct companies. Tharp's work of creating modern dance for ballet companies was an important milestone for 20th-century modern dance and ballet. Her works include:

- *Deuce Coupe* (1973): This dance combines ballet, postmodern dance, and popular social dances to the music of the Beach Boys.
- *Push Comes to Shove* (1976): Created as a duet for Baryshnikov and Tharp, this work blends classical ballet and jazz into a contemporary style.

In the last two decades of the 20th century, postmodern dance expanded in even more directions, including site-specific works, social commentary, multimedia works, and cross-cultural works. Multimedia works included movement, video, and sound in varying proportions (determined by the choreographer or the dancers). When one or more of these elements come together unexpectedly, they create a new, instantaneous, and unpredicted experience for the dancers and the audience. Cross-cultural dances often included choreographed dances or dances created with stylistic cultural elements and music from different cultural sources.

BILL T. JONES (1952 -)   Raised in upstate New York, Bill T. Jones studied African dance, ballet, modern dance, and jazz. In the 1980s, Jones and Arnie Zane began making works that incorporated narrative, video, and autobiographical information into movement. Jones continues to create works that reflect social issues as part of a fusion of dance and theater. Signature works include the following:

- *Intuitive Momentum* (1983; with Arnie Zane): A series of short dances to music by jazz musicians.
- *Last Supper at Uncle Tom's Cabin/The Promised Land* (1990): Was an evening-long dance about freedom and racial topics.

Many of the choreographers who began their careers in the latter part of the 20th century moved into the mainstream of contemporary dance after the turn of the millennium.

MARK MORRIS (1956-)   Born in Seattle, Mark Morris studied ballet, folk, and flamenco dance as a child. He moved to New York in the mid-1970s and performed with the companies of Feld, Tharp, and Dean, among others. In 1980, he formed the Mark Morris Dance Group and by 1991, his company was considered one of the leading modern dance companies. Morris is a prolific choreographer whose works range from large to small works with eclectic music choices. His style is a blend of ballet, postmodern dance, and court dance with other cultural dance genres. His early works include *Dido and Aeneas* (1989) and *The Hard Nut* (1991). Morris created *Beau* (2008) for the San Francisco Ballet. This playful ballet for nine men features them dancing to a 20th-century harpsichord.

TRISHA BROWN (1936-)   From Washington state, Trisha Brown went to school in California before moving to New York to continue her studies. She was a founding member of the Judson Dance Theater and explored games, improvisation, and the spoken word in her site-specific works. In 1971 she performed her *Roof Piece* in New York, which led to other experiments with gravity, mathematical layer phrases, and other possibilities for movement. In her work she has collaborated with visual artists and musicians. After 40 years, she and her company continue to expand her movement ideas by creating new works and revisiting some of her timeless pieces. In the 21st century, Brown has stretched her work to embrace technology. She collaborated with a Japanese artist and robotic designer on *I Love My Robot* (2007) to explore humanity and inanimate objects, and other artists continue the interaction between dancers and technology.

Early Twenty-First Century

In the first decade of the 21st century, modern dancers are still stretching the limits of the dance form with the continued addition of media, technology, and diverse performance settings.

Contemporary modern dance has many new faces and talents who are pushing the boundaries of what is dance and how you can use it to express today's ideas.

Since 2000, *Dance Magazine* has published an annual feature listing its choices for the top 25 dancers and choreographers to watch in the future. Check out one or more of these features to get a sense of the wealth of dancers and choreographers who will contribute to the future of dance. Where these artists will be a decade from now is hard to predict. However, it is fascinating to do an Internet search of those chosen a decade ago to so see where they are today.

Creative Processes

In modern dance if the dancer and choreographer are the same person, a deep interaction occurs between the body and mind. Strong physical and intellectual filters gather and sift through movement ideas, research, and information from many sources—sights, sounds, textures, and words—that spark creativity. Personal perceptions guide the movements you choose, along with the style and the focus of the work.

If the choreographer works with a group of dancers, the process involves communication. The choreographer can provide the dancers with a specific movement or leave it open for their interpretation. The movement can be a product of improvisation directed by the choreographer, or the dancers can use a choreographic concept to create a movement. The choreographer can further sculpt the movement to draw out the choreographic intent.

The creative process in modern dance uses a two-directional approach: one part is based on modern dance vocabulary, and the other part stems from your movement exploration repertory as a result of improvisational tasks, knowledge from other dance forms, and movement styles that you have studied. These approaches inform each other. Which approach takes the lead, depends on what type of work you intend to create. The integration of these two approaches in the creative process makes your movement statement, study, or dance your own unique artistic and creative expression.

Improvisation

Improvisation is deeply embedded in modern dance; it provides the initiative or impetus for your creative expression. Exploring and creating movement uses internal stimuli—how you perceive an idea, a theme, and an emotion—to inspire a movement sequence or a choreographic work. External stimuli include ideas, themes, emotions, or historical, political, or societal events or issues that affect you. As you improvise, you express your responses to these stimuli through movement.

ACTIVITY 10.4 EXPLORE

Dancer and Choreographer

Using the ideas presented in the previous section (Creative Processes), select a theme or idea. Create a movement statement of four or more movement sequences that incorporate these topics. When your movement statement is complete, reflect and analyze what you selected and why. As you reflect, determine whether you see other choices you might have made or that you might explore in the future. You may write a summary of this experience and other choices to explore in your journal for future reference.

Participating in both technical and creative projects develops artistic expression. Using improvisation fuels each part of the performance and artistic process.

Somatic Awareness of Movement

Somatic awareness in dance tunes into your body wisdom; you sense your body movement kinesthetically while mindfully moving to gain a deeper understanding of subtle expression. For more detail on somatic body awareness, see chapter 4.

Basics of Modern Dance Class

In the modern dance class, the format is similar to other concert dance forms. The class begins with a warm-up of the body and its parts. These warm-up exercises are done standing or on the floor. After the warm-up, the class practices center exercises and techniques to gain strength, and flexibility on the floor, kneeling or standing. In small groups, dancers perform combinations in the center or traveling across the floor to develop movement coordination and qualities or efforts. An improvisation, movement study, or a longer combination culminates the class work, followed by cool-down exercises to finish. The format of the modern dance class may vary depending upon what technique or styles are taught in the class.

Modern Dance Class Safety

Because modern dance is usually performed barefoot, always practice proper foot care to ensure safe dancing. Studio and performance floors should be smooth, clean, and neither sticky nor slippery. Many dance studios have vinyl dance floors, eliminating many floor problems. Modern dancers often fall, slide, or otherwise come in contact with the floor. Dancers should take precautions to avoid floor burns. Use body lotions or creams sparingly. These lotions or creams could create slick spots where your feet or body come in contact with the floor. As in other forms of concert dance, awareness of personal and group space is essential to safely jumping, falling, turning, or leaping through the studio.

Modern Dance Wear

For traditional modern dance classes, leotards and tights or a unitard are the standard dance wear. Women wear a leotard, a sports bra, and footless tights that may be capri length. Men may wear a dance belt, leotard, and tights or a tee-shirt and dance pants. Your teacher will guide you with a list of approved dance attire for class. If your hair is long, keep it secured away from your face so that you can see and so it doesn't hit you or another dancer in the face. Jewelry is discouraged for safety reasons. Although modern dancers generally perform in bare feet, for some surfaces you might choose to wear dance sandals to protect your feet.

Modern Dance Technique

Modern dance technique focuses on the movement elements of the body, space, time, and energy or effort. During the 20th century, Rudolf Laban created a system for observing, analyzing, and describing movements. See chapter 3 for explanation of effort and effort actions.

The elements of dance form the foundation for modern dance technique. Movement, choreographic, and aesthetic principles are integrated into the movement to create the level of performance and the style you want to formulate as your point of view.

Other dance forms share the modern dance movement vocabulary. Gaining a basic vocabulary and command of modern dance technique gives you a lot of material from which to select as you create or learn to manipulate movement.

POSITIONS OF THE LEGS AND FEET　Modern dance exercises use parallel and turned-out positions of the legs and feet. See chapter 9 for turned-out position descriptions and basic positions of the arms. There are five parallel foot positions. First, second, and fourth parallel positions are the ones most currently used in modern dance.

first position parallel: The legs and feet face forward of the body and are aligned directly under the hips. The insides of the feet may touch or be slightly apart (figure 10.1).

second position parallel: The legs and feet face forward of the body. The feet are separated about shoulder-width apart; the knees face forward and align directly over the toes (figure 10.2).

fourth position parallel: The legs and feet face forward of the body. The right foot is in front so that the back of the heel is just past the toes of the left foot (figure 10.3). Reverse the foot positions for parallel fourth on the left side

B+ position: Stand with the supporting leg in either parallel or turned-out position. Bend the knee of the working leg, allowing the working leg to extend behind with the toes flexed or pointed and resting on the floor.

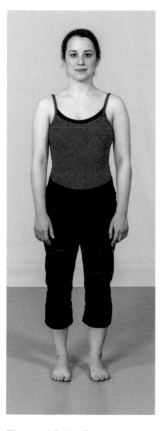

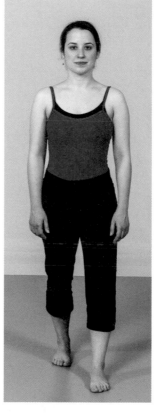

Figure 10.1　First position parallel.

Figure 10.2　Second position parallel.

Figure 10.3　Fourth position parallel.

The foot on the floor or in the air uses these two positions: The *pointed foot* extends from the ankle. The forefoot and toes may flex to continue the curve of the foot in the air. The *flexed foot* begins with a strong flexion from the ankle; the heel presses forward and the toes may pull up to complete this position.

BASIC MOVEMENTS Modern dance uses the elements of space, time, and energy. You can express the elements using these effort terms: space (direct or indirect pathways), time (sudden or slow), weight (light or strong), and flow (bound or free). Modern dance movements include nonlocomotor (axial) and locomotor.

Nonlocomotor movements are body parts moving around a stationary base. The base can be the feet, knees, buttocks, back, front, or side of the body. Axial movements include body extension, rises, falls and recovers, twists, or turns in place.

> *body bends:* These movements include bending at the neck, upper back, waist, hips, knees, ankles, and feet. Bends can be forward, to the side, or back.
>
> *extensions:* The body, or one or more body parts such as arms and legs together or separately, extend forward, backward, or on diagonal planes from body. These types of body or body part extensions contribute to lengthening body line as part of creating an entire body shape.
>
> *rise:* The body changes level upward. For example, you might begin by lying on the floor, then move to sitting, kneeling, demi-plié, standing, relevé, or in the air. The pathway can be straight or in a spiral pattern.
>
> *fall:* The body changes levels downward. Often beginning with a jump into the air, you move through standing, to kneeling, sitting, and then lying on the floor. The pathway can be straight to the front, side, back, or in a spiral pattern. The movement can be quick or slow.
>
> *recovery:* The body's return from a fall. Beginning at the ending position of the fall, you move upward to a sitting, kneeling, or standing position. The pathway can be straight or in a spiral pattern. The movement is fast or slow.
>
> *twist:* Body parts turn or twist around the torso or a body part. Some body parts will extend while others bend.
>
> *turn:* The body moves as a unit around an axis. The base can be the foot, the knee, or the hips. You can do turns in place or moving.

Locomotor movements move the body through the space using steps that range from everyday movements to those from dance and other movement forms. These movements may use either parallel or turned-out foot positions. Many of these locomotor movements can vary in their directions and levels, and they can be large to small.

> *walk:* Includes a natural walk (heel, ball, toes), a dance walk (toes, ball, heel), or high walk (on three-quarter relevé; see chapter 9).
>
> *run:* Fast walks with or without an air moment (pause in the air) and performed in a variety of styles.
>
> *jump:* A spring into the air with an air moment from two feet to two feet, two feet to one foot, one foot to two feet, or one foot to the other foot (such as coupé; see chapter 9).
>
> *hop:* A spring into the air from one foot to the same foot.

prance: A change of weight from one foot to the other quickly in parallel position.

leap: The transfer of body weight from one leg to the other. A leap has an air moment when both legs are in the air before the transfer to the other leg.

gallop: Step or slide forward in demi-plié, then pull both legs in the air. Land in the position you start the gallop.

chassé: The front foot slides out, then the other foot pushes the body into the air where the legs come together or cross. Landing on the second foot, the first foot slides out again.

skip: A step-hop movement that has an extended air moment.

triplet: In this movement, you take three steps, first a step forward into demi-plié, next a step forward onto three-quarter relevé with the second foot, and finally a step forward again onto three-quarter relevé with the first foot. The next triplet begins with the second foot.

grapevine: In this movement you first step to the side, then cross the other foot in front of or behind you, then step to the side again with the first foot to repeat the step. On the repeat, the other foot crosses back or front (opposite to the first time the step was executed) to continue in that direction.

Some basic locomotor movements and exercises cross concert dance forms. In modern dance, these are some of the exercises that are executed in both parallel and turned-out positions:

foot exercises (foot presses, foot pedals, point and flex, flick and press)

demi-plié

grand plié

battement tendu

battement dégagé

battement développé

grand battement

See chapter 9 for descriptions of these exercises.

Body Shapes

Beginning modern dance alignment starts with good posture, but it includes other alignments and body shapes, too. Good posture is the basis for good dance alignment, which supports technique and style and helps you move efficiently.

contraction: In this shape, the entire torso takes a concave shape from the shoulders through the hips (figure 10.4). An upper-body contraction uses the chest and shoulders.

tilt: In this shape, the torso stretches on an angle forward, to the side, or backward from vertical alignment (figure 10.5).

Figure 10.4 Contraction.

Bandaloop

Modern dancers have danced in many types of performance spaces. Contemporary dancers seek out new spaces to perform their works. Bandaloop is a modern dance company that has taken dances to new heights and spaces. For over 20 years, they have been pioneers, using integrated rock climbing skills with modern dance to perform in vertical space such as mountain walls or existing built walls all over the world. Some of their first works were done on the sides of mountains, where the dancers wore climbing gear. Now the company performs on the sides of historical buildings or the newest skyscrapers.

Figure 10.5 Tilt.

release: A return to the aligned position or an upper back tilt following a contraction, a tilt, or another body shape.

Experimenting with modern dance components before selecting those that you think are part of a dance work will help you use them effectively.

Thinking Like a Dancer

Modern dance centers on expressing your emotions and ideas through movement, and conveying meaning to an audience. This dance genre allows you to find your values and passions and then, with reflection, articulate your views in ways that

✔ ACTIVITY 10.5 ASSESS
Evaluate Your Performance

In this activity, you evaluate your modern dancing. Use the combination you created earlier or one that your teacher creates. Using the modern dance rubric on the web resource, you can do a self-check or ask another classmate to view your combination. Review your completed rubric and any notes you made. Reflect by mentally running through your performance. Then write a paragraph in which you identify what techniques you did well and any rubric descriptors that were challenging. Make a list of at least three items on the rubric that you plan to improve. If you worked with a classmate, next review the classmate's rubric appraisal. Write a paragraph to respond to each of the indicators checked for your performance. Add a summary paragraph about the experience, and determine whether you should incorporate any feedback from the review into your goals.

will connect to the viewer. In other words, you think like a dancer through deep exploration, experimentation with movement, and thoughtful decision making.

Summary

Modern dance lets you describe who you are and what you believe through movement. It is a very powerful language. This chapter provided an overview of the language of modern dance, its history, and some major artists. It also introduced you to the creative process and explained basic movements of modern dance. Once you become fluent in this language, your possibilities for expression are endless.

PORTFOLIO ASSIGNMENT

Your teacher will provide you with several visual images of nature or the natural environment. Select one of these images to stimulate your imagination to create a movement sequence. Your movement sequence should be your interpretation of a story or a feeling about nature or moving in a natural environment. Your teacher will determine the length of the movement sequence and other details about it. After you have rehearsed your movement sequence, then find music or a soundscape that complements it. In small groups, take turns presenting the movement sequences. After your presentation, explain your story or point of view about nature or a natural environment to the group, and show the visual image you used as a stimulus.

Prepare a summary and write an e-journal entry to outline your process for this movement activity. Include why you made the selections you did in your movements and music and the process you went through to create the story or feeling expressed through the movement sequence. Include the stimulus photo, and list the music or soundscape you used and why. Determine whether you are pleased with your outcome. How would you refine your movement sequence? What did you learn about nature or a natural environment from this activity? How do the arts interact with nature or the natural environment? How do nature and natural environments support people in this century? You may need to do additional research into a variety of topics to inform you and help you form opinions. Include the research sources that support your opinions, findings, and conclusions.

REVIEW QUESTIONS

Multiple Choice

1. _____Modern dance technique is based on
   a. ballet
   b. folk dance
   c. elements of dance

2. _____Contemporary modern dance could be described as
   a. abstract, blended movement styles, underlying technique
   b. free flowing, personality-centered movement invention
   c. task, nontechnical, improvised, group developed

3. _____Who coined the term *modern dance*?
   a. Isadora Duncan
   b. John Martin
   c. Martha Graham

4. _____A contraction can be described as
   a. vertical stance
   b. curved torso
   c. released back

5. _____Locomotor movement includes all but which of the following terms?
   a. grapevine and run
   b. skip and gallop
   c. rise and fall

True or False

1. Martha Graham created dances about the American Southwest, mythology, and cosmic themes. _____

2. Merce Cunningham and John Cage were choreographers who experimented with chance dances. _____

3. Katherine Dunham was an anthropologist, a dancer, and a choreographer. _____

4. The four pioneer modern dancers used American historical topics as the focus in their new dances. _____

Matching

1. __E__ Isadora Duncan
2. __A__ Ruth St. Denis
3. __B__ Ted Shawn
4. __C__ Martha Graham
5. _____ Doris Humphrey
6. _____ Hanya Holm
7. _____ Charles Weidman
8. _____ José Limón
9. _____ Katherine Dunham
10. _____ Merce Cunningham
11. _____ Alwin Nikolais
12. __G__ Alvin Ailey
13. __P__ Twyla Tharp
14. _____ Bill T. Jones
15. _____ Mark Morris
16. _____ Tricia Brown

a. Dancer who created a series of dances based on Oriental deities.

b. Choreographer inspired by Native American culture and dances from around the world.

c. Early dances expressed the inner conflicts within man.

d. Dances that explored man's conflict with the environment and included strong social content.

e. Dancer who used classical music and created abstract dances inspired by Greek art to express emotions.

f. Choreographer and teacher who incorporated Wigman's and Laban's ideas into the work.

g. Choreographer who blended African, European, Afro-Caribbean, and American dance forms into choreographic works.

h. Choreographer who used strong literary or dramatic themes for dances.

i. Choreographer who created dance events to explore immediacy while performing a work.

j. Choreographer who used motion, color, light, and electronic sound.

k. Choreographer whose style used Horton technique, African overtones, and social jazz dance with blues, spirituals, and gospel music to accompany high-energy choreography.

l. Incorporated narrative, video, and autobiographical information into works that reflect social issues as part of a fusion of dance and theater.

m. Choreographer who predominately used a mix of dance, mime, and comedy but created some pure movement works, too.

n. Founding member of the Judson Dance Theater who explored games, improvisation, the spoken word, mathematic layer phrases, and other possibilities in site-specific works.

o. Prolific choreographer whose works use eclectic music choices in a style that blends ballet and postmodern dance with other dance genres.

p. Created modern dance works for ballet companies, and choreographed on the Broadway stage and the movies.

To find supplementary materials for this chapter such as worksheets, extended learning activities, and e-journaling assignments, visit the web resource at www.discoveringdance.org/student.

Jazz Dance

ENDURING UNDERSTANDING: Jazz dance is an American classic and contemporary dance genre used in entertainment, media, and concert dance.

ESSENTIAL QUESTION: How does jazz dance help me express myself as a dancer?

LEARNING OBJECTIVES

After reading this chapter, you will be able to do the following:

- Recognize major jazz dance works, styles, and jazz dance artists in history.
- Execute basic jazz dance technique, use jazz dance vocabulary, and perform combinations.
- Apply jazz dance etiquette and dance safety while dancing.
- Evaluate and respond to classical and contemporary jazz dance performances.

VOCABULARY
forced arch
isolation
jazz dance

"Don't dance for the audience; dance for yourself."

Bob Fosse, 20th-century American jazz dancer, choreographer, and director

Jazz movement is quintessentially American. Its movement can be both smooth and strong, and its varied rhythms and accents create powerful movement styles for personal expression. Jazz grew out of the popular dances of the early 20th century. Throughout its development, this genre has absorbed many dance forms from society and the stage or has been influenced by music and trends of an era of history. Dancers and choreographers continue to blend jazz with other dance genres to create a dance genre that links personal perceptions with styles of movement.

Jazz dance is versatile; it can adapt to social, concert dance, musical theater, and entertainment styles. Jazz dance has specific techniques, a language of dance that stretches from 20th-century historical social to contemporary dance steps, and styles developed by jazz dance artists and teachers. Similar to some other dance genres, jazz dance absorbs and discards movement styles as fashion, popular music, and society move on.

This chapter provides ways to study the genre of jazz dance to support your dancing experiences in the classroom. You will learn about jazz dance history, dancers and choreographic artists, the major styles and works of this genre, structure of jazz class, and terminology, and you will view selected works from jazz dance performance literature.

Discovering Jazz Dance

Jazz dance has several roots and influences that have intertwined during its development. Dancers, choreographers, and musicians use these characteristics of jazz dance along with their own creativity to create unique works. Jazz dance can combine movement, body shapes, and dynamics to create a personal expression of you.

Exploring Jazz Dance

Although jazz dance contains improvisational and creative movements that blend with jazz dance techniques, it also has some techniques that connect it to other forms of concert dance. Jazz dance artists and choreographers studied or danced many dance genres. These artists took their knowledge of dance, selected from it, and expanded it in new directions to express themselves through jazz dance styles or fused jazz with other forms. For example, hip-hop is a cultural dance form (see chapter 8), but it can also combine with jazz dance styles. Popular dancing has continued to make its way into and out of jazz dance styles. This constant evolution of various dance styles and forms into jazz dance is what keeps it contemporary—and alive.

History of Jazz Dance

Both jazz dance and jazz music are American, but their roots reach back to the African continent. African slaves brought their dances to the Americas. African dance characteristics include a grounded stance, percussive rhythms, isolated body parts, and movement initiated from the torso that transferred into various social dance forms.

From colonial times through the 19th century, dances and theatrical entertainment absorbed African American dance characteristics. On colonial plantations,

---

! ACTIVITY 11.1   DISCOVER

Experience Jazz Dance

To discover jazz dance, you have to feel the movement and hear the music. Your teacher will provide the class with one or more jazz dance combinations to perform. These combinations may explore body isolations, movement sequences across the floor, or center floor movements using basic jazz dance vocabulary. After you have danced these combinations, follow up by writing a journal entry to describe the movement using dance element terms and explain how the movement and the music are related. What was your overall opinion of your jazz dance experience, and why?

owners did the latest dances from Europe. Slaves created dances that blended continental court dances and African dance styles. By the 19th century, African American influences were absorbed into the popular entertainment such as the minstrel shows, *The Black Crook* (see chapter 5), and vaudeville.

The early 20th century became a gathering point for the development of both new music explorations and dance. New art and music styles, such as ragtime, continued social and concert dance innovations. In the late teens and 1920s the jazz age arrived in full force. Harlem led the way with the Savoy Ballroom and others to introduce music and dances. In the 1920s, the Charleston and the Black Bottom became the rage in ballrooms, in dance halls, and onstage.

Beginning in the 1930s *talkies* (the first movies to include sound) were popular, as were the new movie musicals such as those that starred Ginger Rogers and Fred Astaire. Their dancing spread exhibition, social, and show dancing through hometown movie theaters across the nation. The Savoy Ballroom in Harlem became the home for Big Bands that inspired new dances such as the Lindy hop. Adding air movements, the Lindy moved into mainstream, becoming the jitterbug with solo improvisations in its athletic style. Celebrated musicians such as Duke Ellington and Louis Armstrong and Big Band leaders such as Glen Miller and Artie Shaw performed in clubs while radio stations tuned people into jazz music across America. Jazz music, popular social dances, and show dancing funneled into a form of entertainment that appealed to audiences, dancers, and choreographers alike.

The 1930s and 1940s

In the 1930s the Ziegfeld Follies dance director, Ned Wayburn, and then in the 1940s George Balanchine, Jack Cole, Jerome Robbins, and other dance artists, took their experiments in contemporary dance to a new home on the Broadway stage and in the movies.

Ballet choreographer George Balanchine created *Slaughter on Tenth Avenue* and *On Your Toes*. He worked with tap dancer Herbie Harper to blend rhythm tap with ballet.

JACK COLE (1911-1974)   Born in New Jersey, dancer, choreographer, and teacher Jack Cole is considered the father of theatrical jazz dance. His experience with Denishawn led him to continued studies in *bharata nātyam* (a form of classical Indian dance), Afro-Caribbean, and Spanish dance genres. Cole began inserting elements of these dance genres into his solo dances and those of his company. In the 1930s Cole appeared in nightclubs from coast to coast. His unprecedented blend of Indian dance forged his unique brand of movement. As a choreographer he created dances for almost 30 films for movie stars and dancers during the 1940s and 1950s. On Broadway his choreography included *Kismet* (1953), *A Funny Thing Happened on the Way to the Forum* (1962), and *Man of La Mancha* (1965).

Over the next several decades, Broadway and touring musical theater dance choreography continued to absorb popular social dances, developing techniques of dance artists, and their stylized movements.

Katherine Dunham and her dancers performed on stage, in films, and on Broadway. (For more information on Katherine Dunham, see chapter 10). At her New York School, dancers studied her blend of African and Haitian dance with isolated body movements and complex rhythmic patterns that build in tempo to the drumming. Her dance technique contributed to the development of theatrical and educational jazz dance.

JEROME ROBBINS (1918-1998)   Dancer, choreographer, and director Jerome Robbins studied ballet, modern dance, Spanish dance, and other dance forms. During his career he choreographed ballets, Broadway musicals, and movies. His dance sequences in the musical *On the Town* (1944) were based on Robbins' full-length ballet *Fancy Free*, produced by Ballet Theatre (later known as ABT) that same year. In 1950 he joined New York City Ballet (NYCB) and became associate artistic director. While he created ballets for NYCB, he continued to choreograph and began to direct Broadway musicals and films. In 1958 he started a short-lived company producing jazz-flavored ballets. (For more information on Jerome Robbins, see chapter 9.) Some of his musical theater triumphs included the enduring *West Side Story* (1957), *The King and I* (1951), and *Fiddler on the Roof* (1969), for which he received a Tony Award for best direction and choreography. Robbins' work began consolidating the roles of choreographer and director in musicals.

PETER GENNARO (1919-2000)   Louisiana-born Peter Gennaro was a dancer and choreographer who made his Broadway debut in 1948. He danced in *Kiss Me, Kate* (1948) and *Guys and Dolls* (1950), and he was a specialty dancer in "Steam Heat" in *The Pajama Game* (1954). Gennaro collaborated with Robbins on *West Side Story*.

Gennaro danced and choreographed for television shows. He and his company made regular appearances on the *Ed Sullivan Show*. For many years, Gennaro choreographed for Radio City Music Hall and staged the Rockettes.

The 1950s

In the 1950s, the term *jazz dance* generally focused on classes in social dances from the first half of the 20th century, while terms such as *freestyle, musical comedy*, and *Afro-Cuban dance* referred to movements and techniques from Broadway shows that began to move into dance studios. In the 1960s, the impact of *West Side Story* spread across the nation, and jazz dancers were in demand to teach at dance teacher conventions. As a result, jazz dance took its place as a dance form in studios throughout the United States. By the 1970s, jazz dance courses began to appear in college dance programs (Mahoney 1998). Dance artists and master teachers Matt Mattox, Louis "Luigi" Faccuito, and later Gus Giordano and others would train the next generation of jazz dancers.

MATT MATTOX (1921-2013)   Born in Tulsa, Oklahoma, Matt Mattox danced on Broadway and movie musicals, and he choreographed for television and variety shows. Originally trained in ballet, Mattox studied with Jack Cole. In Hollywood, Mattox was a specialty dancer in the movie musical *Seven Brides for Seven Brothers* (1954). He appeared in *There's No Business Like Show Business* (1954) and other movies. Mattox developed his technique for freestyle dance (his term for jazz dance). In his New York classes, accompanied by a single bongo drummer, he incorporated Cole's style into his ballet training and included improvised combinations. His style showcased strong technique and fluid to percussive movements. He moved to France, where he founded a company and taught his technique. Mattox's teaching and technique contributed to the development of American jazz dance.

EUGENE LOUIS "LUIGI" FACCUITO (1925-)   Known as "Luigi," Eugene Louis Faccuito came from Steubenville, Ohio. After World War II, Luigi went to Los Angeles to pursue a movie musical career. As a result of a near tragic accident, Luigi started a stretching routine that enabled him to return to dance class. Luigi danced in over 40 films, including *An American in Paris, Annie Get Your Gun, Singin' in the Rain,* and *White Christmas.* In the late 1950s he moved to New York and appeared on Broadway as a dancer and assistant choreographer. In the 1960s, he began touring the United States and teaching, which led to studios and colleges using his technique. His technique built on his stretching exercises and ballet movements, which flow to a single percussionist's accompaniment (Mahoney1998).

GUS GIORDANO (1923-2008)   A dancer, choreographer, and master teacher, Gus Giordano was born in St. Louis, Missouri. He studied ballet and theater dance. In New York he took classes with modern dancers Hanya Holm, Alwin Nikolais, and Katherine Dunham. Giordano performed on and off Broadway, in film, and on television. He danced in the Broadway shows *Wish You Were Here, Paint Your Wagon,* and *On the Town.* In the early 1950s he moved to Chicago and opened a studio. Ten years later, he formed the Giordano Jazz Dance Company. In the 1970s, Giordano wrote *Anthology of American Jazz Dance,* which outlined his style of jazz dance technique. In the 1990s, Giordano founded the World Jazz Dance Congress. Held in Chicago every two years, this event attracts jazz dancers from all over the world. In 2005, he received the Heritage Award from the National Dance Association for his contributions to dance education. Giordano's daughter, Nan, inherited his positions as artistic director of the Giordano Jazz Dance Company and the World Jazz Dance Congress.

New Directions for Jazz Dance

On both the East Coast and West Coast of the United States, jazz dance began to take new directions. The work of modern dancer-choreographers such as Lester Horton, Alvin Ailey, and Talley Beatty contributed to the continuing evolution of jazz dance.

LESTER HORTON (1909-1953)   Lester Horton performed in concert settings, in nightclub reviews, and later in movie musicals. His technique influenced West Coast jazz dance through the strong, versatile dancers that were to carry on his legacy. (For more information on Lester Horton, see chapter 10.)

ALVIN AILEY (1931-1989)   Alvin Ailey studied and performed with Lester Horton. His choreographic style used Horton technique, African overtones, and social jazz dance components. (For more information on Alvin Ailey see chapter 10.)

TALLEY BEATTY (1918-1995)   Born in Chicago, Talley Beatty was a dancer and educator. Beatty studied with Katherine Dunham and Martha Graham. His choreography used a blend of social jazz, ballet, and Dunham-influenced movement. His works focused on social issues and African American life.

Jazz on Broadway and Beyond

On Broadway, famous musical theater choreographers such as Bob Fosse and Michael Bennett drew audiences' and dancers' interest in jazz dance. In the 1990s, hip-hop and other street dances, pop dances, lyrical dance, contemporary dance, modern dance, and ballet continued to influence the everchanging styles of jazz dance.

ROBERT LOUIS FOSSE (1927-1987)   Robert (Bob) Fosse was a dancer, but his claim to fame was as a choreographer and then director in musical theater and film. He made his Broadway debut as a dancer in 1950. His debut as a choreographer was in the film *The Pajama Game* (1954). His 1968 directing debut was for the film version of a Broadway blockbuster musical called *Sweet Charity* (1966). Later he went on to choreograph the musical *Chicago* (1975), which he also choreographed and directed for film. He both choreographed and directed *All That Jazz* (1979), which was somewhat autobiographical. Fosse's style was unique and innovative. He used turned-in knees, rolled shoulders, and quirky moves. Fosse dancers used props such as hats or canes. He won eight Tony Awards for choreography and one for direction, and was nominated for an Academy Award four times. Fosse is considered one of the most influential choreographers of the 20th century.

A Fosse-style jazz dance pose.

MICHAEL PETERS (1948-1994)   Born in New York, Michael Peters danced with Talley Beatty and Alvin Ailey. Peters danced, choreographed, and directed for stage, television, movies, and music videos. Peters won a Tony Award for co-choreographing the Broadway musical *Dreamgirls* (1981) with Michael Bennett. However, he is best remembered for his choreography of Michael Jackson's music videos *Beat It* and *Thriller.*

MICHAEL BENNETT (1943-1987) Born in New York, Bennett (his stage name) was a dancer, choreographer, and musical director. From dancing in a production of *West Side Story*, he moved on to become a choreographer-director of Broadway shows. *Promises, Promises* (1968), *A Chorus Line* (1975), *and Dream-girls* (with Michael Peters, 1981) are among his most notable works. *A Chorus Line* was Bennett's concept. It became one of the longest-running musicals in the history of the Broadway theater. During his career, Bennett received seven Tony Awards.

DANNY BURACZESKI Danny Buraczeski grew up in Pennsylvania. After his dancing career on Broadway in such musicals as *Mame,* he formed his company, JAZZDANCE in 1979. His company toured the United States, Europe, and the Caribbean. His works show a deep understanding of jazz dance and music heritage. His music is eclectic from decades past to created scores for his works. Buraczeski's work has been supported by national arts organizations. He has set works on ballet companies, repertory dance companies, and universities. Regarded as a leading jazz dance choreographer, he has taught at several universities and received awards for his artistic achievements.

BILLY SIEGENFELD Billy Siegenfeld is artistic director, choreographer, and founder of Jump Rhythm Jazz Project, a Chicago-based company that tours nationally and internationally. Siegenfeld's technique uses body music (rhythmic percussion) and vocalization. Dancers, actors, and singers use his system of training, which is called the Jump Rhythm technique. This fusion technique is the foundation for his choreography. He has won an Emmy Award for the PBS documentary on the Jump Rhythm Jazz Project, and the Jazz Dance World Congress acknowledged him for his contributions to jazz dance. A Fulbright Senior Scholar, he has produced his work in Europe, Finland, and with U.S. companies. Siegenfeld is a professor at Northwestern University.

Over the years, jazz dance has borrowed technique and terminology from modern and ballet. Jazz dance is contextual—it captures current societal trends and movement styles and superimposes them into jazz dance technique. This continual layering effect leads to absorbing or discarding one style for another.

ACTIVITY 11.2 RESEARCH

Social Dance Influences

From the 1920s on, do a web search to create a timeline of social dances that influenced jazz dance. Do you see any of these social dance influences in the past decade? Do you know a couple of these dances? Think about how you could incorporate some of the social dance movements or styles into a jazz combination. Experiment, and see what works best. Then show your movement sequence to another classmate or your group.

Basics of Jazz Dance Class

Jazz dance classes vary, but the general format for the parts of the class is similar to other concert dance forms.

Jazz Dance Class Safety

Jazz dance kicks, leg extensions, big jumps, leaps, and fast-moving combinations make awareness of space essential. Jazz dance safety in class begins with appropriate dance wear and footwear selections and personal grooming. Similar to other dance classes (see chapters 9 and 10), what you wear and how aware you are of your movement in relation to the space around you should always be on your mind as you dance. Dancers should take precautions to avoid floor burns. Jazz dancers should use body lotions or creams sparingly. They could create slick spots where their feet or body come in contact with the floor.

Jazz Dance Wear

You have a wide range of dance wear and footwear options for this genre. Your teacher will provide you with the guidelines for dressing for jazz dance class. Usually people wear leotards and tights or jazz pants of various lengths worn with tank tops or tee-shirts. You will want to wear comfortable clothes you can move in, but baggy clothing is generally discouraged. Jazz footwear can be low-heeled, flexible-soled jazz shoes with or without laces, or they can be jazz sneakers. Sometimes people are barefoot for part of the class. Some styles of jazz dance use soft boots, and some women wear heeled character shoes. As in other dance classes, keep your hair away from your face so that it doesn't interfere with your or others' movements. For safety, keep jewelry to a minimum.

Warm-Up

The jazz class begins with a series of warm-up exercises that include both total-body movements and isolations. Isolated body actions warm up each part of the body beginning with the head, then moving to the shoulders, ribs, hips, and legs. Usually you warm up in the center of the studio, doing standing or floor exercises. Sometimes a jazz dance class may warm up at the barre.

ISOLATIONS   An **isolation** is an exercise in which you move individual parts of the body while the rest of the body stays still or moves in a different way. Isolations begin with the head, then move to the shoulders, rib cage, hips, and other body parts. In isolations a body part moves from an aligned neutral position forward, backward, to each side, in a circular path, or moving upward and downward, as in these exercises:

head isolations: Begin with the head centered and facing directly forward. The head turns from side to center to side to center. The head moves up, center, down, and center. The head tilts to one side with the ear directly in line with the top of the shoulder, tilts back to center, then tilts to the other side, and back to center. Then, the head slowly and gently moves from the facing the side, rotating down and around to face the other side before reversing the direction of the movement.

shoulder isolations: Begin with both shoulders facing the front and in a neutral position.

shoulder raises: Raise and lower the shoulders in a neutral position.

shoulder alternation: One shoulder raises as the other lowers, and then they alternate.

shoulder isolations front and back: The shoulders move forward and center (neutral position), then back and center.

These different directions might be combined so that they move forward, up, back, and down several times, then reverse direction:

hip isolations: With the body in alignment, demi-plié in parallel position. Begin with the hips centered, and move them side to side or front to back, ending in neutral position. In each of these directions, the hips can do a series of quick pulses in the direction they are moving.

hip-lift isolations: Lift one hip, and return to neutral position; then lift the other hip, and return. Later this isolation combines with steps such as different types of walks.

STANDING EXERCISES Standing exercises are similar to standing exercises in other concert dance genres. Following is just an overview of the many exercises that could be included in this part of the class.

demi-plié: These exercises are done in first, second, and fifth position in parallel and turned-out leg and foot positions.

battement tendu, battement tendu with demi-plié, or battement dégagé: As in other concert dance forms, they are performed in parallel and turned-out positions. The working leg moves to the front, side, or back in the en croix position.

battement développé: Done in turned-out and parallel position, the working leg moves up the supporting leg and extends front, side, or back.

leg swing: From first position or B+ derrière, with the working foot pointed on the floor, the working leg swings front to back or side to side.

contraction: These body shapes are similar to modern dance (see chapter 10). A jazz dance contraction's initiation, timing, and qualities may be different than contractions in modern dance.

tilt: This body position or shape is the same as in modern dance (see chapter 10).

FLOOR WORK Floor work includes some conditioning and stretching exercises that prepare you for increased abdominal strength or flexibility. You may have done some of these exercises in modern dance class, such as crunches, push-ups, body stretches, contractions, tilts, or the jazz split.

⬙ ACTIVITY 11.3 EXPLORE

Create a Jazz Dance Warm-Up

Choreograph a jazz dance warm-up of isolations, standing exercises, and floor exercises. Write out your warm-up combination, and divide it into three or four sections. In a small group, form a circle. The first person presents the first section of his or her warm-up. The other dancers execute the leader's movements. Then, the second person presents his or her first section, and then the next person goes, and so on.

On the second round, the second person leads the group in the second section of the warm-up, followed by the other members of the group. After you have completed this activity, go to the web resource to complete the accompanying journaling prompt.

Jazz Dance Technique

The next section of the class is a series of technique exercises. These exercises often use ballet or modern dance as a basis for the jazz dance techniques studied. Some of the exercises are done standing or on the floor to increase strength and flexibility. Your teacher will present specific technique exercises for your class.

POSITIONS OF THE FEET Jazz dance uses both turned-out and parallel positions of the feet. To review turned-out positions, refer to chapter 9; for parallel positions, refer to chapter 10. The foot positions in jazz dance use the same numbering system as in ballet and modern dance (first, second, third, fourth, and fifth). These foot positions are done as full-foot positions and in three-quarter relevé, similar to other concert dance forms. Unique to jazz dance is the **forced arch** position: The supporting foot is in three-quarter relevé with the knee bent (figure 11.1).

Figure 11.1 Forced arch position.

POSITIONS OF THE ARMS Positions and movements for the arms give you long, extended lines. The positions are similar to ballet and modern dance positions, yet they are distinctly recognizable as jazz dance or relate to a specific jazz style. All positions of the arms include various forms of jazz hands (discussed in the next section).

> *second position:* Your arms extend to the sides below shoulder level, and palms face either forward or down (figure 11.2).

Figure 11.2 Second position of the arms.

Figure 11.3 Overhead position of the arms.

overhead position: Stretch both arms upward with the shoulders down; your hands can face different directions (figure 11.3).

opposition: Stretch one arm forward and the other in second position at approximately shoulder height (figure 11.4*a*). Or, one arm is bent in front of the sternum and the other to second position (figure 11.4*b*).

hands on hips: Place your hands low on your torso where the hips meet the legs. Rest the hands flat on the front of your body (figure 11.5). The elbows are directly to the side. Thumbs can be either in front of or behind the hips.

jazz hands: Flatten your hands with your fingers either stretched apart or together. The palms may face up, down, or forward. Hand positions include fists, soft fists, relaxed, or stretched hands, or they may include styles from a specific historical era (figure 11.6).

Combinations

The entire class or small groups execute jazz dance combinations in the center of the studio or moving across the floor. Generally you practice walks, elevation steps (jumps, leaps, kicks) and turns. These combinations are central to learning and practicing jazz dance steps and techniques in various ways. Usually a final combination is an extended choreographed section as practice for learning complete dances. Similar to other concert dance forms, the class ends with a cool-down to review steps and stretch out the body.

Figure 11.4 Opposition: *(a)* one arm stretches forward and the other is in second position at shoulder height; or *(b)* one arm is bent in front of the sternum and the other is in second position.

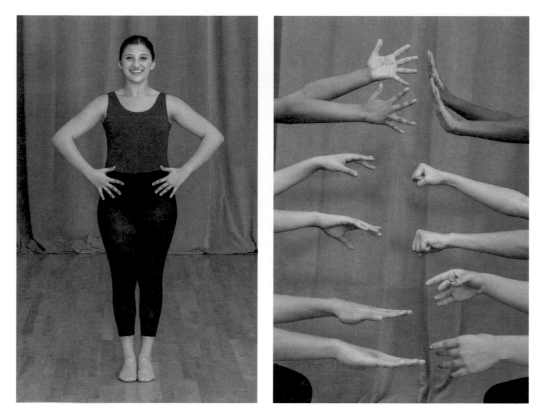

Figure 11.5   Hands on hips.

Figure 11.6   Jazz hands: fists, soft fists, relaxed, or stretched hands.

Jazz movements are either slow or fast. The movements can be syncopated in relation to the music or different parts of the body, as when you do polyrhythms (for example, where one body part moves slow and other parts move fast). Jazz dance qualities can be percussive, lyrical, or fluid movements that are often juxtaposed to keep them interesting.

Center and Across-the-Floor Steps

Jazz technique includes a wide variety of walks to discover and learn. You can do the *dancer walk* (toe, ball, heel) in turned-out or in parallel first position. Walks using levels can be full-foot, in relevé, or in demi-plié. Adding isolations, a hip lift, or a shoulder isolation before a step either front or to the side changes the style of the movement. Additional walks are often associated with styles or eras of jazz dance.

STEP COMBINATIONS

step, touch: Step on one foot; touch the other foot lightly to the floor without weight front, side, or back.

cross, touch: Step over one foot, and touch the other foot to the side.

step, ball-change: Step the right foot forward to a full-foot position (*step*), transfer weight to the ball of the left foot (*ball*), then step the right foot to a full-foot position either front or side (*change*). The step alternates to the other side.

step, kick: Step on one foot, and kick the other leg from the knee either forward or to the side.

kick, ball-change: Kick the right leg from the knee either forward or to the side, step on the ball of the right foot, then step to the full-foot position on the left. This step alternates to the other side.

pas de bourrée: Step on relevé behind the front foot, step side on relevé, and step front to a full-foot position. This basic pas de bourrée step has many variations. You can do it in place, to the side, or turning.

jazz square: Step forward on the right foot. Cross the left foot over the right, put your weight on it. Step back with the right foot, then step side with the left foot.

TURNS   Jazz turns include a number of types. Some basic turns include the paddle turn and the three-step turn.

paddle turn: On the count the right foot steps into demi-plié to the side to prepare for turning to the right. This is the supporting and pivoting leg. On the "&" count, the ball of the left foot steps directly behind the front foot. The back foot action releases the front leg for the next step to continue the turning action. The combination of the first foot moving in a new direction and the second foot taking the weight allows the front foot to continually turn in place.

three-step turn: The right foot steps and the body turns facing the right side. The left foot steps to the right and body turns facing the back wall. The right foot steps so the body turns to the front. The three-step turn should dissect the turn into thirds. The left foot steps to the left to execute a three-step turn to the left.

step, pivot, turn: Step forward in parallel position, then pivot on relevé either a quarter or half turn; repeat the combination. The working foot is at the ankle or knee in parallel position.

ELEVATION STEPS   Elevation steps in jazz include jumps, leaps, and extended kicks.

vertical jump: Demi-plié, then jump so that the legs fully stretch and the feet point in a parallel perpendicular position above the floor, and land in demi-plié. Your arms can stretch overhead and then return to the sides of the body upon landing.

✦ ACTIVITY 11.4   EXPLORE

Create a Combination

With another person or in a group of three people, create a three- to four-step jazz dance combination that can be repeated beginning on the other side. Teach another person or the group each of your movement sequences. Combine the group's sequences. You can choose AB choreographic structure, or you could do another variation of the two combinations by repeating the first section (ABA), or you could use another choreographic structure. Select a piece of contemporary music with your teacher's guidance. The music should complement the combined movement sequences or create a background or counterpoint to the combination. After you have completed this activity, go to the web resource to complete the journaling prompt.

Mia Michaels

Mia Michaels is one of the most famous choreographers and a judge for the television show *So You Think You Can Dance*. Michaels uses a wide variety of music for her contemporary lyrical jazz works. Born in Florida, Michaels learned dance from her father and sister. She attended Interlochen Center for the Arts and Jacob's Pillow. Her years of intensive training prepared her for winning an Emmy for her television achievements in choreography. She has also won many other prestigious awards for her work in film, commercials, Cirque du Soleil's first tour, and in Las Vegas. Her movements are powerful and demand the dancer's immersion of body and soul to perform them. One of her major successes was Celine Dion's Las Vegas show, *A New Day*. It featured 50 dancers in a 2-hour stage production.

arch jump: At the top of a vertical jump, arch the back under the shoulder blades and stretch the legs behind the body. The body returns to alignment, and you land in demi-plié.

step, hop: Step forward in parallel position on one foot, and hop. The working leg is in parallel passé position during the hop. Arms are in opposition (the right arm is forward if the hop is on the right foot).

jazz leap: The leap is generally parallel to the floor and covers a lot of space. Arms are usually in opposition to the legs; if the right leg is forward on the leap, then the left arm is forward. A variation of the leap includes the stag leap, where the extended front leg bends at the knee at the height of the leap before landing. Running or a chassé (see chapter 9) are two approaches for the jazz leap.

hitch kick: Kick the right leg forward, followed by the left leg in quick succession, landing on the right foot in demi-plié.

Thinking Like a Dancer

Jazz dancers must think fast on their feet as they hear, interpret, and move to music. Studying jazz dance is fun and invigorating. It gives you the opportunities to express yourself within the musical framework. To think like a jazz dancer, you have to learn how to manipulate energy or efforts to bring out the dynamics of a combination. You highlight movement qualities by increasing energy, and you change qualities either abruptly or with smooth transitions. You listen to the rhythm of the music and let it ooze through your body, responding to it as you do the movement. As you continue to listen, you become aware of how the rhythm of the music and your movement complement or contrast each other. This combination of opening up your thinking and senses to possibilities makes your jazz dancing style just as original as you are.

Summary

Jazz is an everchanging creative expression that echoes the life and times of the people in each decade. It has complex roots, and it is intertwined with many

✓ ACTIVITY 11.5 ASSESS

Evaluate Your Jazz Dance Performance

Evaluate your jazz dance performance using the combination you created earlier. You can choose whether to do the basic combination or the jazz style combination. You can do a self-check using the rubric or performance rating scale on the web resource, or you can ask your partner or another classmate to view your jazz dancing performance and respond to it. After you read the rubric you completed and any notes you made, reflect for a moment by mentally running through your performance, then write a paragraph identifying what techniques and steps you did well and other rubric descriptors listed. Then, list at least three items on the rubric that you plan to improve this year.

If you worked with a partner, then next review the rubric appraisal your partner developed. Write a paragraph to respond to each of the indicators checked for your performance. Add a summary paragraph about the experience, and determine whether you should incorporate any feedback from the review into your goals.

other dance genres. This chapter provided an overview of the history of jazz and its major artists. It summarized the basics of a jazz dance class, including steps or movements that are similar to those in other forms of dance. Thinking like a jazz dancer, you understand the layering of rhythms, movements, and style that provide the fun and the challenge of doing jazz dance.

Use the jazz dance combination you created earlier. Change the music to popular music from a past decade, then dance the combination. Download the music you selected with your teacher's guidance to practice and refine or revise your movement and style. How does your movement change to reflect the music? Collaborate on your movement sequence with another person or people who selected the same decade for a dance composition. Find a collective title for the work, and write a one- or two-sentence statement that captures the essence of the work. Each person in the group should identify three to five adjectives that describe the work. Then as a group, dance it, determine what parts you want to revise, and perform the final piece. You can have your performance video-recorded to include in your portfolio. Include your title, group statement, and adjectives in the portfolio. Then, write several paragraphs explaining the following:

- How did movement change with the retro music?
- How did the combination change when it became a group composition?

REVIEW QUESTIONS

True or False

1. Nineteenth-century roots for jazz dance include minstrel shows and vaudeville. _____

2. *The Black Crook* was the first Broadway show that used jazz dance. _____

3. Ballet and modern dance choreographers worked in films and on Broadway as part of developing jazz dance styles. _____

4. Jazz dance safety requires being aware of kicks, leg extensions, big jumps, leaps, and fast-moving combinations in general space. _____

5. The jazz class begins with a series of warm-up exercises that include both total-body movements and isolations. _____

Multiple Choice

1. _____Jazz dance has borrowed attributes such as a grounded stance and isolated movements from
   a. African dance
   b. Asian dance
   c. American dance

2. _____The term *jazz dance* came into use after
   a. 1900
   b. 1940
   c. 1960

3. _____In the early part of the 20th century, jazz dance borrowed its styles from
   a. social dance
   b. square dance
   c. tap dance

4. _____Jazz dance performance combines
   a. improvisation and creative movement
   b. percussive movement and flair
   c. technique and personal style

5. _____A position of the feet that is unique to jazz dance is the
   a. forced arch
   b. pointed foot
   c. relevé

Short Answer

1. List the four types of jazz hands.
2. List the three types of body positions used in jazz dance.

Matching

1. _____Jack Cole
2. _____Katherine Dunham
3. _____Jerome Robbins
4. _____Matt Mattox
5. _____Luigi
6. _____Gus Giordano
7. _____Lester Horton
8. _____Alvin Ailey
9. _____Bob Fosse
10. _____Michael Peters
11. _____Michael Bennett
12. _____Danny Buraczeski

a. Choreographer who was influenced by African and Haitian dance and complex rhythms.

b. A choreographer of freestyle dance who used Cole's style, ballet, and improvisation.

c. Blended Indian, Afro-Cuban, and Spanish dances into his work.

d. His work influenced West Coast jazz dance, used cultural dance forms, and developed strong, versatile dancers.

e. His technique is based on a stretching technique and ballet.

f. This influential musical theater choreographer used turned-in knees, quirky moves, and hats.

g. Choreographer who used Horton technique, African overtones, and social jazz components.

h. Choreographer and director of *West Side Story*.

i. Opened a studio, founded a company in Chicago, wrote *Anthology of American Jazz Dance*, and founded the World Jazz Dance Congress.

j. Dancer, choreographer, and musical director who created *A Chorus Line*.

k. Danced with Ailey and other modern dancers. Choreographed and directed for stage, television, and music videos. Choreographer of *Beat It* and *Thriller* videos.

l. Broadway dancer and company director who set works on ballet companies using eclectic music from the past.

 To find supplementary materials for this chapter such as worksheets, extended learning activities, and e-journaling assignments, visit the web resource at www.discoveringdance.org/student.

Tap Dance

ENDURING UNDERSTANDING: Tap dance is an American dance genre in concert and entertainment media.

ESSENTIAL QUESTION: How does tap dance help me express myself as a dancer?

LEARNING OBJECTIVES

After reading this chapter, you will be able to do the following:

- Recognize major tap dance works, styles, and tap dance artists in history.
- Execute basic tap dance technique, use tap dance vocabulary, and perform combinations.
- Apply tap dance etiquette and dance safety while dancing.
- Evaluate and respond to classical and contemporary tap dance performances.

"Dance is a window through which to view the world. I use it to become a better person. My teacher and friend Lynn Schwab taught me that tap dance is like life. One is constantly learning how to balance, when to exert control and when to let it go, how to listen, how to share, how to adapt, and how to leave space for endless possibilities. Dance is an act of giving and reminds me to maintain a generous spirit."

Jenai Cutcher, 21st-century American tap artist, choreographer, and author

VOCABULARY
Broadway tap
rhythm tap
tap dance

Tap dancers mesmerize audiences. Their rapid explosions of sounds and rhythmic movement can move to slow and casual, controlled sounds and then change again in an instant. **Tap dance** is a series of precise, clear tap sounds created by the metal taps on shoes striking the floor. The dancer's movements and rhythmic tap sounds create the essence of tap dance. Tap dancing can complement or counterpoint music, or dancers can use syncopated rhythmic patterns without accompaniment. The language of tap dance includes a vocabulary of steps. Historically based styles along with personal creativity and expression are important attributes of tap dancing. Overall, tap dance vocabulary includes terms for steps that often can be performed in a variety of ways or styles. This flexible tap dance vocabulary is based on different teachers and with whom they studied.

Tap dance is a versatile dance genre performed as concert dance, in entertainment media, or fused with other dance genres. Tap dance is a vital component of dance in entertainment that includes live stage shows, musical theater productions, movies, television, and videos. People of all ages enjoy tap dancing as recreation or dance exercise or in creative tap jams (group improvisational sessions). Once you discover and explore tap dance, you can use it as a medium for expressing yourself.

Discovering Tap Dance

Tap dance is an indigenous American dance. Beginning almost 200 years ago, tap dance absorbed a number of dance forms from different groups of people who came to America and brought their dances. Tap styles have evolved through its history and continue to expand.

You may have had tap dance classes as a child or learned a tap dance for a variety show at school, or perhaps you have performed tap dance in a musical theater production. Even if you are not familiar with it, tap dance is fun, and the basics are easy to learn.

! ACTIVITY 12.1   DISCOVER

Have a Tap Conversation

Create a tap conversation with a partner or your teacher. To begin the conversation, one person dances a movement sequence. The second person replies by "agreeing"—replicating the first sequence or "disagreeing"—making a different response. And so goes the conversation. Memorize the movement conversation, and share with others in your class.

Exploring Tap Dance

Tap dance is a mix of movement and rhythmic footwork. Tap dance has various styles. The most popular are rhythm tap and Broadway tap. Some other styles are summarized later in the chapter. **Rhythm tap**, in which the dancer's tap sounds make the music and the dance, is sometimes called *jazz tap*. Rhythm tap focuses on the dancer's musicality and improvisational skills. **Broadway tap** is featured in musical theater, entertainment, and other media.

History of Tap Dance

Tap dance has roots back to American precolonial days. Through its history, tap dance has acquired a blend of dance forms of various people, including African American, Native American, English, and Irish cultures. On Southern plantations during the 18th century, slaves were prohibited from using drums. Instead they used their bare feet to create shuffling, percussive rhythms. Watching plantation owners performing European and Irish dances, slaves added new elements to their footwork and rhythms that they often displayed in competitions. Irish step dancers wore wooden clogs and performed on wood floors. They created distinct heel and toe sounds that transferred into tap dance. The creativity and complexity of these and other influences became absorbed in the future development of tap dance.

Nineteenth Century

Throughout much of the 19th century, the minstrel show dominated American entertainment. Daniel D. Emmett, who wrote the song "Dixie," is considered the father of the minstrel show. In the early years of the minstrel show, each company member did steps called the *walkaround* and the *step out* during the show (Kassing 2007). As early as 1840 minstrel performer William Henry Lane (1825-ca.1852) included African steps such as the shuffle slide and the jig step into his syncopated dances. Lane became known as Master Juba (a name reserved for fine minstrel dancers and musicians). He received top billing with white minstrel shows, performed on Broadway, and danced for the Queen of England. Lane is considered one of the most influential performers of American dance during the 19th century.

In the latter part of the 19th century, vaudeville and popular social dances contributed to tap dance. By the 1890s various steps, soft-shoe and sand dancing styles, syncopation, and stop time had become part of this dance form. All types of social dance steps from the cakewalk, strutting, and camel walks became the dance form known as buck and wing, buck dancing, or flatfooted dancing. Earlier names for this form include clog, jig, or step dancing (Sommer 1998).

Early Twentieth Century

Early in the 20th century the term *tap dance* appeared in a public advertisement of Ziegfeld Follies dance director Ned Wayburn (Sommer 1998). Around 1910 a metal plate was attached to the toe and heel of the shoe (IED, vol. 6, p. 99). Tap dance has always had a creative improvisational aspect. Beginning in the 19th century and continuing into the 20th century, *tap-offs* (informal competitions) offered ways to learn and expand tap dance steps. Competitive performers developed their individual styles. These styles were copied, but each dancer's interpretation changed them slightly.

With the expansion of vaudeville and musical entertainment, black and white performers toured on separate circuits. The tap dance chorus lines with dance directors became a staple in Broadway theaters. Vaudeville became the school for tap artists as solo performers or as tap teams. The intense schedules of vaudeville shows produced dancers who had practiced and perfected their dances. From vaudeville several style categories emerged. *Eccentric tap*, which was perfected by Ray Bolger (1904-1987) and others used relaxed body movements while the feet tapped out the rhythms. *Comedy tap* was similar to a vaudeville act; one person performed rhythmic tap like the straight man, while the other person did eccentric tap movements. *Flash tap* dancers incorporated spectacular tricks such as leaps from high platforms and other stunts. The elegant tap team known as the Nicholas Brothers, Fayard (1914-2006) and Harold (1921-2000), integrated these flashy techniques into their acts. *Class acts* were performers such as Fred Astaire in the movies and Charles "Honi" Coles (1911-1992) on Broadway, who danced in formal dress with casual elegance (Sommer 1998). Coles won the NEA American National Medal of Arts in 1991.

During the Harlem renaissance, tap dance was popular in night clubs, in vaudeville, on Broadway, and in film. Bill "Bojangles" Robinson's (1878-1949) style was clean sounds created with minimal heel sounds. His technique created a new standard for tap dance performance. Famous for performing his famous stair dance, Robinson's performance with Shirley Temple in the 1935 movie *The Little Colonel* is an example of his artistry. John W. Bubbles (1902-1986) has been called the father of rhythm tap. He used heel taps to create an expanded repertory of contemporary syncopated sounds. The Hoofers club in Harlem continued improvisational competitions where dancers went to learn from the experts that frequented the club.

In the 1930s the movies took focus and the box office away from vaudeville and other forms of entertainment. During this rich era of tap dance, some of the finest tap dancers' works appeared in film. Eleanor Powell (1912-1982) has been called the queen of tap dancing. On the silver screen, she danced with Fred Astaire in *Broadway Melody* (1940). Tap artists in the movies such Ann Miller, Buddy Ebsen, Eleanor Powell, Donald O'Connor, and Ginger Rogers among others danced their way into the hearts of America. Fred Astaire (1899-1987) from Omaha became the iconic tap star, with an immense range of styles and creative choreography.

Gene Kelly (1912-1996) was born in Pittsburgh, Pennsylvania, and trained in ballet. He had his break on Broadway as a lead in the musical *Pal Joey* (1940). Kelly went on to make his film debut in 1942, which led to him dancing in and codirecting *On the Town* (1949). Kelly's ballet training blended with his athletic style and his innovative choreography to reach the zenith in his career with such productions as *An American in Paris* (1951) and *Singin' in the Rain* (1952).

Late Twentieth Century

Beginning in the 1940s, various dance forms merged into Broadway productions. Tap dance continued to entertain people through the rerun of tap films from the past, on television variety shows, or in a few night clubs. The Rockettes' tap dances continually attract people to tap dance.

The tap dance revival began when hoofers (professional tap dancers) from the past appeared in the early 1960s at the Newport Jazz Festival. They astounded audiences with their artistry. Broadway show revivals such as *No, No, Nannette* (1971) with tap star Ruby Keeler, *The Wiz* (1975), *42nd Street* (1980), and other shows breathed life into tap dance. During this same period, tap dance entered the concert stage and the academic world as a performing art form. Master tap artists from the past became the teachers of this new generation. During the 1980s, a new generation of dancers combined jazz, modern dance, and tap dance. Brenda Bufalino, a tap artist and innovator in tap and jazz dance, created numerous tap events, including tap festivals. In the last two decades, national tap festivals have become meeting places for dancers, master teachers, dance scholars, and other people interested in the art. Gregory Hines starred in *Sophisticated Ladies* (1983) and then in *Jelly's Last Jam* as well as films such as *White Nights* (1985; with

Baryshnikov) and *Tap* (1989). Hines was a role model who attracted many new African American dancers to tap dance. In the 1990s, Savion Glover blended tap with hip-hop and funk to create a unique style that revolutionized tap dance and is still popular today. Power tapping created riveting fast, rhythmic sequences. Glover and George Wolfe created a collaborative work called *Bring in 'da Noise, Bring in 'da Funk,* which opened on Broadway in 1996.

Tap dance spans a spectrum of dance media from entertainment to concert dance. A staple dance genre of musical theater productions, commercial entertainment, and concert ensembles, it is a versatile American art form that continues to gain international appeal.

Basics of Tap Dance Class

Tap dance classes vary, but this general format for the parts of the class is similar to the formats for other theatrical dance forms:

1. Warm up the feet and body at the barre or in the center.
2. Practice exercises and steps to review or learn new steps.
3. Execute various types of combinations in the center or traveling across the floor.
4. Learn dances (routines) in various tap styles to gain tap dance experience, and rehearse the dances to polish performance qualities.
5. Perform cool-down exercises at the end of class.

Tap Dance Class Safety

Ensure that you use tap shoes safely. Beginning tap dancers should buy shoes with taps firmly attached to the shoe. Tap shoes come with buckles, laces, or another fastening. Check shoes often to make sure they are fastened. Double-knot tap shoes with laces.

Slippery floors and dancing on certain flooring materials are considerations for tap dance. Some dance floors are specifically designed for modern dance and ballet and may not support tap dancing. If you are unfamiliar with the space, then check to ensure the floor is not too slippery before dancing on it.

Be sure to stay in your personal space at the barre, while moving in the center of the studio, and moving across the floor.

Dance Wear

Tap dancers wear comfortable clothing. Usually men wear a tee-shirt with pants or shorts. Women wear a leotard and tights, or they wear a tee-shirt and jazz pants or shorts. Tap shoes come in many styles. You can find oxfords with low heels, or you might see higher heels, which advanced dancers might wear.

Various tap shoe styles for men and women.

Tap Dance Class Etiquette

In addition to general dance class etiquette, tap dancers need to keep their feet still when listening in class or when other groups are performing combinations or routines. When leaving the studio, walk quietly or remove your tap shoes.

Tap Dance Techniques

Tap dance technique includes footwork, rhythm, sound techniques, and arm movements.

Footwork includes being able to move individual parts of the foot—the toes, ball, heel, full foot, and tip of the foot. All of these parts of the foot then combine in different sequences and rhythms to create steps. As footwork becomes more intricate, so does the coordination of sounds and movements. The footwork used in different combinations provides the ingredients for creating new rhythms and steps.

Rhythm, in tap dance, is specific and entails producing tap sounds with your feet in relation to the beat of the music. In tap you move on the *&*, or the *&* beats before a measure. You also create sounds that counterpoint the music. You make syncopated sounds with your toes, heels, hand claps, and snaps or slaps to the body as accents.

Sound techniques in tap steps include executing single sounds, double sounds, and triple sounds or more with the feet. Sound techniques also include additional syncopated sound accents such as hand claps, snaps, or slaps in various rhythms.

Arm movements give you balance and complement body and foot positions, or they represent a specific tap dance style. In some styles, when the focus is all on the footwork, the arms move naturally. In other styles, the arms coordinate or complement the footwork. Arm movements can be in opposition to the foot movements such as tap runs where the arms move in opposition to the forward leg. Sometimes the arms do natural movements so that the primary focus is on the dancer's performance. Arms complement travelling or turning steps.

Some tap dance steps travel across the floor.

Steps and Exercises

When you learn and practice basic tap dance steps, you usually do a step four or eight times. Most often when repeating the step, it may alternate beginning with the opposite foot. Another approach is to repeat each step either three times or seven times (for a 4-count or an 8-count step sequence, respectively). You end with either a stomp or a break (on count 4 or 8) before starting the repeat of the step on the other side. Before dancing, warm up the ankles to ensure they have the flexibility to execute quick movements. Here are the basic steps:

step: The full foot transfers weight completely from one foot to the other.

stomp: The full foot strikes the floor and accepts the weight.

stamp: The full foot strikes the floor and then quickly releases.

toe drop: The toes and ball of the foot strike the floor. Generally you follow a toe drop with a heel drop.

heel drop: The heel drops to the floor following a toe drop.

heel dig: The heel strikes the floor and then quickly releases off the floor.

toe tap: The toes and ball of the foot tap the floor and then quickly release.

toe tip: The tip of the shoe strikes the floor and quickly releases off the floor.

brush: Beginning with the working foot raised off the floor, the toes and ball of the foot brush the floor and lift into the air. Brushes are executed forward or backward. When performed together, they retain their separate sounds.

shuffle: The toes and ball of the foot brush forward and back as one sound. The hyphenated term *shuf-fle* expresses the two joined sounds.

ball-change: The toes and ball of the back foot briefly take the weight behind the front foot on the *&*. The front foot steps in place on the count.

flaps: Brush forward, then take the weight on the toes and ball of the foot; repeat, starting with the other foot. Alternate feet doing flaps moving forward, and then try flaps moving backward.

Buffalo: leap (right), shuffle (left), step (left), with the right leg bent and right foot in front of the lower leg. The Buffalo moves to the side. Repeat the Buffalo to the right. Then practice it to the left.

time step: The time step is a series of steps, and it has many variations. The single time step is the basis for learning other time steps. A time step can begin in several ways. One way is with a stamp. Another way is with a shuffle hop step. If the time step is new to you, begin it using the stamp. If you have done a time step previously, then you could go for the shuffle-hop-step version. If you are moving up from the stamp version, then practice the shuffle-hop-step separately before adding it as the beginning of the time step.

Count	Footwork
&-1	Shuffle (right) or stamp
&	Hop (left)
2	Step (right)
&-3-&-4	Shuffle (left), hop (right), step (left)

Repeat the shuffle, hop, step 7 times, then add a break.

Tap Combinations

Try this series of simple one- or two-tap steps as a combination to get you moving. After you have done the combination starting with the right foot, repeat it starting with the left. Then repeat the combination again, starting with the left foot and then the right. Practice the combination four times, replace the final step with a stomp, with a hop, or add a clap on the stomp. (If you have had previous tap dance experience, you may count the footwork differently, or your teacher may present a different way to count the footwork.)

Counts	Footwork
1	Step (right)
2	Step (left)
3	Step (right)
4	Stomp

Next try a *shuffle, step* combination. Begin with the right foot. Repeat the combination three more times, then start the combination with the left foot. You can replace the final step in the combination with a stamp. You will have to hold the working leg in the air for the last count. Then you are ready to begin the combination doing a shuffle with that foot.

Note: in a stamp the full foot hits and releases from the floor. In a stomp the full foot hits the floor and accepts the weight.

Shuffle, Step

Counts	Footwork
8	Right foot in the air
& 1	Right shuffle
2	Step
& 3, 4	Left shuffle, step
& 5, 6	Right shuffle, step
& 7, 8	Left shuffle, step to finish, or stamp and hold the 8 in the air to start the step again

If you stamp, then you have to hold & 8 with the left foot in the air.

Step, Ball-Change

Counts	Footwork
1	Step (right)
&	Ball (left)
2	Change (step, right)

With the weight on your right foot, you are ready to step on your left foot to start the left side. Repeat the step three more times.

After you have practiced the *step, ball-change*, you can change it up to a *brush forward, ball-change* or *shuffle, ball-change.*

Brush Forward, Ball-Change

Counts	Footwork
Right foot up	
&	Brush forward (right)
1	Step (right)
&	Ball (left)
2	Change (step, right)

Start the step to the left. Repeat the step three more times.

Shuffle, Ball-Change

Counts	Footwork
& 1	Shuffle (right)
&	Ball (right)
2	Change (step, left)

Start the step to the right. Repeat the step two more times, and count 7 step, count 8 hold (and shift weight to the right). Then you can repeat the combination with the left foot.

breaks: Transitions to change weight, direction, or to connect combinations or finish a combination. Breaks include

- stomp;
- flap, clap;
- shuffle hop, step; and
- ball-change.

turns: In tap dance, you can pivot or paddle turn.

- *pivot:* Step (right), ball (left), and turn a half turn.
- *paddle:* Step (right, touch the left toe) to the side and continue alternating these two steps while you move in a circle around yourself.

ACTIVITY 12.3   EXPLORE

Create Your Own Tap Combination

Practice and review the tap steps. If you have experience with tap dance, you may want to add to some of these basic steps. By yourself or with a partner create an 8- or 16- count tap combination to music, then rehearse and perform it for another group or share it with the class.

Tap Dance Styles

In addition to Broadway tap and rhythm tap (see History of Tap Dance section), many other styles of tap dance have evolved throughout the history of the genre, including the following:

buck and wing: A flashy dance style combining Irish and British clog dancing; it uses African rhythms.

classical tap: A style that combines tap, ballet, and jazz dance with acrobatics. This style is also referred to as *flash* or *swing tap.*

soft-shoe: A light, graceful dance style with rhythmic footwork performed in a smooth and leisurely cadence with soft-soled shoes.

These styles and many others are still practiced today.

SPOTLIGHT

Tap Dogs

Tap Dogs is a tap dance company from Australia. Created by Australian dancer and choreographer Dein Perry, he claims his work is a reinvention of tap. The company has danced all over the globe. Their high-energy, electrifying tap dancing has toured for more than 18 months at a time. Tap Dogs have won international awards for their work and for the opening ceremony of the Sydney Olympic Games in 2000. The dances of Tap Dogs are unique, from their I-beam dance (in which the group dances on a series of I beams set up as their dance space where they create metallic, synchronized sounds with their taps) to other inventive ways to tap. Tap Dogs represents a contemporary style of tap dance.

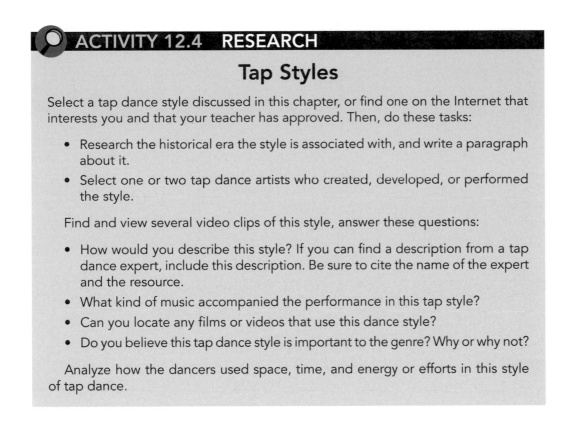

ACTIVITY 12.4   RESEARCH

Tap Styles

Select a tap dance style discussed in this chapter, or find one on the Internet that interests you and that your teacher has approved. Then, do these tasks:

- Research the historical era the style is associated with, and write a paragraph about it.
- Select one or two tap dance artists who created, developed, or performed the style.

Find and view several video clips of this style, answer these questions:

- How would you describe this style? If you can find a description from a tap dance expert, include this description. Be sure to cite the name of the expert and the resource.
- What kind of music accompanied the performance in this tap style?
- Can you locate any films or videos that use this dance style?
- Do you believe this tap dance style is important to the genre? Why or why not?

Analyze how the dancers used space, time, and energy or efforts in this style of tap dance.

Thinking Like a Dancer

Tap dancing requires you to make clear, concise sounds while moving to a rhythm. Practicing tap dance enhances your ability to hear rhythms and sounds and replicate them accurately with your body. To think like a tap dancer, you have to use your vision to watch the foot movement being demonstrated. Even more important, you have to use your listening skills to hear the tap sounds and connect the sound with the name of the step. For example, you need to hear the difference between a step, a stomp, and a stamp. While listening to the sounds

ACTIVITY 12.5   ASSESS

Evaluate Your Tap Dance Performance

Evaluate your performance of the combination you created earlier. You can choose whether you want to do the basic combination or the tap style combination. Using the rubric on the web resource, you can do a self-check. Or, you may ask a classmate to view your tap dancing performance and use the rubric to respond to it. After you read the rubric you have completed and any notes you made, reflect a moment by mentally running through your performance. Then write a paragraph in which you identify what techniques and steps you did well, and comment on your performance of the other rubric descriptors listed. List at least three items on the rubric you plan to improve on this year. If a classmate reviewed your performance, read your classmate's responses to the performance. Write a paragraph to respond to each of the indicators your partner checked for your performance. Add a summary paragraph about the experience, and determine whether you should incorporate any feedback from the review into your own goals for improvement.

and rhythm of a shuffle or a flap, you recognize the quality of each sound and its relationship to other sounds that are parts of the step. This distinction between the more prominent and less prominent sounds is what gives a step its quality. The rhythm and quality of the step must remain the focus, even while interacting with music. Tap sounds and foot movements of one step become more complicated when there are several steps in a combination. Each step in a combination has to be clearly performed with the right amount of energy or effort and timing; each step is a distinct part. Applying your watching, listening, and movement skills to each new combination is both challenging and fun. As you gain experience in tap dance, meeting these challenges increases the depth of your thinking like a tap dancer to enhance your performance.

Summary

An American dance form, tap dance has embraced many dance elements from various people and their dances. This chapter provided a summary of its rich history and an overview of tap dance techniques and basic steps. Tap dance has been and continues to be a staple in musical theater dance, dance entertainment, education, and recreation for people of all ages.

The International Tap Organization provides a web page that celebrates the legends of tap and today's leaders in the genre. It gives you a list of tap dance artists to jump-start your tap dance artist research. Select a tap artist and write a one- to two-page paper about that artist. Include a brief biography of the artist and include their contributions to tap. Identify what style of tap they were known for and one or two tap dance works they are famous for. Cite your sources at the end of the paper.

Based on your research and report, create a poster or media presentation about the tap dance artist you selected. Include photos, video clips of the dancers and dance style, and music from that historical era.

REVIEW QUESTIONS

Multiple Choice

1. _____Tap dance is a dance genre from
   - a. Africa
   - b. Ireland
   - c. America

2. _____One of the most influential dancers on the 19th-century stage was
   - a. Ned Wayburn
   - b. William Henry Lane
   - c. Daniel D. Emmett

3. _____Famous tap dancers who were labeled *class acts* because they wore formal dress and performed sophisticated dances were
   - a. Astaire and Coles
   - b. Temple and Robinson
   - c. Glover and Hines

4. _____How many break steps are there to choose from?
   - a. 2
   - b. 3
   - c. 4

5. _____A Buffalo step could be described as
   - a. a combination of steps that moves to the side
   - b. leaps and jumps
   - c. a set of shuffles

6. _____A contemporary African American tap dancer famous for his work on Broadway and in the movies is
   - a. Gene Kelly
   - b. Gregory Hines
   - c. Savion Glover

True or False

1. Rhythm tap is a style of tap dance featured in musical theater and entertainment. _____

2. Three dances in the minstrel show were the walkaround, the step out, and the shuffle. _____

3. An early 20th-century tap dance director, Ned Wayburn, created all-girl tap lines in the Ziegfeld Follies. _____

4. Tap dance safety depends on securely fastened shoes and a floor that is not slick. _____

Short Answer

1. Name the five parts of the tap dance class.

Matching

1. _____ step
2. _____ stomp
3. _____ stamp
4. _____ brush
5. _____ shuffle
6. _____ ball-change
7. _____ flap
8. _____ time step
9. _____ rhythm tap
10. _____ tap dance

a. Shuffle, hop, step, brush, ball-change.

b. The full foot strikes the floor and accepts the weight.

c. The toes and ball of the foot brush the floor and lift into the air.

d. The full foot transfers weight completely from one foot to another.

e. Precise, clean tap sounds made by taps on toes and heels striking the floor.

f. The toes and ball of the foot brush forward and back.

g. The full foot strikes the floor and quickly releases.

h. Movement of brushing the toes and ball of the foot, taking the weight.

i. The toes and ball of the back foot brush the floor before the front foot steps in place.

j. A style of tap dance that uses heel taps and creates syncopated sounds.

To find supplementary materials for this chapter such as worksheets, extended learning activities, and e-journaling assignments, visit the web resource at www.discoveringdance.org/student.

Dance as Entertainment

ENDURING UNDERSTANDING: Dance as entertainment may focus on one or more dance genres to create a unique performance for audiences to enjoy.

ESSENTIAL QUESTION: How does dance as entertainment provide ways for me to express myself as a dancer?

LEARNING OBJECTIVES

After reading this chapter, you will be able to do the following:

- Recognize specific forms, styles, and dance artists in the history of dance as entertainment.
- Execute dance entertainment techniques, use dance vocabulary, and perform memorized combinations or created movement sequences.
- Evaluate and respond to dance entertainment and specific dance forms and media.

"Then come the lights shining on you from above. You are a performer. You forget all you learned, the process of technique, the fear, the pain, you even forget who you are. You become one with the music, the lights, indeed one with the dance."

Shirley MacLaine, American musical theater dancer, actress, director, and author

VOCABULARY
commercial dance
dance or drill team
dance for the camera
musical theater dance

Any day of the week, if you turn on the television and surf the channels you could tune into dance shows. These shows feature reality dance programs, dance competitions, sitcoms about dancers, documentaries on dance artists and choreographers, special dance events, and even commercials that use dancers to sell products. DVDs and Internet sites present timeless dance movie classics of the 20th century, contemporary dance films, and music videos as entertainment. The Internet's huge collection of articles, blogs, videos, audio clips, opinions, and documents can provide hours of pastime discovering dance, learning how to dance, or learning about dance.

In the community, musical theater productions feature dances as part of the show. Your school's dance or drill team performs routines at sporting events or at competitions. At amusement parks, dancers perform dances as characters; they enact historical or thematic dance sequences to entertain audiences. On cruise ships and at casinos, dancers present stage shows to delight audiences in entertainment settings. Dance in entertainment or commercial entertainment is big business. It contributes to the national economy because it sells products, employs dancers, and contributes to society as an enjoyable leisure experience.

Dance genres from society and the concert stage relate to dance as entertainment throughout history. If you think back to earlier chapters, it is easy to see how many of the dance artists from various genres contributed to dance as entertainment. Some dance genres are supportive, collaborative, or the focus of dance entertainment forms. In dance as entertainment, the choreographer creates live or recorded media performances to match the entertainment setting and the theme of the production. Dance as entertainment ranges from schools and studios to professional dancers. Dance as commercial entertainment, performed both live and in recorded media, projects an image, provides a medium to sell a product, or enhances delivery of a message.

This chapter provides ways to study dance as entertainment to support your dancing experiences in the classroom. You will learn about dance entertainment by exploring dance or drill team, musical theater dance, and dance for the camera. In each in-depth exploration, you will learn about dance terminology, history, dance forms, and dance artists. You will also view selected works from each dance form so that you can experience dance as entertainment.

ACTIVITY 13.1   EXPLORE

Dance in Commercials

Many television commercials use dance to sell products or services. To begin this exploration, spend some time surfing television channels. Select two of your favorite commercials that include dance. Write a one-page paper about one of the commercials. Describe the dancers, the setting, the dance, and why they are dancing. What message do you think is being communicated through the dance? Are the music and dialogue effective parts of the commercial? What product is being featured in the commercial? Do you think the dancing makes connections to the product to sell it effectively? What appeals to you (or doesn't appeal to you) about the dance and the commercial? Write a paragraph to critique the commercial. Search for this commercial on the Internet. In your paper, include a photo and a link for viewing the commercial online.

As a class, share your commercial review papers in the classroom or on the school or class's webpage. If several people selected the same commercial, post them together. Then select two other commercials posted that you did not view but capture your interest. In a class discussion, determine the top three dance commercials, and provide a rationale for these choices using the same criteria you used for your commercial review. On a sheet of paper or the board, post these "awards" with that group of commercial reviews.

Discovering Dance as Entertainment

As you read the introduction to this chapter, you may have recognized some of the forms of dance as entertainment that you knew or have even taken part in. Some of these forms are live performances, and others are performed for recorded media, yet others focus on **commercial dance**. Your first activity is an exploration of a form of commercial dance.

Exploring Dance as Entertainment

Dance entertainment is a vast topic and an important component of dance. As a viewer of dance entertainment, you see the collaboration between dance artists, directors, and media or live production staff. These collaborators create ways to use dance choreography to entertain audiences or sell products or services in various settings. To prepare for dancing in commercial or entertainment settings, you have to be versatile as a dancer. You must study social dance, folk dance, cultural dance, street dance, ballet, modern dance, jazz, and tap dance. When you explore the section on dance unions in chapter 15 and on the web resource, you will see job listings that outline the dance genres a dancer needs to have for these jobs. A job can be for a one-performance event, or it might last for years, such as a musical theater performance on Broadway or a yearlong touring show. Commercial dancers who go from job to job are called *dance gypsies,* because their work is constantly changing from one show to another.

History of Dance as Entertainment

Professional dancers have worked as entertainers since prehistory. In ancient Egypt, the first recorded professional dancers, along with acrobats and musicians, entertained royalty. In ancient Greece dance was part of theater. From medieval times through the renaissance, dance was entertainment and amusement for nobles and peasants alike.

During modern history as dance moved onstage, dance as entertainment was part of other art forms or as interludes between dramas and operas. In the 19th century, dance continued to gain stature through entertainment such as minstrel shows, circuses, spectacles, fairs, variety shows, and vaudeville performances. Dance performances took place outdoors, in music and variety halls, theaters, and arenas. When the transcontinental railway system linked the nation from coast to coast, dance as entertainment exploded. Entire troupes or stock companies or self-contained companies who performed all types of entertainment forms, traveled the country by train; they stopped in cities and small towns to entertain people for the night. These companies were made up of versatile *triple threat* performers—those who did all the acting, dancing, and singing roles required in an evening's entertainment.

In the 20th century, the love of dance as entertainment grew in new directions. Broadway revues evolved into musical theater productions. With the invention of motion pictures and then television, dance moved into entertainment mass media.

For Broadway shows, dance artists and choreographers from ballet and modern dance companies created dances in early-20th-century follies (elaborate shows with music, songs, and dances), revues, and then musicals. As musical theater dance developed, it continued to absorb the styles of dance genres such as tap dance, ballet, modern dance, and jazz dance. Each musical theater production had its unique choreography using blended styles. Broadway shows tour throughout the world, bringing classical and contemporary musical theater productions to millions of people.

Dance movies have been popular since the early days of film. Producing these movies took hundreds of dancers, such as in the work of Busby Berkeley in the 1920s as a Broadway dance director and in 1930s movies where he directed musical numbers which led to his fame. Dance movies became an important area of commercial dance. Dancers and choreographers have entertained and educated audiences in historical dramas, animated movies, movie musicals, and science fiction movies alike. Animated movies in which characters danced were the invention of Walt Disney and his creative staff. Characters such as Snow White and the dancing dwarfs, princesses, and all kinds of creatures perform animated dances. In the 1950s, Gene Kelly bridged the gap between animation and live characters when he danced with an animated mouse in the film *Anchors Away* (1945).

With the advent of television, dance moved into variety shows, such as the *Ed Sullivan Show*. They showcased a wide variety of dance artists and choreographers and made them household names across America. As television programming expanded, so did the opportunities for dance shows. The popular *Dance in America* series brought ballet and modern dance companies to homes across America. Public Broadcasting Service (PBS) continues to provide diverse programming of dance as art, entertainment, and education.

Over the last decade, reality dance shows such as *So You Think You Can Dance* and *Dancing With the Stars* have expanded dance audiences and their appreciation of dance. Televised dance or drill team competitions and other associated dance competitions present another aspect of dance as entertainment. Television programming now includes an array of dance entertainment, including sitcoms and documentary series on dancers, their personal lives, musical theater, and dance genres from around the world.

After Disneyland opened in the 1950s, amusement and theme parks became another mass entertainment medium. Dance became an important feature in theme parks across the nation and the world. Dancing characters from the movies reside in different areas of these parks. In each park, one or more companies of dancers perform short entertainment shows throughout the day, every day. Dancers perform blended historical, cultural, or social dance styles to entertain park visitors. The Disney concept of performers—being in character and onstage while walking in the park or dancing—spurred an entire entertainment industry. Other live entertainment settings, including cruise ships, casinos, and resorts, provide multiple dancing stage shows as entertainment for guests.

When Internet technology expanded, another entertainment site emerged that would support dance films, recorded dance performance, and ways to interact in real time with dancers and choreographers across the globe. In the 20th century the term *dance for the camera* was coined to describe dance that was filmed as art, education, or entertainment. Productions of dance for the camera include documentaries of dancers and choreographers, historical and educational movies, concert and cultural dance companies, and performances of choreographed artistic dance films. These dance films are broadcast on television, shown in schools, or shown as fine art films. On the Internet, anyone can post a personal dance video to be viewed by the class, the school, and often the entire world. Dance for the camera has expanded into a whole new dimension that requires understanding dance as well as the art of filming it. To create dance for the camera, you need to grasp the artistic and production values, choices, and processes that are part of creating a filmed work.

EXPLORE MORE

You can see from this brief overview that there is much to explore in dance as entertainment and its commercial sector. The Explore More sections on the web resource will explore three dance entertainment genres: dance or drill teams, dance in musical theater, and dance for the camera.

Dance or Drill Teams

Dance or drill teams range from students in middle school, high school, and college to professionals who perform at local sporting events to televised professional sports. Halftime shows for many sports feature dance or drill teams. Dance or drill teams perform for school games and community functions, and they take part in dance and drill team competitions. Their routines showcase their ensemble technique, spirit, and enthusiasm for the crowds. Training for dance and drill team requires athleticism and artistry. Dance and drill teams began as a Texas phenomenon that has spread across the United States and around the world. Visit the chapter 13 on the web resource to explore more about dance and drill teams.

A dance team moves together to create a powerful effect.

Learn a Drill or Dance Team Combination

For this activity, your teacher or a classmate teaches one or more basic drill or dance combinations to the class. After everyone has learned and practiced the routine to music, take a few minutes to reflect on the experience. In your journal, write about what you enjoyed in the routine, what was challenging, and which type of routine you preferred and why. Share it with another student or in a group discussion.

Dance in Musical Theater

Musical theater dance spans school musicals, professional productions on the Broadway stage, and touring companies that travel to cities across the world. Becoming a musical theater dancer takes versatile dance training and other performing arts skills such as acting, music, and voice. The challenge in every musical theater production is to blend dancing, acting, and singing to portray your role. Visit the web resource to explore more about musical theater dance.

Musical theater productions feature a blend of singing, dancing, and acting.

Dance for the Camera

Dance in film, television, music videos, and other media forms provides entertainment for audiences. It also provides choreographers and dancers more media choices for presenting dance as an art form. **Dance for the camera** is term that covers entertainment, artistic, and multimedia forms of presenting dance. Filming dance has been instrumental in documenting its artists and works for the public to enjoy. Further, dance media has expanded dancers' views about how to complement or enhance a live performance. The final Explore More section investigates the types of media used in dance for the camera.

ACTIVITY 13.3   EXPLORE

Dance in Musical Theater

Choose a musical from the list provided by your teacher. Form a small group with other students who chose the same musical theater production. Together, search the Internet to find a video of a major dance sequence or dance combination from that musical. Your teacher may provide you with a list of dances from which to choose. View the dance number, then answer these questions:

- Identify each main character, and write a sentence or two about each person to describe their personality.
- Where does the dance take place?
- What inspires the characters to do this dance?

Describe the dance, the music, and whether it includes a song that is part of the musical number.

Collaborate as a group to develop, write, and present a 1- or 2-minute oral summary or a media presentation to the class to cover this information:

- Provide the story line (plot) of the musical.
- Identify the choreographer and give a very brief summary (two or three sentences) of the individual's contributions to the field.
- Indicate the main characters by writing a two- to three-sentence biography about each person.
- Describe the dance, the music, and the song in the musical number that you viewed.

Post a one-page summary of your group's information in the classroom or on the class web page. Add a picture that captures the meaning of the musical, or take a photo of your group in a memorable pose from the dance you researched. On your media presentation and one-page summary, cite the sources for your research.

ACTIVITY 13.4   EXPLORE

Dance on Camera

In a group or as a class, view two short dances or dance sequences from the Internet. (Note that you should choose professionally produced videos.) First watch each dance. Then view each dance again, this time thinking about how the camera was used to record the dance. Share a description of the dance with the group or the class. Then share and discuss how the camera was used to record the dance. If you were the camera person, are there ways you would record the dance differently than what you viewed? Then as a class contribute a list of findings from this activity.

Thinking Like a Dancer

Entertainment and commercial dancers have to be quick on their feet and have a repertory of movement vocabularies from many dance genres. To think like a dancer in entertainment, you must think quickly in order to pick up the choreog-

SPOTLIGHT

Riverdance

Since Riverdance began performances in Dublin in 1995, the show has…

- Played 10,000 performances
- Been seen live by over 22 million people in over 350 venues worldwide, throughout 40 countries across 4 continents
- Travelled 600,000 miles (or to the moon and back!)
- Played to a global television audience of 2 billion people
- Sold over 3 million copies of the Grammy Award-winning CD
- Sold 10 million *Riverdance* videos

And there have been…

- 1,500 Irish dancers
- 14,000 dance shoes used
- 12,000 costumes worn
- 200,000 gallons of water consumed
- 60,000 gallons of Gatorade consumed
- 1,650,000 show programs sold
- 1,500 flight cases used
- 12,000 stage lighting bulbs used
- 40,000 boxes of tissues used
- 16,250 guitar, bass, and fiddle strings replaced
- 284,000 t-shirts sold
- 39 marriages between company members
- 20,000 cumulative years of study in step-dancing by Irish dancers
- 45,000 rolls of self-grip tape used by company physiotherapists
- 15,000 hours of rehearsals on tour
- 5,500,000 pounds of dry ice used on stage
- 60,000 pounds of chocolate consumed (for energy!) by the cast

rapher's movement, perform it, and incorporate the style required. Professional dancers in entertainment or commercial shows are on the clock to learn the dances in the show, rehearse them, and be ready for an audience. A lot of the preparation time depends on whether the show is being built from a script or an idea or if the show is restaged with a new company.

To learn more about this process, attend or participate in an audition or mock audition, or view one online. A list of search terms is provided on the web resource.

✔ ACTIVITY 13.5   ASSESS

Evaluate Your Dance Performance

Your teacher will teach you a combination or select one for you to perform. The combination will come from a dance or drill team or a musical theater combination in a jazz, tap, or hip-hop style. In a group, perform your combination and video-record your performance. After your performance, you can do a self-check using the rubric on the web resource. Or, ask another classmate to use the rubric to evaluate your performance. After you read the completed rubric and any notes you made, reflect for a moment by mentally running through your performance. Then write a paragraph in which you identify what techniques and steps you did well and other rubric descriptors listed. Make a list of at least three items on the rubric that you plan to improve.

Next, review the rubric appraisal your classmate did. Write a paragraph to respond to each of the indicators checked for your performance. Add a summary paragraph about the experience, and determine whether you should incorporate any feedback from the review into your goals.

Summary

This chapter defined the many areas of dance as entertainment and summarized its history. Dance in entertainment and commercial settings presents vast opportunities for dancing, choreography, direction, and associated careers. To be successful in this field, you must be versatile, know traditional and the latest dance trends, and be able to think on your feet. Dance as entertainment continues to expand and offers many opportunities for dancers.

PORTFOLIO ASSIGNMENT

The entertainment and commercial settings listed in this chapter are just a starting point for you to learn more. Perhaps you are interested in dance in theme parks, dance that sells products in industrial shows (for example, featuring new cars or the latest hardware from a national chain), dance stage shows, dancing on cruise lines, or another of the many settings for dance as entertainment. Here is your chance to do some research about what dancers do in another setting of dance entertainment.

First find a topic that sparks your interest from this chapter. Or, go to the dance websites for theme parks, cruise ships, industrial shows, and other settings. Your teacher will provide you with some specific websites that list dance entertainment jobs to spark your interest.

As you begin your research, you can use the basic questions of who dances (union or non-union dancers), what dance genres are necessary for this entertainment or commercial medium, and where some of the locations are. Write a two-page report about this type of entertainment or commercial dance. Cite your Internet sources on the paper.

If a dancer you know or a graduate from your high school works in entertainment or commercial dance, e-mail or talk with the person. Find out what the person likes and dislikes about working in entertainment or commercial dance. Then add a summary of your communication to your paper.

REVIEW QUESTIONS

True or False

1. Dance genres from society and on stage relate to dance as entertainment beginning in the 20th century. _____

2. Many dance genres and artists from various genres contributed to dance as entertainment. _____

3. Cruise ships, casinos, and resorts provide many dance shows as entertainment for guests. _____

Multiple Choice

1. _____The innovator for developing theme park mass entertainment dance shows was
   a. Busby Berkeley
   b. Ed Sullivan
   c. Walt Disney

2. _____The term *triple threat* originated from performers who could act, sing, and dance in
   a. 19th-century theater stock companies
   b. 20th-century musical theater reviews
   c. follies, films, and television shows

3. _____Dance productions that document the work of dancers and choreographers, historical dance, concert dance, cultural dance companies, and performances in various forms of electronic media are called

    a. dance films

    b. dance for the camera

    c. dance media

4. _____Dance as entertainment at a sporting event is known as a

    a. dance or drill team

    b. dance sport team

    c. marching band

To find supplementary materials for this chapter such as worksheets, extended learning activities, and e-journaling assignments, visit the web resource at www.discoveringdance.org/student.

Dance Performance and Production

ENDURING UNDERSTANDING: Performance and production are the products of dance.

ESSENTIAL QUESTION: How do performance and production help me express myself as a dancer?

LEARNING OBJECTIVES

After reading this chapter, you should be able to do the following:

- Understand the timeline and processes for dance performance and production.
- Describe the roles of the various production staff members in creating a dance performance.
- Comprehend the design concepts and technical requirements that contribute to dance performance.
- Apply theater and backstage etiquette, knowledge, and safety rules as a member of an audience, cast, or crew.

"After I perform, I hope the audience is excited, inspired, and taken away from their everyday grind or work. Perhaps even inspired enough to get up and dance themselves."

Lenore Pavlakos, international teacher and former principal dancer with the Dance Theatre of Harlem

VOCABULARY

artistic director
costume designer
crossover
curtain call
dress rehearsal
ellipsoidal reflector
   spotlight
Fresnel
gel
house manager
light trees
lighting designer
mark
master calendar
PAR lights
performance attitude
performance presence
proscenium stage
scoop lights
site-specific dance
   spaces
spike marks
stage manager
strip lights
technical director
theater-in-the-round
wings

"**Ready—curtain,** lights, sound. Set. Go curtain . . . Go lights . . . Go sound." These words signal that a performance is about to start. Reaching this moment just before a dance performance requires many months of planning, creativity, and dedication of artists and technicians. Before dancers perform onstage, artistic and theater personnel have done their preliminary work as designers. Technicians work before, during, and after the performance. This collaboration of artistic and technical aspects of a dance performance ensures a unified dance production for audiences to enjoy.

Attending a dance concert is similar to attending a music concert or a play. You are seeing the product of what performing artists have choreographed or staged and rehearsed. The dance work comes alive with production elements such as lighting, costuming, settings, music, media, and other additions to give you and other audience members a memorable experience.

In this chapter you will explore what dance artists and members of production teams do to prepare for performance. A dance evolves from an idea to

an onstage performance through different points of view—the dancer and the artistic and production teams. The dancer auditions, learns, and rehearses the dance for performance, and the artistic and production teams design, create, and produce the performance.

Discovering Performance and Production

Dance performances can be part of professional, community, or school productions. They can be concert, entertainment, or cultural dance genres. Dance can be staged as a formal event in a theater, a less formal event in a school auditorium, an informal presentation in a dance studio, or in a variety of settings in the community such as museums, shopping malls, parks, and outdoor areas.

Theaters and Other Performance Spaces

Although dance can be performed in all types of settings, some stages offer more advantages for presenting dance for audiences.

In the traditional proscenium arch theater, the stage and the audience are separated by a proscenium arch, which creates a frame for the stage space. The arch can be an architectural element, or it can be created by curtains. The **proscenium stage** is a rectangular space that can either be higher or lower than the audience (figure 14.1). The orchestra area (pit) is located in the space between the stage and the audience seating.

Modern theaters may include stage extensions to the proscenium theater. The apron (front of the stage area) extends into the audience area. The thrust stage is a three-sided performance space that stretches into the audience area. In the **theater-in-the-round**, the audience sits on all sides of a stage in the middle. This type of theater style is the most challenging for the choreographer, whose work must support audiences viewing the dance from all sides.

Alternative spaces for producing dance can be the studio space or enhanced studio spaces. Some dance studios have the infrastruc-

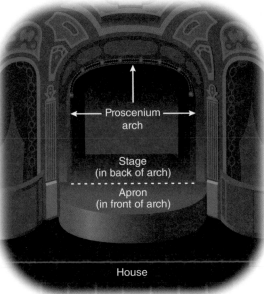

Figure 14.1 Proscenium theater.

ture for curtains, lighting equipment, and other capabilities so that the studio can transform into a performance space.

Dancers and choreographers have been inventive in finding spaces in buildings and places out of doors to perform dance. These **site-specific dance spaces** are located in a wide variety of places such as concert halls, art or other museums, lofts, and shopping malls. Dance performances can occur in outdoor spaces such as parks and natural environments or in sculpture gardens. The choreographer and the dancers have to adapt the choreography for the site-specific settings and the audiences' seating arrangements.

Orchesis

Orchesis comes from Greek and means "to dance." In the 20th century, colleges, universities, and later high schools began orchesis groups. Sometimes orchesis could be a class or an extracurricular activity. The purpose was for students to dance and produce their dances in concerts. Students took the artistic, technical, and business staff roles to produce the concert. These concerts expanded to tours or outreach educational opportunities to schools in the area or community organizations. Today, orchesis groups remain in both high schools and colleges. In some regions of the country they have become dance ensembles or companies.

Stage Draperies

In a proscenium and other theater types, draperies at the front, side, and back outline the stage space. At the front of the stage is the main curtain (also called the *grand curtain*). This curtain is closed when the audience enters the theater; it opens before a performance begins. At the sides of the stage are two or more **wings** (open pathways on- or offstage). Wings are created by stage drapery known as *legs*. At the back of the stage are a variety of draperies, a cyclorama (also called a *cyc* for short), a scrim, black curtains, or other types of backdrops.

Most stages have a narrow corridor between the backdrop and the back wall. This passageway is called a **crossover**; it connects one side of the backstage area to the other. The crossover provides a way for cast and crew to move from one side of the performing space to the other for entrances during a performance.

Flooring

School and community dance companies may purchase portable vinyl dance flooring to transform a studio, gym, or other floor into a dance performance space. Traditional theaters may use this flooring, too. Often, academic or community dance company members participate in laying the portable dance floor in the performance space. They prepare the stage floor, sweep it clean, lay the portable floor properly, and get the wrinkles out. This ritual is hard work that needs willing hands and strong muscles. Taping the flooring strips correctly so that they don't move is critical to dancer safety and floor longevity. After the performance, taking up the floor and rolling it up properly is equally important. Once the floor is taped for a performance, then a centerline and center stage and other spatial marks can be taped on the floor in relation to the audience area. These **spike marks** are tape marks in the stage space that help dancers find center, quarter, or other places on the stage accurately and consistently when they perform.

ACTIVITY 14.1   RESEARCH

Stages and Performance Spaces

View some websites for local theaters or other performance spaces. Find information about the stage space, the number of seats in the audience, and the rental fees for rehearsal and for performance. Then summarize your findings about each performance space and place them on a continuum from the least expensive to rent for a performance to the most expensive. Determine what performance space would be the best choice for a student dance production. Then write a one-page proposal to the artistic director (your teacher) justifying which is the best choice for a student dance production.

Exploring Performance and Production

The performance is the end product of choreographing and rehearsing a dance with the addition of production elements. The production elements may be simple or complex. Variables of any production hinge on the setting selected for the performance, the type of performance (professional or student), the time for producing the work or works, and especially the budget. These production elements are all part of a formula for determining what type of performance it is.

A dance performed in practice clothes in the studio has entirely different production values and requirements than a dance performed at a major city theater with the latest technology or a dance performance on television or the movies. A dance performance enhanced with stage lighting, costuming, makeup, live music, and other elements gives the dance work the supporting artistic components it needs in order to be viewed as a work of art. Regardless of the level of sophistication of a dance performance, the production elements remain the same.

To produce a dance concert for an audience, you need to understand the process of preparing a dance for performance, the roles of the people involved, and the production elements that interface with that process.

Planning for Performance

Months of planning and preparation and many people are involved in a dance performance. From planning to completion, many components contribute to a dance production so that every aspect of the performance comes together seamlessly. Planning, designing, and executing the elements of a performance require the work of numerable artists and dancers. Behind the scenes, simultaneously designers and technicians plan and produce the technical theater aspects of dance performance. Meanwhile, the business staff monitors the budget, and design and marketing staff create advertising, promotional, and public relations to get audiences to buy tickets to the dance performance.

Creating a dance performance starts with a strategic plan. The production plan usually begins with selecting a performance date and then working backward to schedule the artistic, design, and technical components required to make it happen. With the performance goals in mind, the artistic, design, and production staff create a **master calendar** to ensure they have all the artistic and technical components done at just the right time to ensure a successful production. The production team is actually made up of three teams—artistic, technical, and business—who contribute their skills to preparing for a dance performance.

Roles of Artistic, Design, and Production Staffs

Behind every performance is the artistic staff and production staff. The artistic director of the dance company has a vision for a performance. This artistic vision must meet the mission, vision, and budget of the company. The artistic director and staff determine the performance date and which choreographers, dances, and dancers will be part of the program. The artistic, technical, and business staff create rehearsal schedules, hold production meetings, and set deadlines to make sure various elements of the production are completed at the right times.

The artistic staff includes the artistic director, one or more choreographers, the dancers, the understudies, and the rehearsal assistants. The **artistic director** selects and may book a performance space and sets a date and time for the event. The choreographer envisions a concept for the dance, researches ideas, and determines how long it will take to teach, rehearse, and polish the dance before moving into the theater. After the audition, the dancers receive a rehearsal schedule indicating how many rehearsals and weeks they have until the performance.

The theatrical **design staff** includes the lighting designer, costume designer, and sound designer. The **technical director** runs the preproduction operations. During the final technical and dress rehearsals, the **stage manager** calls the show from back stage, while the **house manager** oversees the audience's safety and comfort.

Lighting Designer

The **lighting designer** creates the lighting design and light plots for the dance performance. When you think of lighting for dance, picture the dancers moving within in a three-dimensional space, somewhat like a fish tank. The lighting designer wants to present the three-dimensionality of the body moving in that space. So, the lighting designer uses overhead lighting, front lighting, and side lighting to create the design for the dance. To achieve a lighting design for a dance, the lighting designer talks with the choreographer and the artistic director, and attends rehearsals to gain a vision of what the dance is expressing. Lighting design concepts include the following:

- Illumination of the dancers moving through space
- Environment or mood for the dance
- Intensity and direction of the lighting

The lighting designer draws a light plot and places the lighting instruments to achieve the design concepts. Many dance concerts use a **repertory lighting design**—one design that will accommodate all of the dances on the program (figure 14.2). Then specials (specific lighting instruments) are added into the lighting design along with a variety of colors so that each dance has a unique environment or mood.

The master electrician and lighting crew hang and then focus the lighting instruments indicated on the light plot. The crew connects the instruments into electrical circuits that run to a lighting board. The lighting board is a control console with a series of dimmers to adjust the lighting intensity from off to full and gradations in between.

The lighting instruments hang by clamps attached to battens (long metal rods with electrical outlets that hang from the ceiling over the stage). Battens connect through the theater's wiring system to the lighting board. **Light trees** are vertical stands that hold lighting instruments in the wings or at other places in the theater. These positions are especially important for lighting dance performances.

Lighting instruments have specific functions for illuminating dance productions. See the repertory light plot (figure 14.2) to identify the figure for each of the instruments described, then find them on the plot in figure 14.2 where they are positioned.

- A **Fresnel** is a lighting instrument that produces a wide beam of light with soft edges. It is used for covering large areas onstage.
- An **ellipsoidal reflector spotlight,** often referred to as a Leko, produces a sharp cone of light. The instrument has built-in shutters to shape and direct the beam of light.
- **Strip lights** are a series of lights housed as a single instrument. They are hung on battens across the front of the stage, or they provide general illumination of the stage.

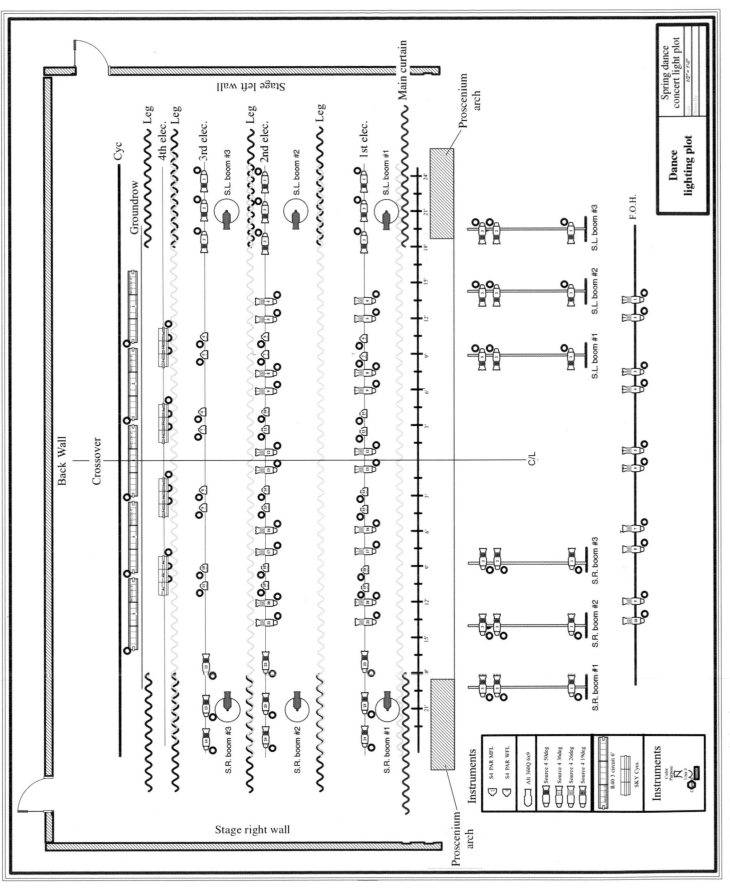

Figure 14.2 Repertory light plot.

- **PAR (parabolic aluminized reflector) lights** are a lamp and a lens in a cylinder or can-like container. PARs produce an oval pool of bright light with unfocused edges that can travels over long distances. This affordable lighting instrument used in theatrical and live music shows uses common lenses from very narrow to wide. The PAR light is often used for special effect lighting and uses gels.
- **Scoop lights** are large scoop-shaped instruments directed to illuminate large areas, such as the backdrop.

Lighting instruments have gel frames where **gels** (colored plastic sheets) are inserted. The colored sheet tints the light beam produced by the instrument. The lighting designer selects these colors to create the mood or environment for the dance.

Costume Designer

The **costume designer** designs costumes for dances. The costume designer is an artist who draws and colors or renders the design for the costumer to construct. Part of the design is determining the fabrics to be used, which is critical in dance. Costume design concepts for dance include the following:

- Movability
- Shape of the costumes
- Color
- Texture

Dance has specific requirements that the costume designer must integrate into the design. The design should enable the dancer to move effectively in it, flatter all body types in the dance, and capture the essence and style of the dance. The costumer and costume crew can build the costumes for the performance. Costumes are often purchased from a costume supplier. Often companies refurbish previously built or purchased costumes for new dances.

The costume designer may design the dancer's makeup, especially if it must coordinate with the costume to create a unified look. General dance makeup design is based on standard stage makeup with some modifications depending upon the dance genre. Makeup for smaller performance spaces can be enhanced street makeup. For large performance spaces, the dance uses heavy stage makeup that may be somewhat exaggerated. Makeup design concepts involve the following:

- Ability to see the dancer's face and facial expression
- General, dramatic, or stylized to relate to the dance
- Enhancing the dancer's eyes and best facial features

The object of makeup is for the dancer's face and facial expression to be seen by everyone in the audience.

Scenic Designer

If the production requires a complete set (as in classical ballets) or set pieces (as in some classic modern works), the **scenic designer** creates the set or set pieces for the dance. If the scenic designer is doing a new production, similar to the lighting designer, he talks with the artistic director and the choreographer, listens to the music, and watches dance rehearsals. If the scenic designer is creating a set design for a well-known dance work, such as *The Nutcracker*, then he may watch a video and talk with the artistic director and choreographer to determine the style for the production.

After creating the design for the dance or production, the scenic designer presents them to the artistic director and the choreographer. Once the designs are approved, the designer continues, drawing specifications for how the set or set pieces are built. Led by the master carpenter, the construction crew builds the set or set pieces for the production or the dance. They put the pieces of the set together, and they paint it. The construction crew ensures the set or set pieces are built and secured for safety.

Stage Manager

The **stage manager** is the person in charge of the stage and backstage areas before, during, and after a performance. She coordinates the cues for each transition and makes the elements of the production come together in a performance. She calls the dancers to backstage and alerts them about when to get ready for the start of their dance. The stage manager cues the lights, sound, and other technical elements, as well as the curtain before, during, and at the end of each dance.

The stage manager prepares for a performance weeks in advance. First she attends dance rehearsals of the work. She confers with the choreographer and artistic staff to understand the curtain, light, and sound cues in relation to each dance and the entire performance. With this information she prepares her script for each dance. The stage manager's cue book lists the sequence of curtains, lights, sounds or music, and each cue for each dance in the program. To write this complicated series of cues, the stage manager needs to know what happens as the stimulus for the actual cue. The stage manager must know the technical aspects of running a show, including the music that accompanies each dance on

A stage manager collaborates with many people to make a production happen.

the program. Most important, the stage manager must know the dance movements or poses in order to call each cue at the right time.

For technical and dress rehearsals and for performances, crews (sometimes called *running crews*) set up lighting and sound equipment, props, sets, costumes, and accessories for each dance on the program. Technical rehearsals enable the production staff to have dedicated time to run and make adjustments for the curtain, light, sound, and other cues in their sequence throughout each dance on the program. In dress rehearsals, dancers wear costumes and makeup to perform the dances. Lighting designers, costumers, set designers, the stage manager, and crews make final changes in cues during technical and dress rehearsals. Choreographers and the artistic director collect and give final changes and notes to dancers and other production personnel.

In many academic and community settings, students often work as backstage crew members on productions. Learning dance production hands on is the best way to understand the teamwork involved in all the parts of a production.

Front-of-House Staff

A second production staff area is the front of the house. It includes the lobby, audience seating, and other areas the audience members visit during the performance. Several production teams serve the front of the house.

The **house manager** supervises the lobby, assists audience members, answers questions, and ensures safety before, during, and after a performance. The **box office manager** and box office personnel oversee ticket sales of purchased and reserved tickets being picked-up for performance. *Ushers* greet audience members at the entrance to the audience seating area and give them a program.

When the house manager gets the stage manager's cue, he dims the house lights to prepare for the performance. During the performance, the house manager monitors the house to ensure cell phones are off and that no photos or videos are taken of the performance. To signal intermission, the house manager turns up the house lights and ushers open the doors to the lobby. To signal the end of intermission, the house manager gives a light signal or a recorded chime in the lobby to remind people to return to their seats. After the performance, the house manager checks the house, and other visitor areas in the lobby, and locks the facility.

Business Staff

The **business staff** includes the business manager, publicity and public relations staff, and graphic and web designers. The business staff develops the publicity materials, the programs, and the tickets for the performance.

The *business manager* projects the budget, then monitors expenses and revenues throughout the production. *Marketing personnel* provide publicity, promotional materials, and public relations for the company to the media. They determine ways to reach core and extended audience segments to buy tickets. The promotional and publicity materials present a coordinated design for the production. *Graphic designers* create the advertisements, announcements (print and electronic), tickets, and programs to publicize the performance.

Each team creates a worksheet timeline (figure 14.3). Together these timelines plot different components that need to be completed by a certain time on their performance schedules. The worksheet includes these different perspectives on how much time it takes to produce a dance performance. These components are then placed on a combined master schedule for each performance and then a complete master schedule for the company's season of performances.

Figure 14.3 Sample Production Calendar

Pre-Planning

- Type of performance (informal or formal)
- Number of performances and times of day
- Budget projection for single and multiple performances

Artistic staff	Collaboration	Production staff
Master calendar connects to the school or university calendar and facility calendars (dance rehearsal and theater availability)		
		Supervisory, janitorial fees
		Lighting equipment, set or set pieces build or rental fees
		Dance floor (availability or rental fee)
		Drapes, scrim, cyclorama, backdrop (availability)
		Costumes (build, refurbish, purchase, or rent)
Spaces and times: dance spaces, theater rehearsal and performances, other production elements availability or related fees		
Auditions		Production personnel selection
Choreographers		
Number of dance works		Number of dance works
Dancers and number of dancers in each dance		Number of designers
Rehearsal assistants, musicians, other staff		Crews to produce the dance performance
Estimated budget for each dance and entire performance	Estimated business office (publicity, programs, posters, tickets), associated business operational expenses	Estimated budget for designers, production budget, technical staff and crew costs (hourly and for entire performance)

Pre-Production Schedule

Production meetings and budget tracking throughout

Artistic staff	Business staff	Production staff
Rehearsal scheduling	Artistic, business, and production budget approval	Design approvals
Supervising and mentoring on progress for completing dances	Design, supervise, and develop for the concert	Build time
Programming	Programming	

(continued)

Figure 14.3 *(continued)*

Artistic staff	Business staff	Production staff
Sound recordings	Publicity plan: Website development Public relations and public service announcements Programs and advertisements tickets	
Studio showings		Sound recordings
Photo calls	Publicity: photos, videos, media	Hang and set-up time

Move Into Performing Space

Spacing rehearsals		Dry technical rehearsals
	Cue-to-cue dance and technical rehearsals	

Dress Rehearsals

Warm-ups for performing		Technical rehearsals with lighting, costumes without makeup
Pacing yourself: rest, nutrition, and self-care	Final dress rehearsal and preview performance	Rehearsals with lighting, costumes, and makeup

Performances

	Evening, matinee, or morning shows	
	2-a-day performances	
	Performance videos	

Post-Performance

Costume return		Strike
Remove dance floor		Remove dance floor and store equipment
Clean dressing room and other spaces		Clean theater
Post-performance analysis by artistic, business, and production staff Artistic values Financial analysis Audience counts		

In small operations, all tasks described are completed by one or two versatile people and student crews. Learning dance production is much like learning dance; it is a hands-on activity. In dance production you may be assigned to a crew to learn what that crew does to help make the performance possible. This old theater adage is applicable: *There are no small parts, only small actors.* It applies to production, too. Everyone in the production is essential in making the performance a success.

✦ ACTIVITY 14.2 EXPLORE

Analyze the Elements of a Dance Performance and Production

You have probably seen dance performances on television or the Internet and live dance concerts at your school or in your community. View a performance at your school or on the Internet, and identify the elements of costuming, lighting, scenic backgrounds, music, and other aspects that contributed to the dance performance. Evaluate how you believe each of the production elements contributed to the performance. Then determine whether they all support the dance.

Dance Production Etiquette and Safety

When participating in a production, everyone involved—dancers, backstage crew members, and the audience—must follow theater etiquette. Dancers and crew members have certain responsibilities when they are in a theater. Following etiquette is a measure of professionalism and helps to keep the performance safe and enjoyable.

Backstage Etiquette and Safety

Backstage etiquette and safety procedures are key ingredients for dance production. Some general rules for the cast and crew who work backstage include the following:

- Be on time for your cast or crew call, and sign in when you arrive at the theater.
- Talking backstage is prohibited, unless it is a critical communication, in which case speak very softly. The audience can hear you.
- Before the performance, check that you have all of the equipment or supplies you need for the entire performance.
- When the announcement is made that the house is open, don't peek through the curtains.
- Stay alert and prepared to move quickly to perform your crew assignment so that the audience does not have to wait too long between dances. Remember, most often the audience is sitting in the dark.
- If you are asked to do something, do it immediately.
- Stand out of the way of cast and crew and out of the wings, but be available for doing your job.

- Do not handle costumes or props unless it is part of your job.
- Be careful not to drop equipment or make other sounds during a performance.
- Complete all of your tasks, and put all of your equipment away so that it's ready for the next performance.

To avoid being seen in the dark, the crew should dress in black shirts and pants. They should wear closed-toed, sturdy shoes that do not make any sound when walking; tennis shoes will work. Crew members carry a flashlight, a pair of gloves, and possibly a crescent wrench. The backstage area during a show is basically dark. A crew member's flashlight is covered with blue gel to dim the beam. Gloves are necessary if you have to replace gels in lighting instruments between dances or if you have to pull the curtain. A crescent wrench is an important tool if your crew assignment includes adjusting a lighting instrument.

Safety in dance production is foremost on everyone's mind during a performance. Many areas and equipment backstage require constant monitoring before, during, and after a performance to ensure safety.

- Battens with heavy lighting equipment move up and down, so if someone in the stage area calls *Heads up,* everyone in the area should respond to it immediately.
- The dance floor should be taped down securely to prevent trips and falls.
- Glow tape should mark the edge of the stage areas, stair steps, and other similar features.
- Cables running across backstage floor areas should be taped down to avoid trips and falls.
- Cables hanging from a batten should be high enough to be out of the way of cast and crew moving though the space, especially in the dark.
- Lighting stands should be weighted properly so they do not fall.
- Lighting equipment and parts such as gel holders become very hot. Be aware of getting too close when working near lighting equipment. Wear heavy gloves if working on the lighting crew.
- Individual and large groups of people may enter or exit the stage at one time. Other cast and backstage crew members must be aware of these dancers entering and exiting.
- Crossover spaces and all backstage areas should be free of clutter and extra equipment. They should also have a safety light (a gel-covered light positioned to illuminate the corridor for dancers to see the crossover path).

Backstage Etiquette for Dancers

Waiting backstage to enter for a dance requires using backstage etiquette. Read the call board (a bulletin board in the backstage areas for cast and crew schedules, call times, sign-in sheet, and other important information related to the production and performance schedule). On the call board you can find out what time you need to arrive at the theater. Sign in and go to the dressing area. "Quiet backstage" is the mantra of the state manager, who calls you from the dressing room to wait backstage for your dance to begin.

Standing backstage, the rule is that if you can see the audience, they can see you, which is unprofessional when it happens. When you stand backstage, stay out of the way of dancers entering or exiting the stage or technicians changing gels in lighting instruments.

If the stage space has a crossover, sometimes it can only be used at certain times so that the audience doesn't see or hear dancers moving behind the backdrop. Exiting the stage, use the movement to take you all the way off stage. Don't just stop at the curtain. After the dance, leave the backstage area immediately and quietly.

Curtain calls can be after a dance or at the end of the concert. The purpose of the **curtain call** is to take a bow with other dancers for your performance and to acknowledge the choreographer, the conductor, and the artistic director onstage while accepting the audience's applause. Practicing the curtain call is critical for the cast to assemble quickly onstage. Know from which side of the stage you need to enter and where your group lines up onstage, the bows and the order in which you line up, and when you should exit or if you remain onstage until the final curtain closes.

Receiving friends and family backstage is only allowed after the performance has ended. The stage manager or your teacher will tell you specific protocols. After the performance, hang up your costumes and clean your space in the dressing room so that it's ready for the next performance.

Etiquette in the Theater

Theater etiquette ensures that everyone in the audience can enjoy the performance. As an audience member, you should arrive and be seated with adequate time to enjoy the atmosphere before the house lights dim. In most theaters, food or beverages are not allowed at a performance. Cell phones and cameras are prohibited. Applause should be saved for after each dance and at the end of the performance.

If you arrive after the house lights have dimmed and the show has begun, the usher may ask you to wait at the back of the theater. Finding your seat later will not disturb other audience members viewing the performance. After intermission, return to your seat promptly to get settled before the performance begins again. The curtain call gives the audience the chance to applaud the entire performance. It allows dancers and artistic staff to receive these accolades for their work and performance.

Preparing for the Performance

You have experienced improvising, composing, and staging dances for performance in the studio or other spaces. These activities have prepared you for the next steps in preparing a dance for a public performance. In the Discovering Performance and Production section, various types of dance performances were listed from casual to formal. Your director or teacher will select which type of presentation format best suits the dance works being produced.

After you have learned and practiced a dance, you and other dancers have to rehearse and check your performance for movement or step accuracy. If you identify some problem areas, then practice them by yourself or with another dancer to ensure you understand the movements, timing, and spacing.

Along with these elements, you need to monitor the qualities of movement you are using in the dance. You should have a clear idea of how you are artistically expressing yourself through the movement. If you question some of the choreography or your performance, then ask the choreographer or your teacher to watch you dance and help you understand the areas that need further rehearsal.

Being in the moment is important, but preparing for the next dance movement or section or a difficult transition is equally important. In dancing, mistakes happen, but becoming a dancer requires you to accept—and move beyond—the mistake. The dance continues, so don't dwell on the problem or stop; just return to the performance attitude of dancing and enjoying the experience.

A group doing the same movements or synchronized movements is a powerful dance image. Synchronized movements to music create an energy that radiates into the audience. If this is an outcome of the dance work, then your group needs talk about how to make it happen. Using your kinesthetic awareness, including using peripheral vision, helps you and the other dancers sense each other and move at the same time. Sensing and matching the timing, energy, and even breath phrasing of the group's movements are helpful, too. Being a dancer in an experience like this where these attributes just "click" is awesome.

When learning a dance, you must know your dancer directions or body facings in the studio. Dancer directions adjust when the dance moves from the studio to performance onstage. The stage space may be different in dimensions or larger than where you learned the dance. Stage directions help you focus on your movements and body shapes for optimum visibility.

While rehearsing, you cultivate a performance attitude—a way of thinking about dancing and rehearsing that contributes to your level of professionalism in dance. Dancing onstage for large or small audiences requires you to have a certain presence to make a connection with the audience. As you rehearse, practice moving with that sense of presence to prepare for the level needed in performance.

Performance presence must reach beyond the stage, all the way to the back of the house.

Learning Stage Directions

In the studio you learned dancer directions. Onstage, dancers use the same directions as actors and other stage performers.

The stage directions are from the point of view of the dancer (figure 14.4). Stand in the middle of the stage (center stage) facing the audience, or downstage. Stage right is to your right. Stage left is to your left. Upstage is behind you where the back curtain is. These basic directions can combine for designating downstage right or downstage left and upstage right or upstage left.

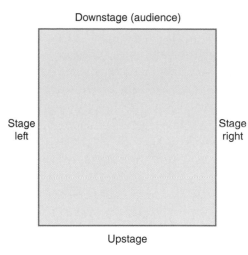

Figure 14.4 Stage directions.

Developing a Performance Attitude

Performance attitude is learning to concentrate on the movement while you are executing it to the best of your ability. With this type of attitude you can create a performance presence in the studio that will transition to the stage. A performance attitude relates to developing a professional attitude; you think and act like a professional. This is an important component in participating as a member of the class or as a responsible dancer in rehearsal and performances.

Performance presence is when you use the movement, the gestures, and the dynamics of the movement effectively so that the performance radiates your dancing through your body and beyond. You may have seen a dancer perform a work in which she radiates her personal presence and movement through space. As an audience member you become connected to the dancer through watching the movements. The performance connects to you kinesthetically and mentally to make a deep and sometimes lasting impression. These memories may become inspiration to you as a future dancer. Often these memories are what dancers use to restage or re-create works from their past.

Types of Rehearsals

In rehearsal you learn the dance and practice it for performance. During rehearsal you practice with other dancers and to music. Dances are usually rehearsed separately and then close to the performance date, and the dances are presented in the order of performance. These *run-throughs* help you get a sense of when you have time to relax, warm up for the next dance, or change roles to a crew position.

On the days you do not have rehearsal, you can do another type of rehearsal, a **mental rehearsal**. Sit down in a quiet place and turn on the music for your dance. Then practice the dance by visualizing yourself doing the choreography perfectly in your mind. This visualization technique is similar to how other performing artists practice. It reinforces your physical practice.

Technical Rehearsals

Technical rehearsals are when the production elements are added to the dance. Some technical rehearsals are done without or with the dancers present. The amount of time you have to rehearse with the production elements depends on the amount of time spent in the performance space.

You have worked with the music since the beginning of the dance. You may have worked with your costume or props during rehearsal. In technical rehearsals, the light board operators practice the lighting design cues to ensure that the dance and the lighting changes come together at just the right moment. During the technical rehearsals, you may **mark, or** move through the spacing of the dance but not do the movements full out or at the same level of energy you would do in an actual performance. Marking the dance onstage allows the light board operator and others to check each cue. Sound operators set the music to start with the dance and with the appropriate volume for the audience and the dancers. If the dance includes sets, set pieces, or a backdrop, the crew makes these changes for the dance.

Dress Rehearsals

Dress rehearsals are final rehearsals before the performance. As the name suggests, you dance in your costume with your hair and makeup done the way it will be in performance. The dress rehearsal helps you get used to moving in your costume and gives you a way to test it out. In dress rehearsals, you wear stage makeup so that the choreographer and technical staff can check it in relation to the lighting design. These rehearsals are the last checks to ensure all of the production elements are integrated into the performance of a dance. Some of the rehearsals are separate, or they can be combined as necessary in the **production schedule** to prepare for actual performance. With all of the technical aspects rehearsed for each dance on the program, the performance is ready for an audience.

Just as for class, preparing for performance means being physically and mentally ready to dance and enjoy the experience. A pre-performance dance class before the house opens and performance begins helps you prepare physically and mentally for dancing. Include time to do your own personal stretches and warm-up exercises that relate to the dance you will perform.

Before performing, some dancers stand quietly to gather their physical, intellectual, and spiritual resources for their dancing. Take time to clear your head of everyday thoughts and go to a neutral place so you can focus on the dance you are going to perform. If you perform more than one dance, then take a moment

SPOTLIGHT

Jean Rosenthal (1912-1969)

Eugenia (Jean) Rosenthal was born in New York City. After studying acting and dance, she became a technical assistant to Martha Graham, who was on faculty at the Neighborhood Playhouse. Rosenthal and Graham developed a lifelong association; Rosenthal designed the lighting of 53 of Graham's works in the company's repertory. Over the course of her career, she designed lighting for over 300 productions with Broadway credits of *West Side Story*, *Hello, Dolly!*, and other musicals. Her artistic work spanned beyond Graham's company to NYCB and ABT. To see her lighting plots and accompanying charts, visit The Lighting Archive website (thelightingarchive.org). Go to Archive > Rosenthal > Martha Graham Dance Company for *Errand into the Maze* and *Night Journey*. One of her many legacies was her book, *The Magic of Light: An Organized Approach to Lighting Dance*.

to clear your mind and your body of the previous movement experience before gathering your resources to perform the dance you are about to do. Practicing this simple technique will help you bring your full mental and physical concentration into the dance experience.

Thinking Like a Dancer

Preparing to perform for an audience, dancers have to tune into a dancer's attitude and mindset. Practicing these attributes of dance begins every day when you step into dance class. First you have to practice becoming a responsible dancer; be responsible for the movement that the teacher gives you, the choreographer presents, or the movement you invent. Being responsible means that you know what each part of the step or movement is, what parts of the body are moving and where you are moving in space, and on which beat in relation to other dancers. This seems like a lot to remember, but dancers develop a movement memory capacity through actively doing and mentally recording the movement. Or, sometimes it just helps to write it down with the counts for when you rehearse the movement.

Performing a dance in a new setting requires adjustments of movement size, how groups move, and how you move within a different space. Changing from a small space to a large space or vice versa takes planning. Walking through the dance in the new space either by yourself or with other dancers helps you to make subtle adjustments needed to perform effectively.

ACTIVITY 14.3 JOURNAL

Your Dance Performance

After you have participated in a dance performance, write a summary of your performance preparation and the roles you played in the dance production. Then identify at least three to five findings of what you learned during the production about yourself as a person or in your roles in the production. Did any parts of the experience prompt you to learn more about a specific area of the production or performance?

Summary

Dance performance and production are two sides of a coin, but both sides collaborate to create a successful production that audiences will enjoy and look forward to attending again in the future. Working collaboratively, staffs, cast, and crews can create productions that attract audiences and make them want to see the next dance performance. Participating as a dancer and crewmember gives you a sense of all the important contributions to the success of a performance, which is everyone's goal.

In past chapters you have created an individual or group dance or responded to either the process or the dance. In the portfolio activity for performance and production, you will take a different focus for analyzing and responding to the experience. Choose one of the movement experiences from previous portfolio assignments to write a report on the rehearsal and performance process. You can outline the process from the beginning of the assignment through after the performance.

Then, write a section on what areas of the process you found challenging and what areas you enjoyed. If you performed a class dance, begin recording the process after you were selected to perform in the dance. If you worked on a backstage crew begin recording the process after you received your assignment and your first crew call.

REVIEW QUESTIONS

Multiple Choice

1. _____Which type of theater space is best suited for dance performance?
    a. thrust
    b. in the round
    c. proscenium stage

2. _____Spaces such as parks and natural environments, art museums, or different places throughout a community are referred to as
    a. site-specific spaces
    b. outside performance areas
    c. alternative performance sites

3. _____The person who coordinates the backstage work before the performance for the elements of lighting and sound is
    a. the artistic director
    b. the technical director
    c. the stage director

4. _____The individual who supervises the lobby, assists or answers questions for audience members, and ensures their safety before, during, and after a performance is
    a. the house manager
    b. the box office manager
    c. the theater manager

5. _____Using peripheral vision helps dancers adjust their movement
    a. to get a sense of their stage space
    b. so everyone's movements are executed together
    c. to gain a sense of the audience's reactions

6. _____Dance costume design concepts include
    a. movability, fit, and comfort
    b. shape, color, and texture
    c. texture, length, and style

7. _____What is the last stage rehearsal before performance called?
    a. run-through
    b. technical rehearsal
    c. dress rehearsal

8. _____The major reason for dancers to use stage makeup is
    a. to see the dancer's face and facial expression
    b. to complement the dancer's costume
    c. for a unified look for all the dancers

True or False

1. A mental rehearsal is practicing the dance by visualizing yourself doing the choreography perfectly in your mind. _____

2. Theater etiquette is what crew and dancers practice backstage during a performance. _____

3. The stage manager calls the cues for each dance. _____

4. The theater manager is in charge of the stage and backstage areas before, during, and after a performance. _____

Labeling

1. On the stage space drawing indicate each of the following terms:

upstage

upstage right

upstage left

downstage

downstage right

downstage left

stage right

stage left

center stage

audience

Short Answer

1. What is the difference between performance attitude and performance presence?

 To find supplementary materials for this chapter such as worksheets, extended learning activities, and e-journaling assignments, visit the web resource at www.discoveringdance.org/student.

College and Career Preparation

ENDURING UNDERSTANDING: Learning in, through, and about dance is learning life skills.

ESSENTIAL QUESTION: What roles can dance play in my career and life?

LEARNING OBJECTIVES

After reading this chapter, you should be able to do the following:

- Understand the meaning and importance of college and career goals.
- Define media literacy, and explain how dance supports learning media literacy.
- Compare dance careers and associated careers.
- Assess and identify your knowledge, skills, and abilities as preparation for college and career goals.

VOCABULARY

artistic literacy

collaboration

communication

creativity

critical thinking

life and career skills

media literacy

multiple intelligences
 (MI)

observation

"Life is hard; it's meant to be a test, but while you are studying for that test, isn't it nice to be dancing?"

Suzanne Farrell, 20th-century American ballerina

What *do you want to be when you grow up?* Since you were a child, you have heard this question asked over and over again. Young children answer this question easily and with passion. You are near a time in your life when you need to consider your interests, your passions, and your possibilities as you prepare for college or a career. So, what do you want to be?

Discovering Dance helps you learn about dance by participating in various dance genres, creating dances, and thinking about dance as an art form. Whether your college or career goals lie in the arts, sciences, mathematics, humanities, or another subject you choose, participating in dance is one way to support these goals. In dance you create, perform, analyze, and respond, which are process tools that align with learning goals to prepare you for college or a career.

In this chapter you will explore the knowledge and skills identified for success in 21st-century careers and life. You will learn how the processes of dancing, dance making, and dance appreciation contribute to that knowledge and those skills. You will have the opportunity to survey dance careers and associated dance and art careers. These careers may spark your interests in new directions.

Discovering College and Career Preparation

Moving in new ways, remembering movement sequences, and executing them in time to music within changing formations and pathways is challenging. Dancing is a complicated process that requires mental and physical coordination, memorization, problem solving, refining, and performing. Like sports and many other fine arts, dancing demands that you juggle many factors to perform at your best. College and careers demand the same.

The processes of dancing, dance making, and dance appreciation fuel the discipline of dance. Across the arts the processes of creating, performing, responding, and interconnecting support other studies. Learning the movement languages of dance genres helps you not only in dance-related studies and careers but also in other arts-related disciplines and in life.

ACTIVITY 15.1   RESEARCH

College and Career Options

Write a list of two or three potential careers in dance, fine arts, or another discipline that you are interested in learning more about. Do an Internet search about each career, and note the following factors:

- Educational requirements
- Skills and abilities needed for this career
- Working conditions (for example, hours)
- Pay range and other benefits
- Personal benefits and values someone in this career would receive

After you have collected the answers to these questions for each career path, write a short descriptive paragraph about each career, and share it with the class.

In another document, write what appeals to you about this career. Also add what you think are your challenges in considering this career. Decide whether this career is a future possibility for further consideration or it is not a direction you wish to pursue.

Exploring Dance and Associated Careers

Imagine you are looking for a job, and you see an advertisement that reads, "Employer looking for creative, innovative, adaptive thinkers. If you are qualified, please apply." As a dancer, you can meet these and other requirements for work in the 21st century. Dancing, dance making, and thinking like a dancer train you in the skills you need for your education and career.

The time since the start of the new millennium has seen tremendous changes at a rapid pace. This quick pace is in part because of advances in technology that affect everyday lives and careers. Near the end of the 20th century, some of the world's greatest thinkers began to investigate what types of knowledge and skills 21st-century workers and citizens would need to be successful. As a result, they identified various types of learning and literacy such as financial, environmental, artistic, and others.

DID YOU KNOW?

Dance Employment

The U.S. Department of Labor Bureau of Labor Statistics posts the *Occupational Outlook Handbook* on its website (www.bls.gov). This handbook includes employment information about dancers and choreographers as part of the country's work force. These government data provide information about work environment, pay scale, and job outlook for the future as well as other information. In 2010 about 25,600 dancers and choreographers held jobs. Approximately 20 percent of dancers in performing arts companies and about 78 percent of choreographers work in a variety of schools and other places (Bureau of Labor Statistics 2012).

Employment of dancers is expected to increase at about 11 percent with a projected employment of 13,700 more people by 2020. This percentage is in the average range of all occupations. Employment of choreographers is projected to increase 24 percent with a projected employment of 16,400 by 2020. This is faster than the average for all occupations. The growing interest in dance as entertainment attracts people to enroll in dance classes. In turn, this growth in enrollment creates employment opportunities in television, movies, and other leisure settings.

Across these categories, a series of broad topics reach from school to work, into the community, and the world:

- Communication
- Creativity
- Collaboration
- Critical thinking

The skills that support these four C's for 21st-century learning are presented in table 15.1.

Scanning the entries in table 15.1 can be overwhelming. Pause a moment, and reflect on the assignments you did in the chapters of this book and your other class work. Then, recall the dance learning processes contained in the items listed. The point to remember is that the four topics contain major knowledge and skills that span dance and other disciplines of study as preparation for college and careers. In table 15.1 you will see that some of the skills identified cross one or more of the four categories. Acquiring these attributes is a long-term process; it can take many years to complete. Reading these ideas gives you an understanding of how learning spans from the classroom through experiences in your community and life. These four C's are deeply embedded in dancing, dance making, and dance appreciation processes:

- **Communicating through dance:** In dance you communicate when you create, perform, or reflect on a dance work. In making a dance, the choreographer, dancers, and associated artistic staff need common arts vocabularies to effectively communicate, analytical skills to solve problems, and negotiation and teamwork skills along with an array of management skills to create and produce a dance performance.

- **Creativity:** When choreographers and dancers analyze and solve movement problems in a dance work, they use the creative process. The choreographer approaches an idea or theme for a dance and creatively seeks a choreographic design through which to communicate a cohesive artistic statement. The audience viewing a dance reflects and analyzes what they perceive as the meaning and the design of the dance work. Their feedback may be communicated to the dancers, choreographer, artistic staff, or the community. These responses can influence the direction of a choreographer's future works, artistic directions, or a company's finances.

- **Collaboration:** Collaboration is an integral part of dancing and creating artistic works with other artists. Improvisational structures and dance compositional forms require that dancers work as a highly functioning team to perform a dance. In dance making, choreographers strategically plan movement for dancers to communicate ideas. Associated artists join forces to present a unified message in an artistic work.

- **Critical thinking:** Through all dance processes, dancers and choreographers, associated artists, and audience members

Table 15.1 Four Cs of 21st-Century Learning

Communication	Creativity	Collaboration	Critical thinking
Oral presentation and writing	Ability to adapt, see options and alternatives	Strategic and deliberate planning	Quick decision making
Grammar and spelling	Analyze	Process planning	Logical reasoning and math skills
Logical reasoning and math skills	Reflect	Problem solving:	Analytical skills
Analytical reasoning	Create a palette for thinking and conceptualizing abstractly	Movement	Multiliteracy skills
Negotiation skills	Representational	Communication	Management skills
Teamwork and cooperation	Gestural	Media interpretations	Multicultural awareness and appreciation
Leadership management skills:	Symbolic	Teamwork and cooperation	Economic and business skills
Time/people		Management skills	Technology skills
Advocacy skills		Stress management	
Multicultural skills		Empathy	
Multilingual skills		Work ethic	
Economic and business skills			
Computer skills			
Telecommunication skills			

use critical thinking. Dancers have to make logical and quick decisions during a dance for safety or for artistic expression. Choreographers use analytical skills along with management and technology skills to make dances that satisfy an artistic mission and to meet business goals. Dance audiences determine whether attending a dance company performance will be a continuing venture.

Dance provides a wide range of professional career options in communities, cities, and around the world. Dance careers span areas of the arts and entertainment, media, fitness, recreation, business, education, technical fields, and other areas.

As you learned in chapter13, dance as entertainment is big business. Dance in education spans from preschool through university and graduate education, and into communities and people's lives across the nation as participation or through education, performance, and advocacy. Dance studios, gyms, recreation centers, and performing arts organizations have expanded their community contributions as more and more people realize the importance and contribution of dance and the other arts to their lives. Dance professional organizations provide continuing professional development for students, educators, artists, scientists, writers, and others interested or involved in dance as profession or associated professions. Dance professionals work as performers and in many roles that support dance performance. Often professionals with a dance background work in associated fields such as dance therapy, kinesiology, production, media, and arts administration. Their presence as dance professionals in these fields brings deeper perspectives to new audiences of how dance can play a role in other disciplines.

Transferring Dance Skills to Life Skills

Life and career skills—the skills you need in order to succeed in work and life—require four characteristics: flexibility, adaptability, taking initiative, and being self-directed. In school, work, and community you should demonstrate cross-cultural and leadership skills. In your school and career, you should be responsible, productive, and accountable for your work. In the dance class you cultivate dancer attributes that then apply in your dancing and personal development.

Your experience in dance develops a number of traits that apply to other life endeavors. Personal development through dance for future career directions beyond dance include these:

- Physical, intellectual, and kinesthetic awareness
- Fine-tuned observation skills
- Enhanced focus and concentration
- Extended self-discipline, responsibility, and empathy
- Perception and sensory awareness of personal movement and others' movement choices and styles
- Versatility, ability to adapt, and flexibility in various situations
- Expanded interpersonal (mental and physical attributes you share with others) and intrapersonal (the internal conversation you have with yourself) communication skills

Observation and Awareness

Observation skills are critical to learning dance and are essential in any career. Observational skills take time to develop. Concentrated observation helps you acquire visual, auditory, and sensory information. As a dancer you filter through this information and determine how it applies to get the desired result.

Dancers learn to coordinate movements of body parts in a step or movement. This complicated coordination of brain and body improves as you move through more complex exercises, combinations, dance sequences, and dances. When you memorize movement you initiate an internal cueing system that engages a complicated synergy of intellectual and body actions with the elements of space, time, energy, or effort. So, what you do in dance contributes directly to your personal development in dance and also to future directions beyond dance. When you take dance classes or perform, you develop these skills:

- Using interpersonal spatial awareness
- Having a physical and intellectual presence in space
- Creating movement as a result of being internally sensitive and intuitive
- Acquiring performance awareness and a professional attitude
- Reading movement and then reproducing the movement (translate it, transpose it) presented by the teacher or choreographer
- Memorizing movements and dances to create a memory bank
- Understanding movement systems, genres, and styles

Creativity and Communication

When composing a dance, you use the creative process to formulate a design and structure for dance movements. You use the creative process in dance when you experiment with the following:

- Determining movement patterns as part of choreography and choreographic designs in space and time using a range of energy or efforts

- Manipulating the order of movements to make a logical statement using seamless transitions
- Using choreographic structures and strategies for augmentations
- Connecting musical knowledge to movement sequences
- Relating visual design elements of patterns, relationships to dance, and identifying styles to apply or augment
- Applying movement, choreographic, and aesthetic principles to dancing and dance composition
- Employing stagecraft and media knowledge in producing the work

Producing a dance is a complicated process that combines design elements, problem-solving skills, and communication with artists and technicians. When you practice these processes, you enhance your abilities as a dancer and create conduits that relate to many associated dance careers.

Media and Artistic Literacy

When you view dances, you develop a visual and mental store of classical to contemporary dance works. Dancers and choreographers have used this system of "recording" to create a memory bank since before the common use of notation systems and electronic recording systems. These mental memories of movements combine with kinesthetic responses you receive from watching dancers perform. Your response to a dance in conversation, discussion, or written forms is also kinesthetic in nature. Translating movement experiences into descriptive and meaningful commentary supports and expands your dance and artistic literacy and your media literacy.

Artistic literacy is the knowledge and understanding required to participate authentically in the arts. Arts include dance, music, dramatic art, visual art, and media. The arts contain content, principles, and applications that are common to them as art forms. In artistic literacy, the processes of creating, performing (in dance, music, or theater), presenting (in the visual arts) or producing (in media arts), responding, and connecting reach across all of the arts. Learning these processes in various art forms contributes to your media literacy and to your experience (State Education Agency Directors of Arts Education 2013).

Media literacy is the ability to access, analyze, and evaluate media content. Viewing and responding to a dance performance includes both deconstruction and construction.

After you reflect upon the dance as a complete work, the next step is to take the dance apart. Deconstruction is analyzing or taking a dance performance apart. It is how you look at the components of the choreography, the dancers' performance, and the production elements of the work. Construction activities use the dance analysis (or deconstruction) as a basis for participating in a discussion about the dance, writing a dance report about a work you have viewed, or summarizing your findings and filing them in your memory bank along with your visual memories of the dance work.

When you attend a dance concert or view a video of a dance performance, you may have been assigned to write a dance report. A couple of strategies are useful for preparing you to write your response. Before you view the performance, read over the items or questions you have to cover in the report. When you view the dance, watch, hear, and feel the performance. Some people suggest reading the

⬖ ACTIVITY 15.2 EXPLORE

Analyzing a Dance Performance

When you view a dance performance, you use your skills in media literacy to analyze it. After you reflect on the dance as a complete work, the next step is to take the dance apart. It is how you look at the components of the choreography, the dancers' performance, and the production elements of the work. When you deconstruct a dance work, think about these questions:

- What do you think is the choreographer's message, idea, and theme?
- Were you able to discern the choreographic structure of the dance?
- How did the music interact or support the dance?
- Did the dancers' technique meet the requirements of the choreography?
- Did the dancers express the style of the choreography?
- Did the production elements of lighting and costuming support the presentation of the dance work and contribute to it as a work of art?
- Was the dance aesthetically moving to you?
- Would you consider this dance a work of art?

program notes about the dance after the concert. Your viewing experience of the dance provides the information from which to write your report.

In past centuries, literacy meant reading, writing, listening, and speaking skills. These skills remain foundational today; they have become the basis of 21st-century skills such as media literacy. When you gain an understanding of a media presentation and its components that create meaning, then you are engaging in media literacy.

Dance literacy includes knowledge of movement, music, theater, and arts terminology. Dance is multilingual through its various genres, their specific terminology, and the application of movement, choreographic, and aesthetic principles. Other facets of dance literacy include knowledge of rhythmic and musical languages, stagecraft and theater vocabularies, arts education, arts media processes, and production terminology. Dance literacy skills contribute to overall media literacy.

Multiple Intelligences

The theory of **multiple intelligences (MI)** and 21st-century educational theories have provided evidence that students acquire many ways of being smart through dance. These intelligences translate to other courses of study and into the workplace.

The theory of multiple intelligences was developed by an educational psychologist named Harold Gardner. Beginning in the 1980s, Gardner's original system of seven intelligences has expanded to nine; it continues to expand. The following list summarizes Gardner's nine intelligences. Your multiple intelligence quotient is really a combination of all of your intelligences. You may rate very high in certain intelligences and not as high in others. Gardner claims that you can strengthen and expand the intelligences that you ignore or challenge yourself (Gardner1983).

1. *Verbal-linguistic intelligence:* Verbal skills and sensitivity to meaning and rhythm of words.
2. *Mathematical or logical intelligence:* Conceptual and abstract thinking skills in both numerical and logic patterns.
3. *Musical intelligence:* Understanding and ability to use rhythm, pitch, and texture.
4. *Visual-spatial intelligence:* Thinking and visualizing using images in spatial and abstract configurations.
5. *Bodily-kinesthetic intelligence:* Moving and handling objects with grace, skill, and artfulness.
6. *Interpersonal intelligence:* Communicating appropriately with other people in relation to their moods, ideas, and directions.
7. *Intrapersonal intelligence:* Self-awareness of feelings, values, and thinking processes.
8. *Naturalist intelligence:* Recognizing and categorizing plants, animals, and other things in nature.
9. *Existential intelligence:* Deep thinking about philosophical and essential questions about life and its meaning.

❗ ACTIVITY 15.3   DISCOVER

Your Multiple Intelligences (MI)

Do you recognize some of your intelligences? The web resource includes a link to an MI test to take for fun and to find out the various ways you are smart. Then you can compare your MI with those of others in the class. Knowing your MI can give you insights into some possible career directions. Your MI can change over time as you develop other intelligences. Documenting your MI can be an interesting way to self-check and track your changes in the future.

Preparing for Auditions

Dance auditions are handled differently, depending upon where the audition takes place. Auditions are how dancers are selected for some schools, programs, or companies. In the professional dance world, auditions are how you apply for a job. In some settings, an informal audition process is a series of classes and learning choreography from which the teacher or dance company director select students for performance. More formal dance auditions are similar to those found in community and other company settings, while professional auditions are similar to what you have seen in the movies or in Broadway shows.

Before you go to a dance audition, read the audition information to understand what the company or production is seeking in the areas of dance genre or style. Audition information should specify the number of men and women needed, dance requirements, and whether additional talents such as singing or playing a musical instrument or ability to do acrobatics are desirable. Having these added talents if requested on the audition sheet may enhance your chance of being selected. Decide if you meet the requirements stated on the audition sheet.

Prepare for the audition like you prepare for a performance. Pack proper shoes for executing all dance genres, and other support materials such as a digital recording of the song or a copy of the sheet music that you practiced for the audition. If equipment for the audition stipulates that you prepare a choreographed dance or sing a song as part of your audition, read and follow the specifications exactly. Prepare for your performance in advance. You will have to be ready to perform when you are called.

At the Audition

Arrive at the audition early so that you have adequate time to complete the paperwork and get your audition number that you attach to your dance wear. Allow yourself adequate time to warm up, and be mentally prepared to dance. For many auditions you will need copies of your dance résumé and several professional dance photos. Find out exactly what is required for the type of audition before you go.

In dance auditions you should expect to perform in one or more dance genres. You may do part of a dance class and then learn dance combinations or choreography quickly, and then perform in groups. The number and dance genre combinations depend on the choreographer and artistic director's needs for the performance. The audition process can take several hours or several days if there are callbacks for specific roles. Each organization has their particular audition process but the goal is the same—to select the right dancer for the right dance and performance role.

A couple of things to keep in mind when attending an audition is that an audition is a learning experience. When you go to an audition, you should focus and compete against one person—yourself. Before you begin the audition or workshop, take a deep breath, clear your mind, and just enjoy the dancing. Giving your personal best with a smile on your face will not only afford you a great experience, but your audition will radiate your enthusiasm for dance. After the audition, review your performance and determine what you learned from the experience that you believe is valuable for you to remember at your next audition. You should keep notes to help you prepare for the next audition.

At a dance audition, the organizers call small groups to perform while others wait for their turn on the sidelines.

Careers in Dance

Dance careers are many and varied. Most people aim for a first career as a performer or choreographer, but these career choices can also combine with other career paths in dance. Education, training, and work experience can often provide the basis for a second career in dance.

Dancers, choreographers, and directors work as professionals in any of the following settings:

- Professional dance companies
- College and university dance companies
- Civic and regional ballet companies
- Industrial shows
- Stage shows on cruise lines, casinos, and amusement parks
- Television, film, and music videos
- Musical theater

Professional dance auditions usually have two auditions or calls for dancers. One audition call is for union dancers, or professional experienced dancers, who are members of one or more dance unions, and the second call or audition is for nonunion dancers. If selected, the nonunion dancer joins one of the dance unions.

Performing artist unions ensure that contracts meet regulations concerning equitable wages and overtime pay, safe working environments, resolution of arguments, sick leave, retirement benefits, and other resources. Dancers join the union associated with the type of media in which they perform, such as:

- American Guild of Musical Artists (AGMA)
- American Federation of Television and Radio Artists (AFTRA)
- Screen Actors Guild (SAG)
- Actors' Equity Association (AEA)
- American Guild of Variety Artists (AGVA)

These unions are all sister unions and members of an organization called the Associated Actors and Artistes of America (4As). For more information about each organization, visit the web resource.

Other dance-associated careers include rehearsal assistant, assistant to the choreographer, artistic director, musical accompanist, musical director, dance physical trainer, therapy staff, and dance psychologists.

Preparation for these careers can include college or conservatory degrees or apprenticeships with professional companies.

Dance Educators

Dance educators teach dance in many settings from preschool through university and in various settings in the community. The National Dance Education Organization (NDEO) supports dance educators in a wide variety of settings. NDEO has developed dance education standards for dance educators and benchmarks for student learning in dance. Other dance education organizations support specific dance genres or dance educators who work in specific areas of dance education.

Dance educators who teach in pre-kindergarten through high school prepare for their careers with a college degree in dance, physical education, or theater with additional education courses. In states with a dance certification, dance educators take a dance test to qualify them for teaching in public schools. Teaching artists are often dancers from a community or regional professional dance company. They present outreach activities and teaching residencies in schools and community settings. Dance educators teach in these settings:

- Public, parochial, or charter schools
- Magnet and magnet arts schools
- Community arts and recreational centers
- Dance studios
- Preschool and day care centers
- Health and fitness centers

In college and university settings, dance educators have an undergraduate degree and one or more graduate degrees. Most often, dance educators in these settings have danced professionally. Sometimes they work with pre-kindergarten through high school dancers before or in addition to teaching in a post-secondary education setting.

Dance educators teach in a variety of settings in schools and the community.

Dance Therapists

Dance therapy has a variety of modalities, including dance and movement that professionals practice in many community settings. The American Dance Therapy Association (ADTA) supports movement and dance professionals in this psychotherapeutic discipline. Generally, people study dance therapy during the graduate level of university education. For a career in dance therapy, students should become proficient in many forms of dance during their undergraduate education and also acquire a major or minor in psychology as preparation for graduate work. After completing the academic requirements, students take an exam to become a registered dance therapist, which qualifies them for entry-level employment positions. After gaining experience in the field, registered dance therapists can take the Board Certified Dance/Movement Therapist (BC-DMT) examination. Passing this advanced exam qualifies a person to become a dance/movement trainer, supervisor for students preparing for the field, or work in private practice. Dance/movement therapists practice in

- hospitals,
- special schools,
- nursing and assisted living facilities,
- group or private practice, or
- university programs as teachers or supervisors.

Dance Notators

Dance notators write dances in various notation systems such as Labanotation, Benesh, and others. Notators preserve major dance works in concert and cultural forms so that performing companies, scholars, and students can access these dance works. The notator can create or interpret a dance score. Using a very detailed system of symbols, the dance score presents movement of the body and its parts in relation to the music that accompanies the dance work.

Labanotators analyze and record movement using a symbol system developed by Rudolf Laban (1879-1958), a dancer, choreographer, movement theorist, and analyst. (For more information on Laban, see chapter 10.) The Dance Notation Bureau in New York and generations of Labanotators have preserved many major contemporary and historical dance works. Notators stage a dance from the written dance score for companies and schools across the world.

Benesh notation is a British system developed by Rudolf Benesh (1916-1975), an accountant with a passion for the arts. Benesh and his dancer wife, Joan, developed the notation system. The Benesh Institute of Choreology was established in 1962 in London. The Benesh system as a result of the work of its first graduates supports a wide variety of dance forms such as ballet, modern dance, folk and cultural dance, historical dance, and choreographic analysis.

Careers in dance notation include the following:

- Dance notator
- Dance reconstructor (notation and historical research)
- Dance notation educator

Dance Writers and Critics

Dance scholars, historians, journalists, critics, and authors produce dance writing that contributes to dance literature. Likely employers for dance writers include critics who write for newspapers, magazines, journals, television, and websites. If you plan to explore a career in dance writing, be aware that it can emerge from many starting places. Many dance writers are not dancers, but have a deep appreciation for and love of dance and choreography. Many dancers and choreographers are dance writers, too. In university circles, dance professors are often expected to produce dance works and write scholarly articles in journals, too.

Major newspapers and dance magazines may have a dance writer or critic review a dance performance. Some of the major dance critics of the 20th century wrote books about various eras or styles of dance and the choreographers who created dance works. To support dance critics, the Dance Critics Association provides conferences for professors who teach dance criticism and other interested dance professionals.

Dance writing and reporting has expanded with its inclusion in online magazines, journal articles, and blogs on various topics that have broadened readership in dance. Dance careers in writing and criticism include the following:

- Dance writer
- Dance reporter
- Dance critic
- Dance historian
- Dance researcher

Theater Production, Arts, and Event Managers

Associated dance career options in theater are in artistic design and technical theater roles. In dance arts management, the artistic direction and management of facilities and organizations offer many opportunities for dance-associated careers. These careers span from community to professional organizations and production companies. Dancers, choreographers, and directors contribute to theater, musical theater, and opera productions. Dance theatrical production, dance arts management careers, and industries that support dance include the following:

- Lighting designer
- Costume designer, costumer, and costume constructor
- Set designer
- Makeup artist
- Stage manager
- Technical assistant
- Crew member (crews build and run the show)
- Business and financial management
- Production designer

Arts management staff includes the following:

- Producer
- Executive director
- Fundraiser or grant writer
- Marketing, publicity, and promotion staff
- Dance company manager
- Booking agent
- Lawyer for the arts
- Lobbyist for the arts

Industries that support dance include the following:

- Dance wear and shoes
- Dance music

- Dance books and media resources
- Dance photography
- Dance videography
- Dance event planning
- Training or seminars
- Media development: photography, video, artist, and company websites

Cultural Dance Professionals

Although cultural dances have traditional, classic, or entertainment dance roots, cultural dance can also lead to a professional career. Studying, performing, recording, viewing, and writing about cultural dance has its foundations in the 20th century. Here are dance careers that focus on cultural dance and have expanded to other disciplines:

- Dance anthropologist
- Dance ethnologist
- Ethnomusicologist
- Cultural anthropologist
- Dancer
- Cultural dance historian
- Cultural dance professor
- Dance notator
- Dance administrator
- Cultural dance musician, or musicologist
- Choreographer specializing in restaging or reconstructing dance works

Cultural dance is supported by many organizations, such as the World Dance Alliance (WDA). It takes a worldwide view of cultural dance from a heritage to contemporary perspective. The WDA is structured as an umbrella organization made up of geographical regional groups to represent all dances of each region.

Recreational Dance Coordinators

In recreational dance forms, the staples of square dance and contradance events continue to grow. Country-western and line dancing have become global phenomena, reaching enthusiasts across Europe to Japan. People realizing the health and social benefits of recreational dance has increased participation in these dance forms that in turn has created the need for more instructors and event managers. Recreational dance coordinator jobs include:

- Square dance or contra dance instructor or caller
- Social dance instructor
- Folk dance instructor
- Social historical dancer, choreographer, or reconstructor
- Company administrator
- Folk arts event manager

Dance Fitness Instructors

Dance fitness took off with aerobic dance, then Jazzercise, and now Zumba and many other styles of dance fitness classes. Dance fitness instructors are associated with these careers:

- Dance fitness classes in a variety of systems
- Dance conditioning trainer
- Pilates instructor
- Yoga instructor
- Massage therapist

Dance Medicine, Health, and Wellness Professionals

The dance medicine, health, and wellness fields have expanded over the past decades. Some college or career preparation options include the following:

- Dance athletic trainer
- Dance orthopedic specialist
- Dance physical therapist
- Dance kinesiology or other scientist
- Dance nutrition counselor or dietitian
- Dance psychologist

Many of these careers have been important for various sports, but they are migrating to dance. These professionals work in private practice, with dance companies, or in universities. Since the late 20th century, dancers became viewed as performing artists but also as dancer-athletes. With the emergence of dance fitness workouts, dance has become linked to the health field, too. This expanded view of dance has led to organizations that support the health, fitness, and wellness for dancers. The International Association for Dance Medicine and Science (IADMS) provides research and education for dance educators, dancers, and dance science, health, and wellness professionals and researchers.

Studying dance includes many benefits and values that relate to skills used in associated dance careers. As a dancer, this means you have many dance-related choices for college and beyond.

SPOTLIGHT

Career Transition for Dancers

Career Transition for Dancers is a non-profit organization with the mission to enable dancers to define their career possibilities and develop the skills necessary to excel in a variety of disciplines. Under the leadership of 20-century dancer and choreographer Agnes de Mille, the organization developed a partnership to present ways to help dancers during and at the end of their careers. The goal was to help dancers make use of their background, skills, and talents on and off the stage for a second career.

Career Transition for Dancers today serves all dancers from pre- through postprofessionals over the age of 16. Offices in New York and Chicago serve dancers throughout the United States.

Thinking Like a Dancer

Considering a college major or minor or a career is a huge decision! Making this decision takes a lot of thinking over time. Before deciding on a major, research the field you are interested in to determine whether this is the profession for you. Talking to a variety of professionals in that career can give you information about working in different settings, getting a sense of what people do on a daily basis and the challenges they face in the field. Shadowing one or more professionals in a daily routine is a good way to find out about a profession. Another part to consider is the cost. Find out what it will cost to prepare for the profession, how much you would make in the first few years of the profession, and then figure out whether you can support yourself on the beginning salary.

The bottom line is to learn as much as possible, then weigh the positive and the negative attributes in your decision-making process.

When you set goals, they give a probable outcome. Setting goals for the next year or longer can help you focus your energies, time, learning, and direction. Often posting your goals in a place that you can see every day reminds you about your targets. Revisiting your goals is important for determining whether they are still as important as you originally believed or if they have changed direction.

ACTIVITY 15.4 JOURNAL

Personal Goals

Your personal goals can be short-term or long-term goals. If you anticipate reaching your goals by the end of the term or the end of 2 or 3 years, you need to add checkpoints along the way. Then you can evaluate your progress toward reaching the goal.

In your journal, write two or three college or career goals. Date the entry. Post a copy of your goals in a place you see every day, such as a mirror in your room. Then you can reread and keep your goals clearly in mind. Include a future deadline for attaining some of these goals, such as before the next term or year begins. Start working toward achieving the goals you have developed. Next time you review your goals, you can determine whether these are still the goals you want, or you can revise or expand your goals, then date and post them again. The continued activity of goal setting gives you insights about yourself as you make future plans.

You can use goal setting effectively in many aspects of your life. You can set dance goals in class, or you can set goals for fitness, test taking, or personal health and wellness. Setting goals gives you a focus and a purpose. Goal-setting can help you achieve your dreams and your ambitions.

Summary

This chapter presented education and career options related to dance. You can't start planning your future too early; college and career decisions are just around the corner. Now is a great time to explore the diversity of dance and associated careers beyond what you learned in this chapter. Talk to people you know who have careers that attract you. Visit with friends and students who have enrolled in college dance programs to learn more about their studies. Read major magazines to gain a sense of the dance profession or associated professions. And, keep setting goals.

Review the various types of dance careers presented in this chapter. Work with your teacher to select one or two careers that are appealing to you. Then, using the career report outline on the web resource, you can research and write a report for one or both dance careers you selected. Prepare a one-minute oral report about one of the careers. Then, write a one-page paper comparing and contrasting two dance careers based on your career research or what you learned in class from other students' oral reports. In your final paragraph, determine which career attracts your interest the most and why.

REVIEW QUESTIONS

True or False

1. Producing a dance is a simple process of selecting movement and design elements, problem solving, and communication with artists and technicians. _____

2. Multiple intelligences are different ways of being smart. _____

3. Associated Actors and Artistes of America (4As) is an organization of dancers, choreographers, and educators. _____

4. Dance literacy includes knowledge of movement, music, theater, and arts terminology. _____

5. Professional dance auditions are either a nonunion or union call for dancers. _____

Matching

Match the four core abilities for 21st-century careers in the right-hand column and their description in the left-hand column.

1. _____collaboration   a. Teamwork and cooperation

2. _____communication   b. Writing and speaking

3. _____creativity   c. Logical reasoning

4. _____critical thinking   d. Seeing options and alternatives

Matching

Match each term listed in the left column with the phrase that identifies or describes it in the right column.

1. _____dance arts manager

2. _____dance educator

3. _____ dance ethnologist

4. _____dance fitness professional

5. _____dance health and wellness professional

6. _____dance industry professional

7. _____dance notator

8. _____dance theatrical production

9. _____dance/movement therapist

10. _____dance writer

a. Costume, lighting, or scenic designer

b. Works in cultural dance and associated fields

c. Pilates teacher

d. Dance booking agent

e. Scientist, psychologist, or nutritionist

f. Produces work in newspapers, magazines, journals, and websites

g. Dance videographer

h. Practices in the community and in health care settings

i. Preserves major dance works in concert and cultural forms

j. Teaches students preschool-age through senior citizens

Short Answer

1. List five dancer skills gained from the dance class that transfer to college or career preparation. Then add a sentence for each skill and indicate how it connects to your college or career preparation.

 To find supplementary materials for this chapter such as worksheets, extended learning activities, and e-journaling assignments, visit the web resource at www.discoveringdance.org/student.

Dance In Your LIfe

ENDURING UNDERSTANDING: Dance is a physical, social, and intellectual pursuit for life.

ESSENTIAL QUESTION: How is dance part of my life?

LEARNING OBJECTIVES

After reading this chapter, you should be able to do the following:

- Determine your dance preferences.
- Recognize dance choices in school and community.
- Decide your interest in dance participation as dancer or audience member.
- Evaluate the role of dance in your life.

"Dance isn't a form, it's a way of life."

Anonymous

This chapter is all about you. It is your chance to look at dance in relation to you. Viewing a dance work is like reading a great piece of literature, hearing a musical masterwork, or watching a major dramatic work. A significant dance work can include all of these experiences in a single piece. Art works can speak to you in many ways—physically, intellectually, and spiritually—and often resonate with you so that they stay in your memory. When a dance becomes a memory, it resides in your body's movement memory. Performing and viewing dances creates a memory bank of dance experiences. These experiences become the foundation for your future artistic creativity, expression, and performance. Together your dance, arts, and other memory banks can influence how you express yourself through your choices in style, demeanor, and outlook of the world throughout your life.

Through previous chapters you have explored concepts, principles, and processes that underlie dancing, dance making, and dance appreciation. You experienced creating, performing, responding, analyzing, and interconnect-

ing to dance, dance works, dance literature, and other arts and disciplines. The purpose of this chapter is to get you thinking about what your dance was before this course, what it is as a result of this course, and your future choices as you move from school to career and throughout your life.

Discovering Dance in Your Life

It is your turn to take your dance experiences from this course and reflect. Begin by setting aside some quiet time to examine the dance you have discovered, explored, experienced, and thought about throughout the book. Take some time to filter these experiences through your physical, intellectual, emotional, and spiritual perceptions and values. Take some more time to dream about what dance could be in your future. Then you can discover, explore, and gather your thoughts about what is your dance.

To help formulate your reflections about the question *What is your dance?*, begin with the following questions:

- What are your dance genre and style preferences?
- What are your dance challenges?
- What dance forms do you want to discover and explore next?

Keep these questions in mind for the future, asking them again and again as you move through life. As you change and as dance evolves, your answers may change, too.

Exploring Dance in Your Life

Have you ever taken a magazine or Internet quiz that asks several questions (or has you select from various options) and then the results give you an idea of how you rate as, say, a runner, cook, or dancer? Begin by selecting your favorite dance categories. Then survey the dance genres. The next step is to evaluate your dance abilities and determine your style of dancing. With these activities, you may be able to discern what your dance is and what it could be in the future.

Chapter 1 presents traditional categories of dance genres. Review the categories with some extensions, as described in the following list, then rate each category according to your level of interest. Here is an example of a scale: 5 = high interest, 4 = above average interest, 3 = average interest, 2 = some interest, and 1 = no interest. Write each category, then list your selection for how your rate your interest.

Concert dance included dance genres that were performed as dance art and generally onstage.

Dance fitness relates to aerobic or other fitness that is either dance based or incorporates dance movements performed to music for fitness benefits.

Recreational dance covers participation in a wide range of dances performed as leisure or social activities as part of a community. Recreational dances include historical dances, folk dances, traditional cultural dances, social dances, street dances, and many other dance genres, forms, and styles.

Cultural dance is traditional to contemporary dances performed in communities or as an art that originated from different places and people throughout the world.

Dance as entertainment can draw from all of the other dance categories. Dance entertainment often blends (fuses) dance genres and styles for the purpose, theme, or type of an entertainment event. Musical theater dance is a prime example of an entertainment category that often incorporates concert, recreational, and cultural forms for a particular production.

Rank the dance categories from your most preferred to your least preferred. Then write a paragraph after each category explaining what you like about the dance category and what you do not like about it. Include a statement about what types of dance experiences you have participated in before this course.

Your Preferences

The chapters in this book covered numerous dance genres in each category, but this is not the total list. Some chapters focused on one or more dance genres or classical and contemporary versions of the genre. In many of the chapters, the Explore More sections (provided on the web resource) included one or more related dance forms. These sections provide a glimpse into dance forms that relate to the dance genre covered in the chapter (see the list that follows). As you may recall, not all dance genres fit neatly into one of these categories. Some dance genres, such hip-hop, can be considered social dance, cultural dance, concert dance, and a major contributor to entertainment and media. Using the dance genres you have studied or expanding to genres or blends not covered in this book, rate your preferences. Some genres may have specific dance forms or styles that appeal to you.

Classical or contemporary ballet

Classical or contemporary modern dance

Cultural dance

Dance fitness

Dance team

Folk dance

Historical dance

Social and ballroom dance

Jazz dance

Musical theater dance

Street dance

Tap dance

What other genres, forms, or styles do you want to explore through dance, dance making, or dance appreciation? After you list your preferences, write a summary paragraph describing why you like or do not like each of the genres listed.

This and other activities may also help you find other dance forms you want to start participating in now. With the gamut of dance forms, it is easy to see that you have the resources to investigate dance as a lifetime activity.

Your Movement Style

The elements of dance are part of each dance genre and style. Some dance genres dictate how you use these dance elements, while some genres offer you the chance to create movement inventions. You may gravitate to one or more dance genres, which in turn will influence how you identify your movement style. Starting with the elements of dance (in the following list), first re-read the descriptions for the major components. Then think about how you use these elements, and jot down how you use each of them.

Body

Space

Time

Energy

Effort

Relationships

Then summarize your movement style findings, and write a paragraph or two that describes your movement style.

Your Motivations

Underlying your dance choices and your movement style, there must be some reasons you spend your time dancing. Characterize these essential reasons that motivate you to dance.

Why do you dance? What benefits do you believe you receive from dance—physically, intellectually, socially, emotionally? What challenges do you face if you decide dance is a college or career direction?

Seeking opportunities and new directions for continuing to learn dance often involves exploring your community or a nearby city or a summer program. Look for classes and other opportunities to dance or choreograph or help produce dance. Explore various opportunities to find your passion.

Motivation may surface for being an audience member, an advocate for dance and arts education. You may be already formulating a direction as an educator who wants to include dance in your courses. Do you want to support dance by volunteering time and skills to dance performance or production, or as an advocate for dance as arts education in your community? Do you prefer participating in or viewing dance as a leisure time activity?

Regardless of your motivation for what role dance can be or become in your life, there are opportunities to support these directions.

Dance in School

School is a time for learning and preparing for careers and life. Dance has so many attributes that it can beneficial throughout your life.

Continued Participation in Dance

Beyond academic courses or programs in dance, you have many other options to explore. Colleges offer outreach courses in dance for their communities. Community theater and dance companies have performances and often classes open to anyone in the community. Other community arts and leisure organizations provide performance and class opportunities for children through adults.

Careers in Dance

Chapter 15 explored both careers in dance and careers associated with dance. Your college or career decisions are personal. Because this is *your* dance chapter, take a second to look at the list of attributes and the work requirements from chapter 15, and ask yourself whether this is a direction you want to pursue. You need to determine whether you have the physical, intellectual, psychological, and other characteristics that would prepare you for a career in dance. List these attributes, and compare them to the list in the web resource for this chapter.

Careers Beyond Dance

You may have other career interests that offer new directions to consider when you combine them with dance. You may want to combine dance with other arts or with business, health and wellness, or another discipline. Chapter 15 identified associated careers. To find other interests related to dance, answer these questions:

- Do your interests lie in the artistic or the technical aspects of producing a performance?
- What other arts attract you?
- Do you do computer architectural drawings as a scenic or lighting designer does?
- Are you savvy in organization and can read music and dance cues to direct the sequence of light and other cues for a performance?
- Are you a leader—a people manager in addition to a performance manager who brings a huge number of variables together in a specific time frame to produce a performance?
- Do you have an interest or experience in business that may or may not be associated with dance or arts organizations?
- Does kinesiology, health and wellness, or nutrition as it relates to dance appeal as a discipline of study or perhaps as a career?

Your Dance Directions

You have many options in dancing, dance making, and dance appreciation. What you decide as one direction today might change in the future. Dance can be your muse, your go-to stress relief, an important part of your life, or an occasional thing you like to do with friends. Best wishes if you choose to reside in the world of dance or have dance as part of your world during different chapters in your life.

Thinking Like a Dancer

Dance uses a large number of integrated skills which, similar to other arts, are part of the creating, performing, responding, and connecting cycle. Thinking like a dancer and learning dance applies to other disciplines you study or will study, and it applies to life, too. It has only been recently that scientists and scholars have identified many of these characteristic traits associated with dance and the arts and how they reinforce learning in other academic disciplines, apply on the job, and in your life. In chapter 15, you assessed how you used the four C's—communication, creativity, collaboration, and critical thinking. Earlier in

❗ ACTIVITY 16.1 DISCOVER

What Is Your Dance?

Collecting the surveys, your summaries, and reflections from this chapter, pull them together to answer the question posed at the beginning of the chapter: *What is your dance?* Your answer can be a written or visual document you share with another student, your teacher, or your class; or it can be something you put away and look at in the future. If it is the latter choice, then put a date on it. When you revisit the question *What is your dance?*, it will be interesting to see whether this was a path you pursued and whether you have any thoughts about striking out in a new direction to explore new dance territory.

this chapter, you compared learning traits from studying dance as they apply to life endeavors. With these two surveys along with the self-quizzes throughout this chapter, it is time to take the next step.

Summary

Dance can be a fun, enjoyable, meaningful activity for a lifetime. Toddlers create their own movements and dances. School-age children dance in their gym and arts programs and in their classrooms. Creative movement and dance integrate and facilitate learning core subjects such as mathematics, sciences, and language arts, and they interrelate with other arts. Extracurricular activities provide activities such as swing choir, pom-pom, dance team, drama, and dance company activities. Community arts offer participation and audience experiences in cultural dance, theatrical arts, and entertainment. Take the time to explore them all. Then, decide what your dance is.

PORTFOLIO ASSIGNMENT

Beginning with chapter 1, you were asked to respond to the questions posed below and then put a copy of your answers in the back of your journal. Before you look at what you wrote at the beginning of the term, do the assignment again. After you have completed this assignment, read your original answers to these questions again. Take some time to reflect on the answers to the questions in these two assignments. Then, on a separate sheet of paper, write a response to each of the questions to compare your original with today's answers. Include the three parts of this assignment in your portfolio.

How do you believe participating in and studying dance will benefit you

- physically?
- intellectually?
- socially?
- emotionally?

Answer each question by writing a paragraph about the benefits of participation and the benefits of studying dance.

Your portfolio is an extended expression of you through what you learned and created during this course. It is now time to compile your portfolio. As you put your portfolio together, set aside some time to reread some of the portfolio activities from when you began your discovery of dance. Once the portfolio assignments are assembled, it may be a collection of your discovery of dance or it may be the springboard to exploring dance in your life.

To find supplementary materials for this chapter such as worksheets, extended learning activities, and e-journaling assignments, visit the web resource at www.discoveringdance.org/student.

accent—In music, relates to emphasis on a beat or group of beats.

AB form—In musical and dance composition, this two-part form is made up of an A section followed by the B section.

ABA form—Includes the two-part form of the A section, followed by the B section, and a repeat of the A section.

adagio—Slow movements. In a ballet class, adagio is the section of the center where dancers practice slow sequences of movements.

aesthetic principles—The components of unity, balance, variety, repetition, and contrast, which create the standard for determining whether a dance is a work of art.

à la seconde—To the side, or second position in ballet.

à terre—On the floor; refers to the location of the foot in ballet.

alignment—Correct positioning of parts of the body for ease and efficiency of movement.

allegro—Ballet term for fast, brisk movements. In the center, dancers do two types of allegro: petit (small) allegro steps and grand (large) allegro steps.

artistic director—Selects and may book a performance space and sets a date and time for the event. Has a vision for the performance that must meet the vision, mission, and budget of the company.

artistic literacy—The knowledge and understanding required to participate authentically in the arts. Arts include dance, music, dramatic art, visual art, and media.

arts processes—Include creating, performing, responding, and connecting to or interconnecting with by analyzing the arts within dance, other art forms, and the community.

asymmetrical—Describes a body shape in which one side of the body is in a different design or pose than the other side.

ballet—A classic, Western dance genre, and a performing art. Ballet is characterized by the outward rotation of the legs and feet, specific poses, and codified exercises and steps.

ballet technique—Includes positions of the feet, arms, and body; poses; exercises; steps; and movement principles.

ballroom dances—Social dances performed in more formal settings, or American and Latin dances performed for exhibition or competitions.

barre—The first part of a ballet class, in which dancers do a series of exercises that prepare for dancing in the center. *Barre* also refers to the rail that the students use in this section of class.

basse danse—A slow, dignified walking processional dance from the later Middle Ages and into the Renaissance.

beat—The underlying pulse of the music.

body actions—When the whole body, body parts, or body shapes move in space.

body composition—What your body is composed of: bone, muscles, body fat, and all other body tissues.

body shape—The body's shape during a dance. Depending on the dance genre, it refers to whether the body is vertical, angular, curved, or twisted during the dance.

branle—A group dance popular from medieval times through the renaissance. Couples performed in a circle with regional differences that often included short pantomimed sections.

Broadway tap—Tap dance featured in musical theater, entertainment, and media.

carole—A circular or processional dance accompanied by song from the Middle Ages. The dance was performed for centuries on church holidays and at festivals.

center—The second part of a ballet class in which the dancers do a series of exercises and combinations of steps in the middle of the dance space or across the floor.

cha-cha—A 1950s popular dance that originated in Cuba. The cha-cha is a lively, fun, and energetic dance.

chance dance—A series of random movements selected by chance by either the dancer or choreographer to create a dance.

choreographer—Person who creates a dance work.

closed position—In social dance, when partners face each other and the leader places his right hand on the follower's center back below the shoulder blades. The follower places the left hand on the leader's upper arm. The leader holds the follower's right hand in his left hand.

collaboration—Working together with others as a team or ensemble to accomplish a common goal.

commercial dance—An umbrella term for forms of live or media dance entertainment.

communication—The process of exchanging ideas, feelings, and opinions.

concert dance—A category of dances you see performed onstage as art and entertainment. These dance genres include ballet, modern dance, jazz dance, and tap dance.

constructive rest—Resting in supine position (on your back with your knees bent, feet on the floor with arms resting across the chest). This relaxed position is a way to improve posture and concentrate on deep and relaxing breathing techniques to stimulate body awareness.

contradance—A dance from the renaissance that became popular in 18th-century England and America.

costume designer—In performing arts, the person who creates the costume designs for performances.

creative movement and dance—Personal movement exploration to understand the elements of dance, and create movement sequences and dance using the creative or choreographic processes.

creative process—The process of gathering information for developing choreographic ideas, experimenting, evaluating, and putting it together to create, and then elaborating on the movement ideas you have selected.

creativity—The ability to use personal inspiration and imagination to create a new idea or way of doing something.

critical thinking—The process of gathering information to analyze and evaluate it for accuracy or as a solution to a problem.

crossover—The corridor behind the backdrop and the backstage wall that connects one side of the backstage area to the other.

cultural anthropology—The study of humans and their culture, which includes social structures, languages, laws, religion, arts, and technology.

cultural clash—Occurs when two cultures resist each other's traditions, arts, and dances. The outcome of cultural clash might be disruption or challenge to the existing traditions.

curtain call—The bow at the end of a performance.

dance or drill team—Students who perform dance or drill team routines for school games and community functions; they often take part in dance or drill team competitions.

dance appreciation—Participation in a variety of dance-related activities as ways to learn about and through dance.

dance categories—General divisions of dance knowledge (i.e., creative movement or dance, recreational dance, dance fitness, concert dance).

dance fitness—A way to increase cardiovascular endurance, strength, and flexibility. A wide variety of dance genres support fitness.

dance for the camera—Includes dance documentaries of dancers and choreographers, historical and educational movies, concert and cultural dance companies, and performances of choreographed artistic dance films viewed on television, videos, and the Internet.

dance historian—A scholar of the history of dance.

dance literacy—Understanding movement, dance genres and terminology, composition design, application of aesthetic principles, and knowledge-related arts that contribute to dance and dance performance.

dance literature—All past and present video, film, books, and resources about dance.

dance making—Composing dances for presentation to audiences.

dance phrase—A short series of movements that connect into a pattern.

dance sport—A type of dance in which elite ballroom dancers perform choreographed dances for competition.

dance wellness—A person's physical and mental dimensions of wellness that contribute to preparing and sustaining dance participation and enjoyment. For example, nutrition and hydration, rest and recovery, and self-care are some components of dancer wellness.

dance works—The products in dance.

dancer directions—Similar to stage directions, they use numbering systems instead. The Cecchetti and Russian methods of ballet used different numbering systems for dancer directions.

dancing—The human body rhythmically moving with energy through space and time.

derrière—To the back.

devant—To the front.

dimension—Spatial element referring to the relative size of a movement.

directions—The basics of moving forward, backward, sideways, on a diagonal, in an arc, in a circle, or up and down.

dress rehearsal—Last rehearsal before a performance, in which you dance in your costume with your hair and makeup as it would be in the actual performance.

dynamics—A combination of movement, energy, and time.

effort—Describes combinations of time, weight, space, and flow in different proportions to create different blends of energy components.

effort actions—Designate types of exertion of sudden or slow movements that are light or strong, and use a direct or indirect path.

ellipsoidal reflector spotlight—Often referred to as a Leko, produces a sharp cone of light. The instrument has built-in shutters to shape and direct the beam of light.

en l'air—In the air.

ethnologist—Someone who lives in a community for several years to record the everyday life of the people and their culture.

ethnology—The study of cultural life of a community. An ethnologist lives in a community for several years to record the everyday life of the people and their culture.

ethnomusicologist—Someone who studies world music from a cultural perspective. Ethnomusicologists may extend their study to dances performed to the music of the culture.

ethnomusicology—The study of a people's music in relation to their culture or society.

farandole—A chain dance performed by peasants and courtiers.

FITT principle—A set of guidelines for creating an effective exercise program; it stands for frequency, intensity, time, and type.

flexibility—The ability to move a joint through its entire range of motion. Also refers to how far a muscle can stretch.

first people—The original people who inhabited a land, dating from millennia ago.

folk culture—The heritage of a group through stories, ceremonies, and cultural practices that include music, dance, food, and language.

folk dance—The dance of the people that represents a specific nationality or group's heritage and values that is passed down from generation to generation.

folklore—A collection of myths, stories, jokes, tall tales, and dramas that are part of a folk culture.

forced arch—In jazz dance, a position in which the supporting foot is in three-quarter relevé position with the knee bent.

four-part suite—A series of court dances performed together: the allemande, courante, sarabande, and gigue.

foxtrot—An early 20th-century American social dance named for Henry Fox.

Fresnel—A lighting instrument that produces a wide beam of light with soft edges for covering large areas onstage.

full-foot position—All five toes, metatarsals, and the center of the heel of each foot connect to create a foot triangle. The body weight should vertically be centered over the center of the foot triangle.

gel—A colored sheet that tints the light beam produced by the instrument.

genre—Class or category of art or dance based on some set of stylistic criteria.

high (haute) dance—Refers to dances that included kicking, jumping, or hopping movements.

historical dance—Refers to dances performed from the renaissance to the 20th century.

house manager—Person who supervises the lobby, assists or answers questions for audience members, and ensures their safety before, during and after a performance.

improvisation—Also known as free movement, body storming, spontaneous movement, and movement invention. In dance, it is used to explore movement ideas.

isolation—Moving individual parts of the body while the rest of the body stays still or moves in a different way. Isolations can be done with the head, shoulders, ribs, and hips.

jazz dance—A 20th-century American dance genre with specific techniques and a vocabulary of steps often related to different dance genres and styles that emerged from jazz dance artists in different eras.

joint—Where two or more bones of the skeleton meet.

kinesthetic awareness—Becoming sensory-aware of bone, muscles, and joints (either nonmoving or moving through space).

kinesthetic sense—An awareness of the body's position or movement in relation to space.

Le Ballet Comique de la Reine—Commissioned by Catherine de Medici, the queen of France, in 1581, this production staged by her court musician, Balthasar de Beaujoyeulx, has since become known as the first ballet.

levels—Describes relative heights of movements in space; levels can be low, middle, or high.

life and career skills—Refers to the four skills needed to be successful in life and work: flexibility, adaptability, taking initiative, and being self-directed.

ligament—A strong band of tissue that connects bone to muscle.

light trees—Vertical stands that hold lighting instruments in the wings or at other places in the theater.

lighting designer—Creates the lighting design and light plots for the performance.

locomotor movements—Movements that travel through space with even or uneven rhythms.

low (basse) dance—A slow dance in which dancers walk or glide across the floor.

mark—To move through the spacing of the dance but not do the movements full out or at the same level of energy you would do in an actual performance.

master calendar—Created by the artistic, design, and production staff to ensure they have all the artistic and technical components done at just the right time during the schedule to ensure a successful production.

measures—In music, groups of beats, separated into intervals with a primary accent.

media literacy—The ability to access, analyze, and evaluate media content fluently.

merengue—A Caribbean dance performed in two styles: Haitian style has a smooth quality; Dominican Republic style uses a shift of weight between one bent and one straight leg.

minuet—A historical dance in 3/4 or other triple meters. The man and woman performed the steps for this dance in S or Z figures.

modern dance—A dance genre and performing art that began in the 20th century and continues today. Modern dance enable the choreographer and dancers to artistically express and perform works with a wide variety of personal viewpoints.

movement principles—Kinesiological and other movement science principles that apply to executing correct dance technique and performance.

movement qualities—A term to describe distinct features of movement that include pendular, sustained, suspension, collapse, vibratory, and percussive or abrupt.

movement sequence—Movement that is longer than dance or movement phrases and is part of creating a movement statement.

movement statement—A group of movements that when joined together express a cohesive view; similar to a sentence in writing.

multiple intelligences (MI)—Howard Gardner's term for different ways of being smart.

musical theater dance—Includes social, folk, cultural, or stage dance genres, styles, or blended styles for characters or chorus in the musical to express an emotion, support, an idea or further the story in the production.

nonlocomotor (axial) movements—Movements in which body parts move around a stationary base and include bending, stretching, and twisting.

observation—The process of perceiving and studying someone or something through the senses.

open position—Social dance position in which the leader and follower stand side by side.

PAR (parabolic aluminized reflector) light—A self-contained lamp and lens housed in a can-like container. PARs produce an oval pool of bright light with unfocused edges that cover long distances and are often used for special effect lighting.

pathways—Routes created by the movement that are straight, curved, diagonal, indirect, or direct. Pathways can combine direction and levels on the floor and in the air.

performance attitude—Learning to concentrate on the movement while executing it to the best of your ability.

performance presence—When you use the gestures and dynamics of the movement effectively so that the performance radiates your dancing through your body and beyond.

prehistory—The time before the advent of writing.

PRICED—Acronym referring to treating minor injuries; it stands for **p**revention of injuries, **r**est, **i**ce, **c**ompression, **e**levation, and **d**ecision of whether it is necessary to consult a health professional.

proscenium stage—In a theater, a rectangular stage space that can either be higher or lower than the audience.

RADS—Stands for **r**elationships, **a**ctions, **d**ynamics, and use of **s**pace.

range of motion (ROM)—The amount of movement you can make at a joint.

recreational dance—Dance form done for recreational activity. It can be traditional, cultural, historical, social, or community dance.

rhythm—The pattern of sounds in music.

rhythm tap—Style of tap dance in which the dancer's tap sounds make the music and the dance.

rhythmic awareness—When you hear and feel the rhythm.

rhythmic competency—The ability to perceive and do the rhythm automatically.

salsa—A popular Cuban or Afro-Caribbean dance form that originated early in the 20th century.

scoops lights—Large scoop-shaped instruments directed to illuminate large areas, such as the backdrop.

semi-structured—Refers to movement experiments or improvisations that solve a problem or answer a question.

site-specific dance spaces—Dance spaces that are located in a wide variety of places such as concert halls, art or other museums, lofts, shopping malls. Outdoor spaces such as parks and natural environments throughout a community.

social dance—A dance genre that often displays styles of a specific historical era.

somatic awareness of movement—Using your body and mind together to bring self-awareness to movement.

space—The area the dancer occupies; *where* the dancer moves.

spike marks—Tape marks on the stage space to help dancers find center, quarter, or other places on the stage accurately and consistently in a dance.

square dance—An American folk dance done with four couples in a square formation from which the dancers create many figures.

stage manager—The person in charge of the stage and backstage areas before, during, and after a performance. This person coordinates the lights, sound, and other technical cues for each transition and makes the elements of the production come together in a performance.

strength—The amount of force a muscle can produce.

strip lights—A series of lights housed as a single instrument hung across the front of the stage.

structured improvisation—An experimental movement sequence that is loosely structured and practiced.

style—A particular kind, sort, or type of dance, as with reference to form, appearance, or character.

swing—A social dance with a variety of styles danced throughout the 20th century. Danced with a partner, swing has simple to complicated footwork and many handholds.

symmetrical—Refers to a body design in which both sides of the body are the same design.

tap dance—An American dance genre performed as concert dance, in entertainment media, or fused with other dance genres, it is characterized by audible rhythmic footwork.

technical director—Coordinates the backstage work before the performance for the elements of lighting and sound.

tempo—The speed of the movement or the music.

tendon—Strong band of tissue that connects muscle to bone.

theater-in-the-round—A theater in which the audience sits on all sides of a stage in the middle.

time—Refers to *when* the dancer moves in relationship to the music. It may also refer to the duration of a dance movement or dance.

transitions—Relate to space, time, energy, or effort that changes between movements, steps, or phrases.

turnout—The outward rotation of the legs from the hip sockets.

two-part suite—An early suite of court dances that included the pavane and the galliard.

waltz—A dance in 3/4 time that gained and maintained popularity in the 19th century ballroom.

wings—The open pathways on- or offstage. Wings are created by stage draperies known as *legs*.

Bennett, John and Riemer, Pamela Coughenour. 2006. *Rhythmic Activities and Dance,* 2nd ed. Champaign, IL: Human Kinetics.

Bergan, Ronald. 1984. *Glamorous MUSICALS: Fifty Years of Hollywood's Ultimate Fantasy.* London, England: Octopus Books Limited.

Billington, Michael, Consulting Editor.1980. *Performing Arts: A Guide to Practice and Appreciation.* New York: Facts on File.

Blankenship, Diane. In press. *Exploring Diversity through Leisure and American Culture: An Interactive Self-Analysis.* Champaign, IL: Human Kinetics.

Bloom, Ken. 2010. *Hollywood Musicals: The 101 Greatest Song-And-Dance Movies of All Times.* New York: Black Dog & Leventhal Publishers.

Bujones, Maria and Zeida Cecilia-Méndez. 2009. *Fernando Bujones: An autobiography with memories by family and friends,* with Zeida Cecilia-Méndez. Doral, FL: Higher Education & Technology Consultants, Inc.

Carter, Paul. 1994. *Backstage Handbook: An Illustrated Almanac of Technical Information.* Louisville, KY: Broadway Press.

Clarkson, Priscilla, PhD, under the auspices of the Education Committee of IADMS. With special thanks to Elizabeth Snell, BSc, RD. 2003-2005. "Nutrition Fact Sheet: Fueling the Dancer." International Association of Dance Medicine and Science. http://www.iadms.org/displaycommon. cfm?an=1&subarticlenbr=2. Retrieved March 28, 2013.

Clippinger, Karen. 2007. *Dance Anatomy and Kinesiology.* Champaign, IL: Human Kinetics.

Corbin, Charles & Lindsey, Ruth. 2005. *Fitness for Life.* 5th ed. Champaign, IL: Human Kinetics.

Driver, Ian. 2000. *A Century of Dance: A Hundred Years of Musical Theatre Movement, from Waltz to Hip Hop.* London, England: Octopus Publishing Group Limited.

Duke, Jerry C. 1998. "Country Western Dance," *International Encyclopedia of Dance*, Vol. 2, p. 258. New York: Oxford University Press.

Franklin, Eric. 2004. *Conditioning for Dance: Training for Peak Performance in All Dance Forms.* Champaign, IL: Human Kinetics.

Franklin, Eric. 2012. *Dynamic Alignment Through Imagery, 2nd ed.* Champaign, IL: Human Kinetics.

"Fosse, Bob." 2001. International Dictionary of Films and Filmmakers, Encyclopedia.com. Retrieved March 17, 2013.

Gardner, Howard. 1983. *Frames of Mind: The Theory of Multiple Intelligences.* New York: Basic Books.

Giguere, Miriam. 2014. *Beginning Modern Dance.* Champaign, IL: Human Kinetics.

Gilbert, Anne Green. 2006. *Brain-Compatible Dance Education.* Reston, VA: AAHPERD/NDA.

Gilbert, Anne Green. In press. *Creative Dance for All Ages.* 2nd ed. Champaign, IL: Human Kinetics.

Hong, Tina. "Developing Dance Literacy in the Postmodern: An Approach to Curriculum." Paper presented at Dancing in the Millennium: an International conference. Washington, DC, July 2000. http://artsonline2.tki.org.nz/TeacherLearning/readings/danceliteracy.php.

Holland, Nola. 2012. *Music Fundamentals for Dancers.* Champaign, IL: Human Kinetics.

Irvine, Sarah, Redding, Emma, and Rafferty, Sonia. 2011. "Dance Fitness." International Association of Dance Medicine and Science. Retrieved: 2/20/2013.

Kassing, Gayle. 2007. *History of Dance.* Champaign, IL: Human Kinetics.

Kassing, Gayle. 2010. "New Challenges in 21st Century Dance Education," *JOPERD*, vol. 81, issue 6, pp. 21-32.

Kassing, Gayle. 2013. *Beginning Ballet*. Champaign, IL: Human Kinetics.

Kassing, Gayle and Jay, Danielle M. 1998. *Teaching Beginning Ballet Technique.* Champaign, IL: Human Kinetics.

Kassing, Gayle and Jay, Danielle M. 2003. *Dance Teaching Methods and Curriculum Design*. Champaign, IL: Human Kinetics.

Keeton, Gladys, O'Neill, Jennifer R., Sardo, Mike, Murray, Tinker D. 2012. *101 Tips and Activities for Dance/Drill Team Directors.* Monterey, CA: Coaches Choice.

Lane, Christie. 1998. *Multicultural Folk Dance Treasure Chest*. Champaign, IL: Human Kinetics

Lane, Christie. 1995. *Christy Lane's Complete Book of Line Dancing*. Champaign, IL: Human Kinetics.

Lane, Christie and Langhout, Susan. 1998. *Multicultural Folk Dance Guide*, volume 1. Champaign, IL: Human Kinetics.

Lane, Christie and Langhout, Susan. 1998. *Multicultural Folk Dance Guide*, volume 2. Champaign, IL: Human Kinetics.

Laufman, Dudley and Laufman, Jacqueline. 2009. *Traditional Barn Dances with Calls and Fiddling.* Champaign, IL: Human Kinetics.

Lawson, Joan. Revised and reprinted 1955. *European Folk Dance: Its National and Musical Characteristics.* London: Sir Issac Pitman & Sons, LTD.

Lewis, Lisa. 2013. *Beginning Tap Dance*. Champaign, IL: Human Kinetics.

Library of Congress. 1999. *An American Ballroom Companion*: *Dance Instruction Manuals.*

www.memory.loc.gov/ammem/dihtml/dihome.html.

Liu-Ambrose, Teresa. 2012. Canadian's Research chair in physical activity, mobility and cognitive neoscience, Warm-up and Cool-downs. www.bottomlinepublications.com/content/article/diet-a-exercise/movements-that-boost-memory?DHN.

Mahoney, Billy. 1998. "Jazz Dance." *International Encyclopedia of Dance*. Vol. 3, p. 600.

McAtee, Robert E. and Charland, Jeff. 2014. *Facilitated Stretching*. 4th ed. Champaign, IL. Human Kinetics.

McCutchen, Brenda Pugh. 2006. *Teaching Dance as Art in Education.* Champaign, IL: Human Kinetics.

Minton, Sandra Cerney. 2007. *Choreography*. 3rd ed. Champaign, IL: Human Kinetics.

National Assessment of Educational Progress. 2008. NAEP Arts Education Framework.

www.nagb.org/.../publications/frameworks/arts-framework08.pdf.

National Dance Education Organization. 2005. "Standards for Learning and Teaching Dance in the Arts: Ages 5-18." Silver Springs, MD: NDEO.

National Dance Education Organization. 2012. "Core Arts Standards Framework for Artistic Literacy." Los Angeles, CA: 2012 NDEO conference.

National Teachers Association for Country Western Dance Teachers. 2012. *Dance Terminology Booklet.* Revised ed. Las Vegas, NV: National Teachers Association for Country Western Dance.

New York City Department of Education. "Blueprint for Teaching and Learning in Dance, PreK-12." http://schools.nyc.gov/offices/teachlearn/arts/blueprint.html.

New York City Department of Education. n.d. Blueprint for the Arts: Dance, Dance Making.

Nicolas Brothers Biography: www.atdf.org/bios/nicholasbrosbio.html. Retrieved March 21, 2013.

Oliver, Wendy, ed. 2009. *Dance and Culture: An Introductory Reader*. Reston, VA: AAHPERD/NDA.

Oliver, Wendy, ed. 2010. *Writing About Dance*. Champaign, IL: Human Kinetics.

Playford, John. 1651. *The English Dancing Master*. www.contrib.andrew.cmu.edu/~flip/contrib/dance/playford.html.

Pomer, Janice. 2009. *Dance Composition: An Interrelated Arts Approach*. Champaign, IL: Human Kinetics.

Reeve, Justine. 2011. *Dance Improvisations: Warm-Ups, Games, and Choreographic Tasks*. Champaign, IL: Human Kinetics.

Robey, James. In press. *Beginning Jazz Dance*. Champaign, IL: Human Kinetics.

Salk, Jennifer. 2010. *Experiential Anatomy.* (DVD.) Champaign, IL: Human Kinetics.

Sefcovic, Nadia, DPT, COMT and Critchfield, Brenda, MS, ATC under the auspices of the Education Committee of IADMS. 2010. "First Aid for Dancers." International Association of Dance Medicine and Science.

Sofras, Pamela. 2006. *Dance Composition Basics.* Champaign, IL: Human Kinetics.

Sommer, Sally R. 1998. "Tap Dance." *International Encyclopedia of Dance.* vol. 6, pp. 98-100.

State Education Agency Directors of Arts Education on behalf of NCCAS (National Core Arts Standards). 2013. A Conceptual Framework for Arts Learning. http://nccas.wikispaces.com.

Taylor, Jim and Estanol, Elena. In press. *The Psychology of Dance Excellence.* Champaign, IL: Human Kinetics.

Texas College and Career Readiness standards. 2010. www.thecb.state.tx.us/index.cfm?objectid=E-AE69736-B39D-F3FF-EA.pdf.

U.S. Bureau of Labor Statistics. 2012. *Occupational Outlook Handbook, 2012-13 Edition, Dancers and Choreographers.* www.bls.gov/ooh/entertainment-and-sports/dancers-and-choreographers.htm. Retrieved *December 4, 2013.*

Weikert, Phyllis S. 1989. *Teaching Movement and Dance.* Ypsilanti, MI: High Scope Press.

Wright, Judy. 2012. *Social dance: Steps to success.* 3rd ed. Champaign, IL: Human Kinetics.

Zona, Christine and George, Chris. 2008. *Gotta Ballroom.* Champaign, IL: Human Kinetics.

Web Resources

Actor's Equity Association: www.actorsequity.org/home.asp.

Alliance for Round, Traditional and Square-Dance (the ARTS). Youth Squares or Teen Square Dance: YOU2CANDANCE VIDEO'S at ARTS & You2candance. www.arts-dance.org.

American Dance Therapy Association: www.adta.org.

American Guild of Musical Artists or AGMA: www.musicalartists.org.

American Guild of Professional Artists: www.agvausa.com.

Astaire, Fred: www.streetswing.com/histmai2/d2astair1.htm See list of movie clips.

Ballet Dancers: So You Think You Can Sleep:

http://sleepeducation.blogspot.com/2009/09/ballet-dancers-so-you-think-you-can.html.

Benesh Notation Organization: www.rad.org.uk/article.asp?id=114.

Burgundian Basse Dance: www.peterdur.com/kwds2007/proceedings/Another-Look-at-Fifteenth-Century-Burgundian-Basse-Dance.htm.

Burns, Ken. *Jazz: A Film.* PBS: www.pbs.org/jazz.

Career Transitions for Dancers.org. www.careertransition.org.

Charlip, Remy: http://remycharlip.org/?splash=1.

Dance Critic's Association: www.dancecritics.org.

Dance Heritage Coalition: America's Irreplaceable Dance Treasures: The First 100. www.dance-heritage.org/treasures.html.

Dance Marathon: http://thelongestlistofthelongeststuffatthelongestdomainnameatlonglast.com/long286.html.

Dance Notation Bureau: www.dancenotation.org.

Dance Planet: www.thedancecouncil.org/content.aspx?page_id=22&club_id=752324&module_id=33013.

Dance Technology: www.dancemagazine.com/issues/December-2007/iDANCE#sthash.WMK0B-TUv.dpuf.

Dance Unions: www.thalo.com/articles/view/85/dance_unions.

Dance Warm-ups: www.fitday.com/fitness-articles/fitness/exercises/5-dance-warm-ups-and-stretches.html#b.

A Dancer's Guide to Better Sleep: www.danceadvantage.net/2012/05/31/get-some-sleep.

Eleanor Powell: www.atdf.org/bios/epowellbio.html.

Etiquette for different centuries: www.americanantiquarian.org/Exhibitions/Dance/etiquette.htm.

Howard Garnder's Use of Multiple Intelligences: www.thirteen.org/edonline/concept2class/mi/index.html.

International Tap Dance Association: http://www.tapdance.org/Leaders.

Jean Rosenthal: www3.northern.edu/wild/jr.htm.

Lloyd Shaw: www.floridasquaredance.com/dixiedancers/lloyd_shaw_page.htm.

Media Literacy: www.medialit.org/reading-room/unesco-international-conference-media-and-information-literacy.

Medieval Dancing for Village Idiots: http://middlegate.atlantia.sca.org/Library/MedievalDance-forVillageIdiots.pdf.

Medieval Music. http://www.pbm.com/~lindahl/music.html.

MyPlate Supertracker: www.choosemyplate.gov/supertracker-tools/supertracker.html.

National Dance Education Organization: www.ndeo.org.

Partnership for 21st Century Skills. 2010: www.p21.org.

River Dance Information: http://events.riverdance.com/entice-clients/facts.

Screen Actor's Guild: www.sagaftra.org.

State Symbols and Dances: www.statesymbolsusa.org/Texas/SQUARE_DANCE.html.

Stress relief and self care: http://peer.hdwg.org/sites/default/files/7a%20SelfCare-PeerRole-Peer_Training.pdf.

Teens and Sleep: www.sleepfoundation.org/article/sleep-topics/teens-and-sleep.

Ten Top Tap Dancing movies: www.denofgeek.com/movies/tap-dancing/25766/10-tip-top-tap-dancing-movies#ixzz2dU5lJlmO.

Texas State Historical Association: www.tshaonline.org/handbook/online/articles/xdg02.

United Square Dance Association: www.usda.org.

Warm-up exercises for dance: www.livestrong.com/article/406653-good-warm-up-exercises-for-dance/#ixzz2K2yzIfk7.

World Dance Alliance: www.worlddancealliance.net.

Note: The letters *f* and *t* after page numbers indicate figures and tables, respectively.